Build-It-Better-Yourself
Country Furniture

Build-It-Better-Yourself Country Furniture

by the Editors of *Family Handyman* Magazine

Rodale Press, Emmaus, Pennsylvania

Copyright © 1987 *Family Handyman* Magazine, The Webb Company

Printed in the United States of America on recycled paper, containing a high percentage of de-inked fiber.

Senior Editor: Ray Wolf
Produced by Scharff Associates, Ltd.
Editors: Lois Breiner, David Caruso, William Casey
Cover Design: Jerry O'Brien
Cover Photo: Mitch Mandel
Cover Photograph Styling: J. C. Vera
Fireplace tools courtesy of Allen Hardware, Allentown, Pennsylvania

Library of Congress Cataloging-in-Publication Data

Build-it-better-yourself country furniture.

    1. Furniture making.   2. Country furniture.
I. Family handyman.
TT194.B85   1986   684.1'042   86-15577
ISBN 0-87857-629-0   hardcover

    6 8 10 9 7 5   hardcover

Contents

SECTION III: CABINETS AND STORAGE UNITS

SECTION IV: ACCENTS AND ACCESSORIES

Introduction

Read the information on this page carefully before building any of the projects. It will help familiarize you with some of the more common tools and materials you'll be working with, as well as the terminology used throughout the book. Remember that taking the time now will enable your work to progress more smoothly later.

- Feel free to change any of the designs to suit your taste.
- The finished dimensions of each component are provided in the cutting lists.
- All cutting list dimensions are actual (not nominal) and are given in inches.
- All measurements are given in the standard order: thickness × width × length.
- The materials lists include all the materials (fasteners, hardware, etc.) needed to build the projects, with the exception of the lumber. Some projects are specific with regard to fastener designation (sixteen No. 8 × 1-1/2" wood screws, twenty 6d finishing nails, etc.), while others are not. In such cases, use your judgment to determine the type and amount of fasteners to use.
- Where available, scale patterns are provided to make templates for cutting the more intricate components.
- Some of the projects require turned legs. If you don't have access to a lathe, the turning can be done at a lumberyard or millworking shop.
- While particular wood types (pine, cherry, etc.) are recommended in some of the projects, feel free to use whatever type of wood you prefer. Depending on where you live, availability will also determine what type of wood is used.
- Some of the projects are not specific with regard to the tools needed. Always use the best tool you have available, keeping in mind that the best method is not always the quickest.
- Assume that all wood screws are the flathead variety unless otherwise noted. When roundhead or other types of wood screws are required, they will be specified in the materials list.
- When wood glue is required, use a good grade of carpenter's glue, including white vinyl or aliphatic resin (yellow).
- While some projects recommend specific methods of drawer construction, feel free to use whatever method you are most comfortable with. Remember to leave a 1/8" gap between the drawer and the frame to allow for expansion of the wood.
- The term *stiles* refers to vertical members; the term *rails* refers to horizontal members.
- Most of the projects do not discuss finishing. For information on this subject, see the special finishing section that begins on page 332.

Section I
Tables and Desks

Because few other items of furniture can so quickly change the entire feel of a room, and because they are so practical, tables and desks are among the most popular building projects. The variety of designs shown here is sure to suit whatever country look you aim for, from Shaker simplicity to a more contemporary look.

In each project, actual finished dimensions are given, but feel free to explore variations that might be more suitable to your taste. Similarly, even though particular wood types are noted in some projects, the choice of wood type must finally depend on your preference and local availability. Since your work is going to bear the marks of your efforts anyway, don't be afraid to shape the projects to your own liking.

Shaker Trestle Dining Table

 haker purity in furniture design was being developed at the same time the outside world was embracing Victorian styles. In mid-19th century, Mother Ann, leader of the Shaker movement, directed her craftsmen to simplify their furniture designs. Functionality was to be its own beauty.

Shaker designs inspired modern furniture makers throughout the Western world. While the Shaker religious sect has virtually disappeared, their furniture has grown more popular.

This trestle table design appeared in many Shaker communities. The table is at once

MATERIALS LIST

Wood screws
1/4″-dia. dowels
120-grit sandpaper
Wedges
Wood glue

CUTTING LIST

KEY	PIECES	SIZE AND DESCRIPTION
A	4	1-1/16 × 7-13/16 × 73 top
B	1	1-1/16 × 7-1/2 × 52-1/8 stretcher
C	2	1-1/16 × 2 × 8-1/2 end pieces
D	2	2-5/8 × 2-5/8 × 27 uprights
E	2	2-5/8 × 2-5/8 × 26-5/8 feet
F	2	2 × 2-5/8 × 25-5/8 supports
G	1	3/4 × 3-1/2 × 25 center crosspiece

elegant in its simplicity, functional in its design, appropriate in its material, and straightforward in its construction.

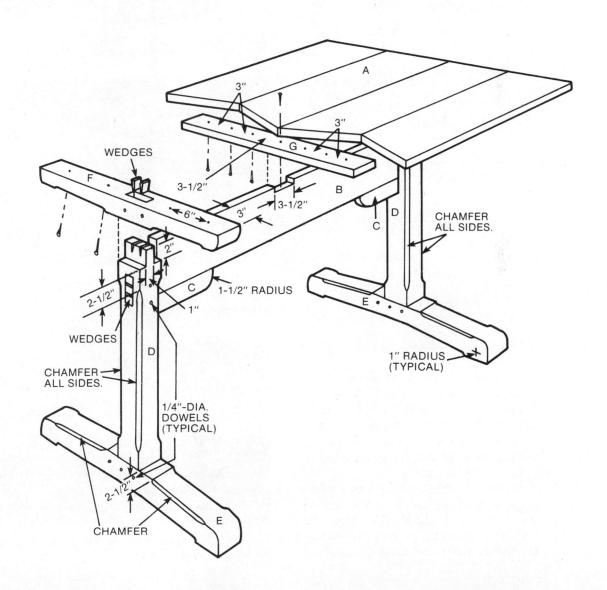

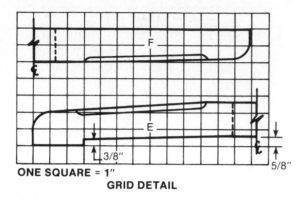

ONE SQUARE = 1"
GRID DETAIL

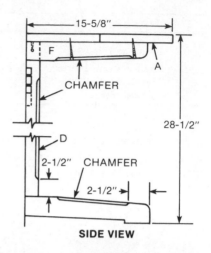

CHAMFER

CHAMFER

SIDE VIEW

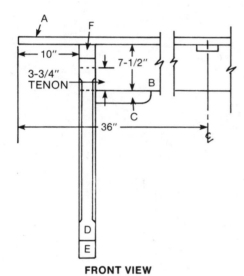

FRONT VIEW

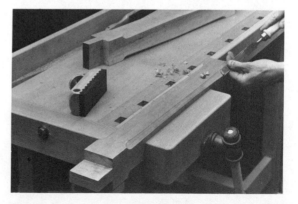

A backsaw is ideal for cutting tenons in the uprights. Cut the tenons at a slight taper (1/16") to accommodate the wedges.

The 3/8" stopped chamfers in the uprights can be cut with a wood chisel.

The Shakers used cherry or maple for the trestle. While a pine trestle would shave costs, their joinery design requires a hard wood. Otherwise the joints will eventually enlarge and make the trestle wobbly. Cherry was popular because of its workability and beauty. If you wish, the top and center stretcher dimensions can be lengthened to accommodate more seating.

Start construction by cutting and surfacing 5/4" pine to 1-1/16" thick for the top (A). Joint the edges to be glued. Then glue and clamp so the top does not bow. When the glue has dried, plane and sand the surface with 120-grit sandpaper. Trim the top to an overall length of 72", then shave the ends smooth with a block plane.

Next, cut and surface the trestle parts to size. Cut tenons in the uprights (D) with a slight taper (1/16") to accommodate the wedges. Cut through mortises in the supports so the tenons will fit tightly.

Round the feet (E) and supports (F) to 1" radius. Cut lower tapers in the foot pieces and save the cutoffs for making the wedges.

Cut 3/8" stopped chamfers in the uprights, feet, and supports with a wood chisel or spokeshave. Cut the stretcher (B) to size, then cut tenons as shown. Mortise each of the uprights to accommodate the tenons.

Cut a 1-1/2" radius on the two end pieces (C) and glue them onto the stretcher. Cut a notch in the stretcher for the center crosspiece (G).

Dry-assemble the trestle for fit. Glue a foot, upright, and support together, making certain the assembly is square. Apply glue and drive in the wedges. Cut off the wedge ends flush. Assemble the other side similarly.

Dry-assemble the stretcher to the two legs. When satisfied with the fit, apply glue to the mortise and wedges. Assemble and clamp. Check the trestle for squareness.

When the glue has dried, bore 1/4"-diameter holes in the uprights and feet for dowels. Insert the dowels with glue. Sand the entire trestle with 120-grit paper. Don't round the chamfered edges.

Screw the center crosspiece to the trestle. Flip the top upside down and set the trestle in place. Mark and bore 3/16" holes in the center crosspiece and 7/64" pilot holes in the top for wood screws. Screw the trestle to the top as shown.

Trestle End Table

Tenon the ends of the bottom stretcher (E) to fit the leg slots. Cut a through mortise in each end of the bottom stretcher to receive a wedge, as shown in the illustration. Next, cut wedges to fit the mortise; the wedges should be tapered slightly thick on their upper end to ensure a solid assembly.

Assemble the legs and stretchers, gluing all joints. Glue the top to the upper edge of the legs and the top stretcher (F). Further secure it in place by driving wood screws through the stretcher as shown in the illustration.

Plug all screw head holes with wood filler and sand smooth. If desired, age and wear can be simulated by adding nicks and abrasions.

MATERIALS LIST

3/4"-dia. dowels
Wood screws
Wood filler
Wood glue

This attractive, easily-made country trestle end table consists of only thirteen parts. Although pine was used in this example, cherry, birch, or maple may be substituted.

Boards for the top (A) are doweled and edge-glued to form a single piece from which an oval is cut. The molded edge is finished with a router or shaper.

Each leg (B) is made from two pieces of stock with the butt joint running vertically on the leg centerline. Before doweling and edge-gluing the leg halves, cut the heart shapes and notches for the stretcher joints. Attach the top and bottom leg members (C, D) with wood screws and glue.

CUTTING LIST

KEY	PIECES	SIZE AND DESCRIPTION
A	3	1-1/8 × 12 × 36 top
B	4	1-1/8 × 6-1/2 × 23 legs
C	2	1-1/2 × 2-1/2 × 21 bottom leg members
D	2	1-1/2 × 2-1/2 × 20 top leg members
E	1	1-1/2 × 2-1/2 × 25 bottom stretcher
F	1	1-1/2 × 2-1/2 × 19 top stretcher

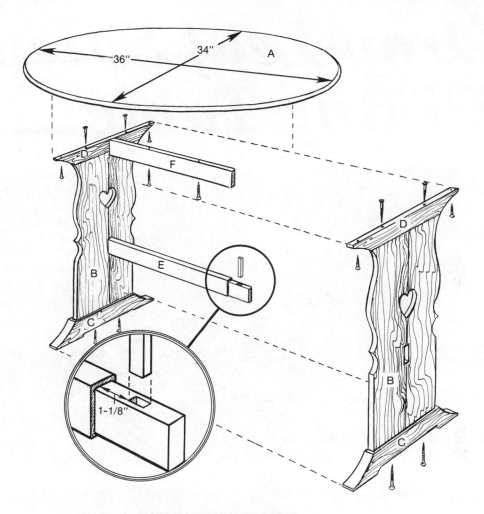

BOTTOM STRETCHER DETAIL

1-1/8"

A

D

F

B

E

C

D

B

C

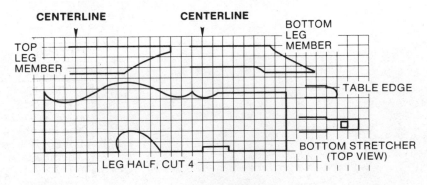

CENTERLINE   CENTERLINE   BOTTOM
LEG
MEMBER

TOP
LEG
MEMBER

TABLE EDGE

BOTTOM STRETCHER
(TOP VIEW)

LEG HALF, CUT 4

ONE SQUARE = 1"   **CUTTING PATTERNS**

Drop-Leaf Salem Dining Table

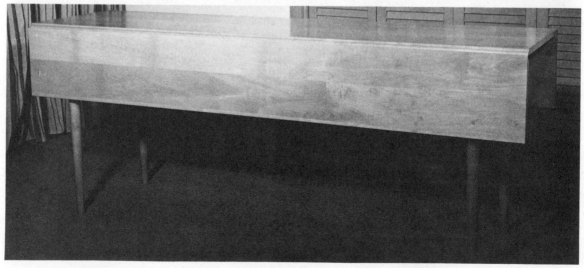

The drop-leaf Salem dining table shown here reaches a width of nearly 40" when the leaves are raised and can accommodate eight people comfortably. Maple, pine, and cherry are all good stock to use to build this table.

To begin, first cut all pieces to size. The side rails (D) must have dadoes cut approximately 8" from each end, as shown in the illustration. Cut these dadoes 1" deep and 1-1/4" wide to accommodate the support slides. Make these cuts before assembling the frame.

Start assembly with the rails (C, D) and legs (E), using mortise-and-tenon joints. Dry-fit the tenons into the mortises, then drill two 1/4"-diameter holes completely through both to accommodate the dowels. Now take

MATERIALS LIST

No. 10 × 2" wood screws
No. 10 × 1-1/4" wood screws
No. 8 × 1/2" wood screws
3/8"-dia. × 1-1/4" dowels
1/4"-dia. × 1-3/8" dowels
Butt hinges (6)
Wood glue

CUTTING LIST

KEY	PIECES	SIZE AND DESCRIPTION
A	1	3/4 × 19 × 72 top
B	2	3/4 × 10-1/8 × 72 leaves
C	2	3/4 × 6-1/8 × 14-1/4 end rails
D	2	3/4 × 6-1/8 × 57-1/2 side rails
E	4	1-3/4 × 1-3/4 × 28-1/4 legs
F	4	1 × 1-1/4 × 16-1/2 support slides
G	2	1 × 2 × 5-1/2 guides

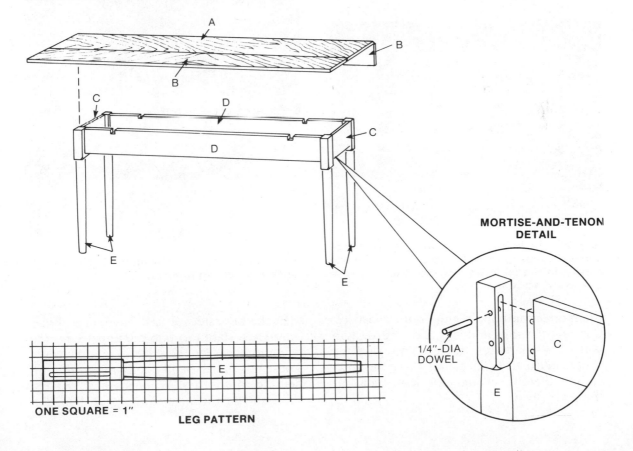

MORTISE-AND-TENON DETAIL

1/4"-DIA. DOWEL

ONE SQUARE = 1"

LEG PATTERN

Support slides and guides are held in position while pilot holes are marked carefully.

With the frame-and-leg assembly centered over the underside of the table, a pencil or nail is used to mark the location for drilling pilot holes to join the two table pieces.

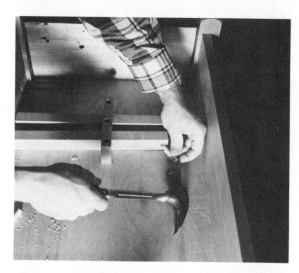

When the guides are fastened, the 3/8"-diameter dowels are driven in place.

After all pilot holes have been drilled, the frame-and-leg assembly is again centered over the underside of the table and fastened with No. 10 × 1/4" wood screws.

them apart and apply glue to the mortises. Connect the rails and legs and secure them with 1/4"-diameter dowels and glue, as shown in the detail drawing. Drive the dowels completely through the legs, then cut them off flush.

Each of the sides should have screw holes bored at a slant through the upper edges to accommodate No. 10 × 1-1/4" wood screws. These edges will be in contact with the underside of the top. When assembling the sides and legs, it is very important that all of these edges with holes face upward. Also, be sure that all of these screw holes face inward.

Because of the size of the table, it is suggested that any sanding, staining, and finishing be done at this point; a good water-resistant varnish is recommended. Do not resume construction until the finish has dried completely.

Attach the leaves (B) to the top (A) using three butt hinges for each leaf. The holes in the hinges should line up with the predrilled pilot holes in the undersides of the leaves and top. Use No. 8 × 1/2" wood screws and be sure to attach the long side of each hinge to the leaves.

Place the assembled top and leaves face-down on the floor. Now place the frame-and-leg assembly exactly in the center of the underside of the table. Insert a pencil or nail in the holes of the rails, and mark the underside of the table for pilot holes. Drill holes not more than 1/2" deep at the same angle as those in the rails. Do not drive screws without pilot holes into the bottom of the top because this may cause it to split. To achieve the proper angle, use a 1/8" drill bit, which is longer than usual for this size. The rails are then fastened with No. 10 × 1-1/4" wood screws.

The final job is the installation of the support slides (F), which hold up the leaves, and their guides (G). There are two support slides under each leaf; insert them in the holes in the rails. The guides have three holes in them and two notches cut to fit the slides. Cut these notches 1" from each end of the guides. The guides are placed equidistant from the side rails with their notches or dadoes over the support slides.

Mark spots on the underside of the table through the holes in the guides. Drill pilot holes at these spots no deeper than 1/2". Attach the two guides with No. 10 × 2" wood screws. Now glue and insert 3/8"-diameter dowels in the sides of the support slides, about 1/2" from the end as shown in the photo. Make certain that these dowels face away from each other; they will prevent the slides from pulling out completely.

Harvest Table ___

There is nothing unusual in the construction of the harvest table, a beautiful country piece that is equally useful and appropriate in the 20th century. The top and frame are made of 3/4″ stock. Boards are doweled and edge-glued together to meet the 24″ width requirement of the top (A) and the 16″ width of the leaves (B).

Glue and nail the frame pieces together, lapping the side rails (D) over the end rails (E) as shown. Glue the corner braces (F) into place. Make the cutouts for the leaf supports (G) and attach these supports with 3/8″-diameter dowels. The dowels should be at least 3″ long to extend all the way through the supports and into the frame. Drill the holes in the supports slightly larger than the holes in the frame so that the supports can

MATERIALS LIST

3/8″-dia. dowels
Strap hinges (4)
Finishing nails
Lag screws
Wood glue

CUTTING LIST		
KEY	**PIECES**	**SIZE AND DESCRIPTION**
A	1	3/4 × 24 × 72 top
B	2	3/4 × 16 × 72 leaves
C	4	3 × 3 × 29 legs
D	2	3/4 × 5 × 48 side rails
E	2	3/4 × 5 × 16-1/2 end rails
F	4	3/4 × 5 × 11-1/2 corner braces (beveled and cut to fit)
G	2	3/4 × 2 × 20 leaf supports

pivot freely. (For best results, use a drill press to make these holes.)

The legs are turned, according to the pattern, then glued to the corners of the frame, and secured by lag screws set through the corner braces. Butt joints are used between the top and leaves. Fasten the leaves to the top with strap hinges. Center the top on the frame; then glue it in place. Be careful not to get any glue on the leaf supports.

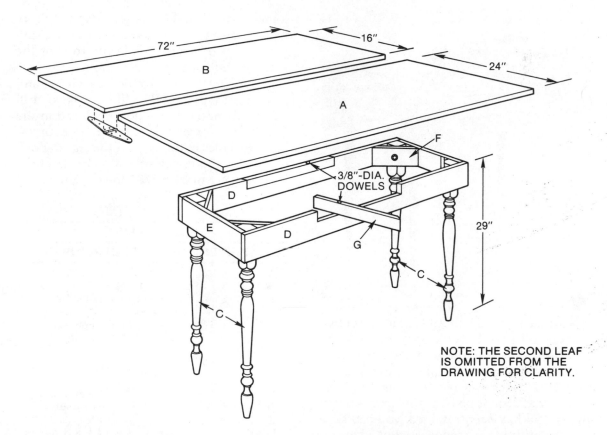

NOTE: THE SECOND LEAF IS OMITTED FROM THE DRAWING FOR CLARITY.

ONE SQUARE = 1"

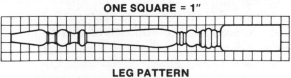

LEG PATTERN

Drop-Leaf Table

sides, end piece, and side support. The dadoes are cut 3/8" in from the corners of the legs, and all of the cuts are 3/8" wide and 1/2" deep for the full width of the piece to be joined to the leg. If the original type of drop-leaf supports is to be used, cut out the supports with beveled ends in the tops of the sides as shown in the illustration.

Assemble the sides to the legs, gluing and clamping them until the glue sets. Next, drill a 3/8"-diameter dowel hole centered in the ends of the lower side support, and corresponding holes in the sides of the legs dadoed to receive the upper side support. Drill the leg holes on a mark 5-5/8" down from the top

The original of this cherry drop-leaf table was built about 1825 in one of two Hancock, Massachusetts, Shaker communities considered by many to have produced the finest furniture of that style. It can be built easily, following the drawings. The original method for supporting the leaves when they're up has been retained; you can save time using modern hardware—but what you gain in time you lose in authenticity.

Cut the stock to the dimensions given in the cutting list. Cut and shape the legs (B) according to the detail provided. Each of the leg tops is dadoed on two adjoining sides to accept the sides (A), end piece (D), and one side support (C). Rabbet the ends of the

CUTTING LIST		
KEY	**PIECES**	**SIZE AND DESCRIPTION**
A	2	3/4 × 6 × 29-1/2 sides
B	4	1-3/4 × 1-3/4 × 27-1/4 legs
C	2	3/4 × 3/4 × 14-1/4 side supports
D	1	3/4 × 6 × 14-1/4 end piece
E	1	3/4 × 6 × 15-1/4 center support
F	2	3/4 × 2 × 4 center support cleats
G	2	3/4 × 1-1/2 × 11 leaf supports
H	1	3/4 × 16-3/4 × 41 tabletop
I	2	3/4 × 9-3/4 × 41 leaves
J1	1	3/4 × 4-3/8 × 14-1/8 drawer front
J2	2	3/4 × 4-3/8 × 14 drawer sides
J3	1	3/4 × 4-3/8 × 12-5/8 drawer back
J4	1	3/4 × 12-5/8 × 13-1/4 drawer bottom
K	2	3/4 × 3/4 × 15 drawer runners

of the leg and 3/8" in from the outside edge of the leg. Then glue and clamp the end piece and side supports to the legs, and nail and glue the center support cleats (F) to the sides. Attach the center support (E) to the cleats with glue. Cut 1/4" × 1/2" notches in one end of both drawer runners (K) and attach them to the legs and cleats with wood screws 3"

down from the tops of the legs. Make sure they are level.

Attach the leaf supports (G) to the sides. If the original style of supports is being used, attach them to the sides with dowel pins at the pivot point indicated in the illustration.

Rout the joining edges of the tabletop (H) and the leaves (I), and hinge them together as shown. Glue and clamp the tabletop to the assembled frame.

Cut a 1/2" × 1/2" groove in the drawer sides (J2) to correspond with the drawer runners.

Assemble the drawer pieces with nailed butt joints. The drawer front is notched as shown so that the sides and nails will not be exposed to view.

MATERIALS LIST

3/8"-dia. dowels
Drawer pull
Drawer hardware
Hinges
Finishing nails
Wood screws
Wood glue

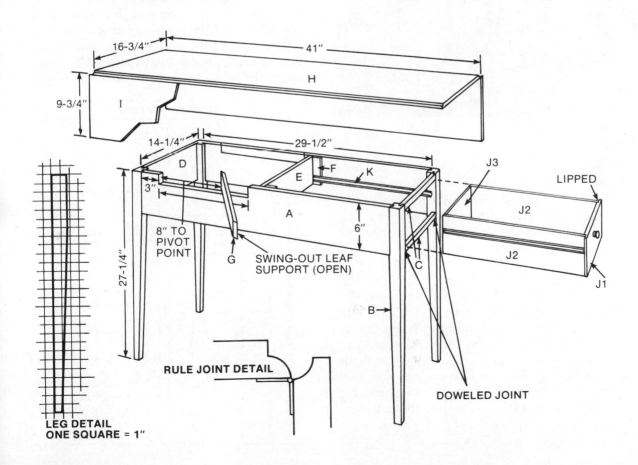

LEG DETAIL
ONE SQUARE = 1"

RULE JOINT DETAIL

DOWELED JOINT

SWING-OUT LEAF SUPPORT (OPEN)

8" TO PIVOT POINT

Drop-Leaf End Table

top (a good guide would be to begin the taper for all six at the notch of the swing-out legs, as suggested by the sketch).

The framing on the long sides of the table consists of full-length inner rails (A) joined to the corner legs with 1/2"-diameter dowels, half-length outer rails (B) and their hinged extensions (C), and drawer runners (D). The double-thickness sides (each 3/4") fit flush with the leg tops. The end (M) is nailed in place between the back legs as shown.

The two swing-out legs, as noted, are notched. Simply cut away half the thickness for a distance that equals the width of the

For an occasional table with country character, this drop-leaf end table meets both decorative and functional needs. When the table is folded compactly against the wall with the swing-out legs tucked in, usable table surface is a very slim 8" × 14". Fully expanded, the two leaves (F) increase the area to a lavish 32" spread. There's nothing, however, to prevent you from making a dimensional change here or there to suit your preference, because the design allows modifications at no expense to appearance.

Cherry or a clear maple are ideal stock for this project. Whatever you select, plan a table height that will serve your exact need; for example, on a level with the couch. And regardless of the height, allow for six legs (L), which taper to 7/8", beginning 4" from the

MATERIALS LIST

Porcelain knob
1/2"-dia. dowels
Finishing nails
Butt hinges (8)
Wood glue

CUTTING LIST

KEY	PIECES	SIZE AND DESCRIPTION
A	2	3/4 × 2-1/2 × 11 inner rails
B	2	3/4 × 2-1/2 × 5-1/2 outer rails
C	2	3/4 × 2 × 3-1/2 extensions
D	2	1/2 × 1/2 × 9 drawer runners
E	1	1-1/8 × 8 × 14 top
F	2	1-1/8 × 12 × 14 leaves
G	2	1/2 × 3/4 × 1 stops
H	2	1/2 × 2-1/2 × 4 drawer front and back
I	2	1/2 × 2-1/2 × 10 drawer sides
J	1	1/2 × 4 × 10 drawer bottom
K	2	1/2 × 2 × 4 drawer supports
L	6	1-1/2 × 1-1/2 × 24 legs
M	1	3/4 × 3-1/2 × 4-1/4 end

full-length rail. Joined to the hinged extensions with 1/2"-diameter dowels, the swing-out legs should fit snugly in place, their notched portions tucked under the full-length rails. In swing-out position, the extensions are halted at 90° by stops, which can be made from scrap.

After assembling all of the rails with wood glue and finishing nails, prepare the top (E) by routing the hinged edges with the classic cove-and-bead typical of the drop-leaf table. The top is simply glued and nailed to the frame.

Butt joints are used to construct the drawer; the height and width are a good 1/16" less, all around, to assure free movement. Attach the porcelain knob; then stain the table as desired.

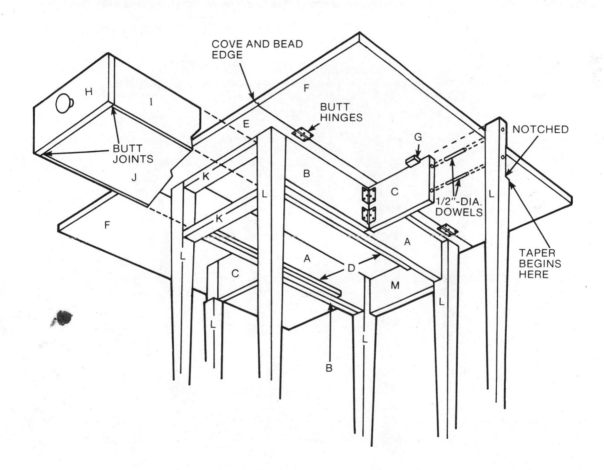

Queen Anne Occasional Table

The design of this table was taken from an 18th century antique masterpiece that comfortably adapts itself to any country decor. Rich walnut stock adds to the table's distinctive look.

Compound cuts on a bandsaw or jigsaw produce the cabriole legs (A). First, make a template by drawing a full-size outline of the leg on a piece of cardboard. Trace the leg pattern on adjacent sides of the stock, mak-

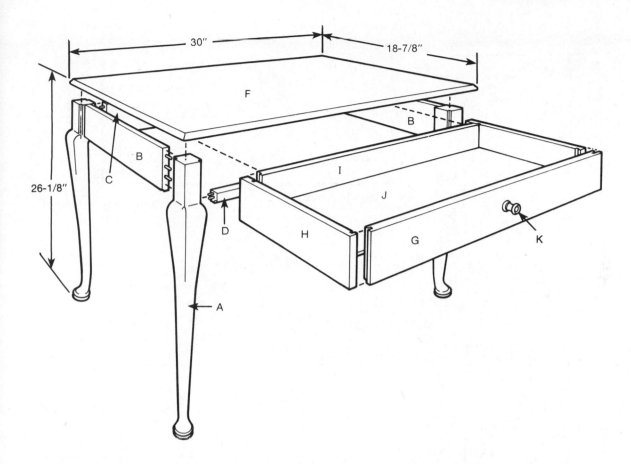

ing sure that the template is turned in the opposite direction when moved from one side to the other, as shown in the drawing.

On the bandsaw or jigsaw, make the cuts on one of the marked sides. Next, tack or tape the cutaway pieces back in their original position; this is done to provide a flat surface necessary for guiding the piece through the saw a second time. If tacks are

MATERIALS LIST

3/8"-dia. × 1-3/4" dowels
5/16"-dia. × 1-3/4" dowels
No. 7 × 1-1/2" wood screws
No. 7 × 1-1/4" wood screws
Masking tape or tacks
Wood glue

CUTTING LIST		
KEY	**PIECES**	**SIZE AND DESCRIPTION**
A	4	2-1/4 × 2-1/4 × 25-3/8 legs
B	2	3/4 × 5-1/4 × 14-7/8 side rails
C	1	3/4 × 5-1/4 × 19-3/8 back rail
D	1	3/4 × 1-1/4 × 19-3/8 front rail
E	2	3/4 × 1-3/8 × 14-3/4 drawer runners
F	1	3/4 × 18-7/8 × 30 top
G	1	3/4 × 4 × 19-3/8 drawer front
H	2	1/2 × 4 × 16 drawer sides
I	1	1/2 × 3-1/2 × 19 drawer back
J	1	1/4 × 19 × 15-5/8 drawer bottom
K	1	1-1/8 × 1-1/8 × 3-1/8 drawer handle
L	1	3/16 × 1/4 × 1 drawer handle pin

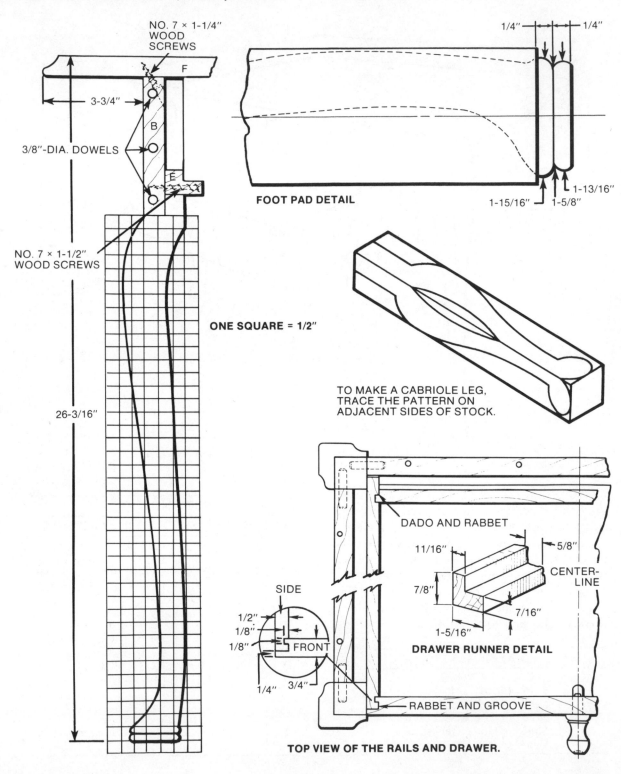

NO. 7 × 1-1/4" WOOD SCREWS

F

3-3/4"

B

3/8"-DIA. DOWELS

E

NO. 7 × 1-1/2" WOOD SCREWS

26-3/16"

ONE SQUARE = 1/2"

FOOT PAD DETAIL

1/4"   1/4"

1-13/16"

1-15/16"   1-5/8"

TO MAKE A CABRIOLE LEG, TRACE THE PATTERN ON ADJACENT SIDES OF STOCK.

DADO AND RABBET

11/16"   5/8"

7/8"

CENTER-LINE

1-5/16"   7/16"

DRAWER RUNNER DETAIL

SIDE

1/2"
1/8"
1/8"

FRONT

1/4"   3/4"

RABBET AND GROOVE

TOP VIEW OF THE RAILS AND DRAWER.

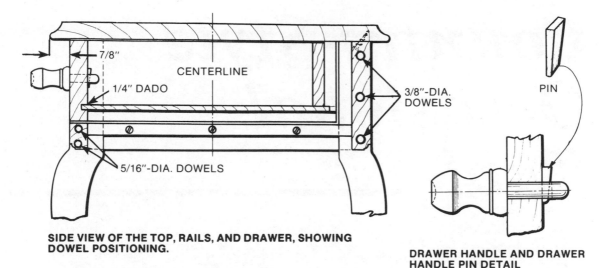

SIDE VIEW OF THE TOP, RAILS, AND DRAWER, SHOWING DOWEL POSITIONING.

7/8"

CENTERLINE

1/4" DADO

5/16"-DIA. DOWELS

3/8"-DIA. DOWELS

PIN

DRAWER HANDLE AND DRAWER HANDLE PIN DETAIL

used, be sure to place them where the saw blade will not come in contact with them or else the blade can be ruined. Then flip the stock so that the adjacent marked side is facing up, and make the cuts.

The remainder of the work on the legs can be done with a chisel or spokeshave while holding the leg in a vise. The only exception is the upper portion of the foot pad, which can be sanded with a sanding drum on a drill press.

For the dowel joints required to hold the legs to the rails, bore dowel holes in the top of the legs on a drill press, using a 3/8" bit. Eighteen 3/8"-diameter dowel holes must be drilled altogether, three for each joint, between a side or back rail and leg. The front rail (D) takes two 5/16"-diameter dowels at each end; the front legs must be drilled accordingly.

After boring all of the dowel holes in the side (B), back (C), and front rails, shape the bottom edge of the rails using a router. Counterbore three pocket holes in the side and back rails for fastening the top to the rails. The holes for the No. 7 × 1-1/4" wood screws are made with a 9/64" drill bit. After the top (F) has been cut to size, it is molded with a router.

The drawer runners (E) are made as shown in the drawings. They are then counterbored and fastened to the side rails with No. 7 × 1-1/2" wood screws. The drawers are made with a rabbet and groove joint at the front (G) as shown. The back (I) and sides (H) are joined with dado and rabbet joints. The bottom (J) is set and glued into 1/4" dadoes in the front and sides. In keeping with the style of the furniture, a turned drawer handle (K) should be made and held in place with a tapered pin (L) as shown.

For a mellow finish, brown mahogany stain is recommended. This should be followed by one or two coats of tung oil.

Country-Style Occasional Table

Magnificent curly and bird's-eye maple was used to construct this table. The dimensions of the piece allow the use of solid stock throughout.

The top (F) is made from two pieces of stock doweled and edge-glued together. It is fastened to the frame with wood screws and glue.

The legs (A) are turned according to the pattern shown, then attached to the sides (B) with mortise-and-tenon joints and glue. The end braces (C1) are attached with similar mortises and tenons. In the original, the legs and sides were pegged together, with the pegs going through the tenons. You can retain this feature, but the version shown here is simpler: just drill 1/4"-diameter holes approximately 1/4" deep into the legs; then plug with short pieces of dowel to simulate pegging. Fasten the drawer runners (E) to the drawer runner guides (D) with wood screws. Glue the center brace (C2) to the tops of the guides and to the sides. The drawers are made with a rabbet-and-groove joint at the fronts (G). The backs (H) and sides (I) are joined by dovetailing. The bottoms (J) are set and glued into 1/4" dadoes in the fronts and sides.

CUTTING LIST

KEY	PIECES	SIZE AND DESCRIPTION
A	4	1-3/4 × 1-3/4 × 26 legs
B	2	3/4 × 5-1/2 × 21-1/2 sides
C1	4	3/4 × 3/4 × 11 end braces
C2	1	3/4 × 3/4 × 10 center brace
D	2	3/4 × 3/4 × 4-1/2 drawer runner guides
E	2	1/4 × 1/4 × 23-1/2 drawer runners
F	2	3/4 × 9-1/4 × 34 top
G	2	3/4 × 3-3/4 × 10 drawer fronts
H	2	1/2 × 3-3/4 × 8-1/2 drawer backs
I	4	1/2 × 3-3/4 × 10-3/4 drawer sides
J	2	1/2 × 9-1/2 × 10-1/2 drawer bottoms

MATERIALS LIST

1/4"-dia. dowels
Wood screws
Drawer pulls
Wood glue

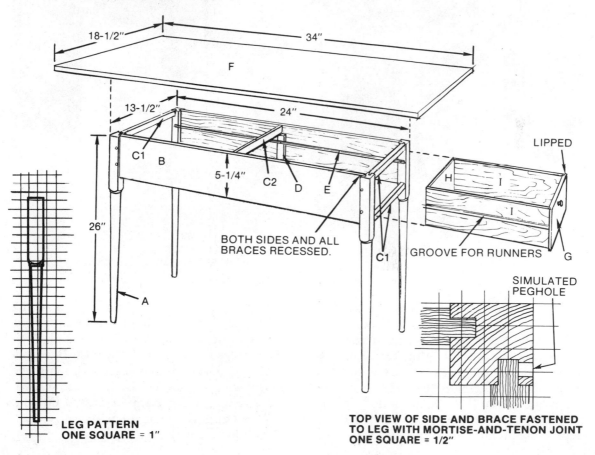

BOTH SIDES AND ALL BRACES RECESSED.

LIPPED

GROOVE FOR RUNNERS

SIMULATED PEGHOLE

**LEG PATTERN
ONE SQUARE = 1"**

**TOP VIEW OF SIDE AND BRACE FASTENED TO LEG WITH MORTISE-AND-TENON JOINT
ONE SQUARE = 1/2"**

Rugged Cocktail Table

The simple design of this rugged cocktail table highlights the natural wood grain, making the piece perfect for living room or den. Use 2 × 4 and 2 × 8 lumber; a less expensive grade will best capture the interesting grain patterns. Note that the screw plugs are made from 1/2"-diameter dowels and may protrude slightly or be sanded flush, depending on individual preference.

Begin construction by cutting all of the pieces to size according to the dimensions found in the Cutting List. Countersink 1/4"-deep holes in the leg members (A, B) with a 1/2" bit. Assemble the legs by joining the members with glue and 2-1/2" wood screws. Square up the three top pieces (C, D) with braces (E) and fasten them securely from the underside with screws.

Next, attach the two apron pieces (F) to both sides of the tabletop. Carefully square up and secure the legs to the tabletop with screws; then cut the screw plugs from 1/2"-diameter dowels and tap them into the screw holes. Finally, sand down the table and finish as desired.

MATERIALS LIST

2-1/2" wood screws
1/2"-dia. dowels
Wood glue

CUTTING LIST

KEY	PIECES	SIZE AND DESCRIPTION
A	4	1-1/2 × 7-1/4 × 14-3/4 leg members
B	4	1-1/2 × 3-1/2 × 14-3/4 leg members
C	2	1-1/2 × 7-1/2 × 41 top
D	1	1-1/2 × 3-1/2 × 41 top
E	2	1-1/2 × 3-1/2 × 18 braces
F	2	1-1/2 × 3-1/2 × 41 apron pieces

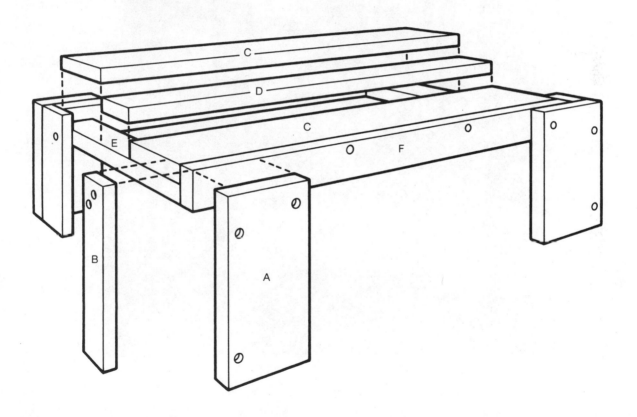

Console Table _____

The sturdy, simple utilitarianism of this table identifies it as Pennsylvania Dutch in origin. Its graceful proportions and well-turned legs suggest that its creator was influenced by the work of some of the re-nowned furniture designers of the late 18th century.

To reproduce this piece, first, dowel and edge-glue white pine boards together for the top (C, D). Clamp until dry; then cut out the semicircular top. As another option, you may simply use a single sheet of 3/4" plywood for the top.

The legs (A) are turned of maple according to the pattern shown.

A 3/4" × 3/4" support frame is composed of two vertical members (E) and one upper horizontal member (F). It is attached to both pine rails (B) with glue and wood screws.

The rails and frames are then centered on the sides of the legs and secured by driving wood screws through the vertical frame members into the legs. The entire bottom assembly is then fastened to the top by driving wood screws through the horizontal frame members into the top.

MATERIALS LIST

3/8"-dia. dowels
Wood screws
Wood glue

CUTTING LIST

KEY	PIECES	SIZE AND DESCRIPTION
A	3	2 × 2 × 28 legs
B	2	3/4 × 5-1/2 × 16 rails
C	2	3/4 × 5-1/2 × 34 top
D	1	3/4 × 7-1/4 × 34 top
E	4	3/4 × 3/4 × 5-1/2 support frame, vertical members
F	2	3/4 × 3/4 × 14-1/2 support frame, horizontal members

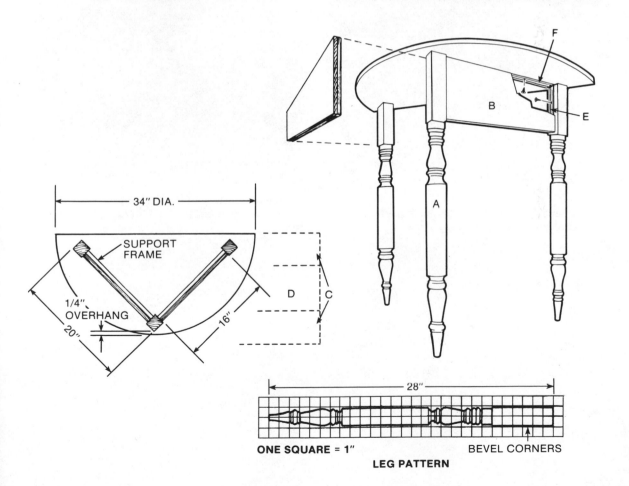

34" DIA.

SUPPORT FRAME

1/4" OVERHANG

20"

16"

D   C

28"

ONE SQUARE = 1"   BEVEL CORNERS

LEG PATTERN

A doweling jig is used to drill the 3/8"-diameter dowel holes in the top boards.

Secure the frame assembly by driving screws through the vertical members into the legs.

Fasten the bottom of the table to the top by driving screws through the horizontal members into the top.

Victorian End Table

This end table is a reproduction of the one President Lincoln's children used as a play table. It has a pine top supported with cherry legs and stretcher.

In the mid-Victorian period, children did their schoolwork on tables such as this. Because the top and stretcher took abuse from pencils and spilled ink, a pine top was a logical choice because it could be replaced easily and inexpensively when badly marred.

This simple table serves nicely as an end table and accent piece in the home.

To begin, make a 1/8″ hardboard template of the leg design. Because the leg is symmetrical, you need only half of the pattern. Lay the template on four pieces of cherry stock to make sure you have enough width from which to cut out the full design. Cut the stock about 1″ longer than required. Joint the edges to be glued; then bore 1/4″-diameter holes for inserting the dowels (see diagram for the approximate locations).

Stack and nail together the four pieces of cherry in the waste areas, then lay out and cut the pattern. After sanding, separate the boards and cut to the proper length. Dowel both sets of legs. Edge-glue and clamp the half-patterns together.

Next, cut out the top pieces (A, B) and stretcher (C). Dowel and edge-glue the top in the same fashion as the legs (D); then clamp snugly and allow to dry overnight. Round the edges of the top and stretcher.

Cut the small battens (F) from scrap obtained from the stretcher before planing it to 3/8″. Cut the large battens (E) to size.

Cut pine and cherry plugs from scraps. Carefully mark and bore plug holes where indicated in the diagram. Next, bore 3/32″-diameter pilot holes through the stretcher and into the small battens. Attach the stretcher to the battens with glue and wood screws. Cover the holes with cherry plugs.

Mark the stretcher position on both legs. Bore 3/32″-diameter pilot holes in the battens and legs. Fasten the stretcher to the legs with wood screws; then cover the plug holes.

Bore pilot holes through the top into the large battens and mount with wood screws and glue. Place the top with the mounted battens onto the legs. Attach with wood screws and glue. Plug all the holes with wood plugs.

CUTTING LIST		
KEY	**PIECES**	**SIZE AND DESCRIPTION**
A	1	1/2 × 7-3/8 × 23-9/16 top
B	1	1/2 × 8-1/8 × 23-9/16 top
C	1	3/8 × 8 × 19-1/2 stretcher
D	4	5/8 × 6-1/2 × 22-3/4 legs
E	2	7/8 × 1 × 12-3/4 large battens
F	2	1/2 × 3/4 × 8 small battens

MATERIALS LIST

1/4″-dia. dowels
Pine and cherry plugs
Wood screws
Wood glue

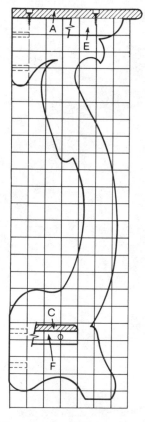

ONE SQUARE = 1″

LEG PATTERN

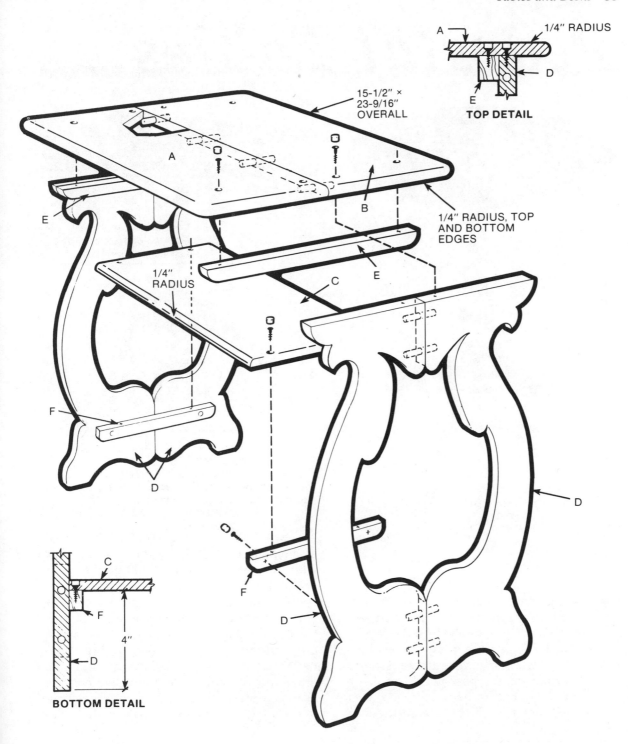

1/4" RADIUS

A

D

E

TOP DETAIL

15-1/2" ×
23-9/16"
OVERALL

A

B

E

1/4" RADIUS, TOP
AND BOTTOM
EDGES

1/4"
RADIUS

C

E

F

D

D

C

F

D

4"

BOTTOM DETAIL

F

D

Pedestal Tables

If you prefer, it is possible to install a rectangular top in the same manner as the round top. The example shown here measures 18″ × 21″.

This handsome cherry pedestal table is a classic expression of the Shaker philosophy of design. Completely devoid of ornamentation, its beauty is entirely the result of its truly utilitarian form. The graceful shape of the turned center post is the result of trimming away excess material where it is not needed for strength; the elegant, tapered curve of the legs provides the most material at the point of the greatest stress—the joint with the center post—and follows the grain of the wood for maximum strength.

From the modern woodworker's point of view, the most difficult part of this project is the dovetailed leg joints. While they can be cut with a router or hand tools by those who have the patience and skill required, simple glued mortise-and-tenon joints will provide adequate strength. However, for those willing to tackle it, the dovetail provides solid construction. Details for both methods are shown, with the easier mortise-and-tenon joint described in greater detail.

To build this table, first, edge-glue the two boards for the top (B). From this piece, cut an 18″-diameter circle; round the edge of the top to the contour of the template as shown.

Cut a cleat (C) as shown in the drawing. Next, make a full-sized turning template for the center post (A), using the squares method. Turn and sand the center post with its bottom end positioned at the right end of the lathe.

Build the mortising jig with finishing nails and glue as shown in the illustration. Be sure to brace both ends to ensure rigidity and strength. Also, if the lathe you're working with has an 11″ swing, reduce the height of the jig to 7-1/4″. Next, rout three 3/8″-wide mortises 9/16″ deep in the center post. To avoid damaging the router, start it on a shallow setting and cut the mortises in stages.

Lay out the pattern for each leg as shown in the detail drawing. Cut a tenon in the end of each leg that fits the mortise in the center post. Make the tenon slightly shorter than the mortise to allow for gluing, as indicated in the detail drawing.

Cut out one of the legs with the pattern drawn on it; then use this leg as a pattern for the other two. (The three legs may also be stacked and cut at one time with a bandsaw.) Sand the legs with 120-grit sandpaper.

Finally, assemble the table. Attach the cleat to the top, across the grain, with wood screws and glue for maximum strength.

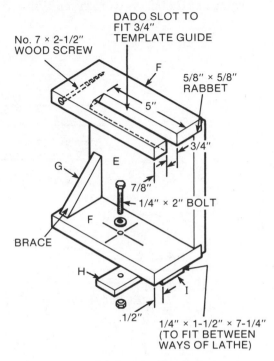

Jig for routing mortises in the center post.

MATERIALS LIST

No. 10 × 1-1/4″ wood screws
No. 7 × 2-1/2″ wood screw
1/4″ × 2″ bolt, washer, and nut
120-grit sandpaper
Finishing nails
Wood glue

CUTTING LIST

KEY	PIECES	SIZE AND DESCRIPTION
A	1	3 × 3 × 18 center post
B	2	3/4 × 9 × 18 top
C	1	3/4 × 3-1/2 × 15 cleat
D	3	3/4 × 4 × 14 legs
E	1	3/4 × 7-1/4 × 7-3/4 mortise jig back
F	2	3/4 × 3-3/8 × 7-1/4 mortise jig top and bottom
G	2	3/4 × 3 × 3-1/2 mortise jig braces
H	1	1/2 × 1-1/4 × 2-1/4 mortise support
I	1	1/4 × 1-1/2 × 7-1/4 mortise support

A word about finishing: Most fairly light stains, especially those with distinct reddish or orange tones, can legitimately be used on Shaker reproductions. Darker woods, notably walnut and cherry, were often finished with linseed oil. If you choose to use linseed oil, wait four or five days before applying a second coat. Allow at least 24 hours drying time between subsequent coats.

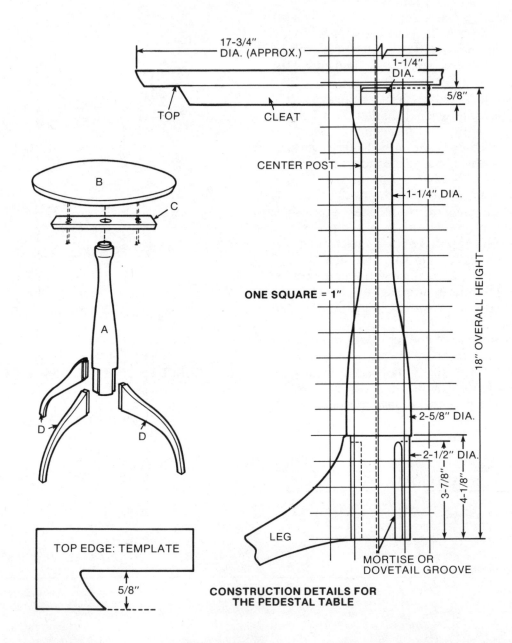

**CONSTRUCTION DETAILS FOR
THE PEDESTAL TABLE**

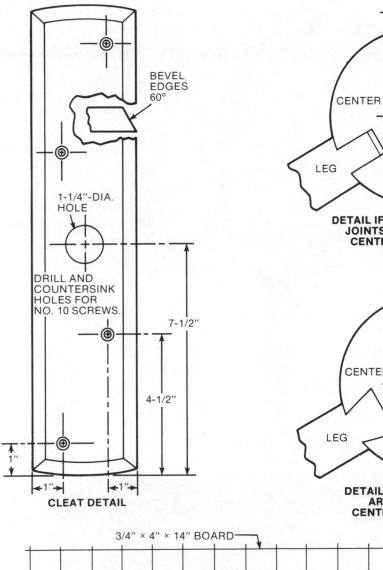

BEVEL
EDGES
60°

1-1/4"-DIA.
HOLE

DRILL AND
COUNTERSINK
HOLES FOR
NO. 10 SCREWS.

7-1/2"

4-1/2"

1"

1" 1"

CLEAT DETAIL

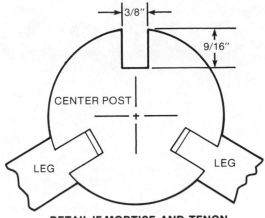

3/8"

9/16"

CENTER POST

LEG

LEG

**DETAIL IF MORTISE-AND-TENON
JOINTS ARE USED FOR THE
CENTER POST AND LEGS.**

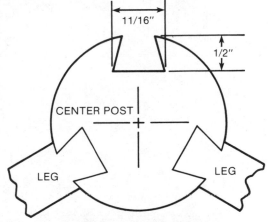

11/16"

1/2"

CENTER POST

LEG

LEG

**DETAIL IF DOVETAIL JOINTS
ARE USED FOR THE
CENTER POST AND LEGS.**

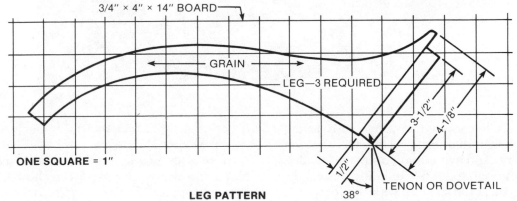

3/4" × 4" × 14" BOARD

GRAIN

LEG—3 REQUIRED

3-1/2"

4-1/8"

1/2"

TENON OR DOVETAIL

38°

ONE SQUARE = 1"

LEG PATTERN

Candle Stand

A candle can give a room a soft elegant charm—if the occasion isn't a power blackout. And even if you don't use candles often enough to justify building this candle stand, you could still find wide use for it as an occasional table that blends in easily with country decor.

Its stick or peg legs and rectangular top make this design unique. Even though the legs are tapered, construction of the candle stand is quite easy. With the exception of the maple top, the entire piece is made from pine.

The top support (C) has a 2"-diameter hole drilled through its center to accommodate the central column (A). The top (D) is joined to the support with wood screws and glue. Then the central column is joined to the top support with glue.

After the three legs (B) are rounded and tapered (a spokeshave is recommended for

this), cut them off at a 45° angle as indicated. The top dotted line shows the angle of the holes in the central column needed to accommodate the legs. After drilling the holes at a 45° angle, attach the legs with glue.

Although the method of finishing is optional, the original piece had a red stain.

MATERIALS LIST

Wood screws
Wood glue

CUTTING LIST

KEY	PIECES	SIZE AND DESCRIPTION
A	1	3 × 3 × 19-3/4 central column
B	3	1 × 1 × 15 legs
C	1	1-1/2 × 5-1/2 × 6 top support
D	1	3/4 × 14-1/2 × 20 top

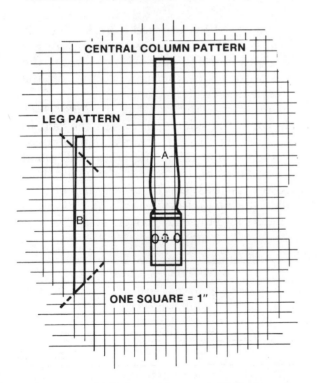

CENTRAL COLUMN PATTERN

LEG PATTERN

ONE SQUARE = 1"

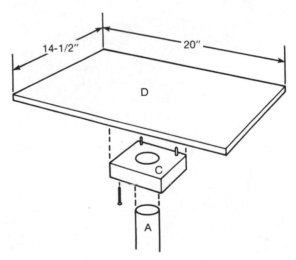

Coffee Table

This coffee table is based on the design of a slicing table, a country kitchen "appliance" of yesteryear. A slicing table enabled the cook to pop a few fresh heads of cabbage into the box and push it back and forth across the blade to produce the makings of a delicious sauerkraut. A bowl placed below an opening at the blade caught the sliced vegetable.

Today, this unusual and clever piece makes a perfect coffee table, with the box serving as a handy compartment for snacks. The plans are for a table faithful in detail to the original, except that the opening at the

slicing blade has been eliminated, and the "blade" is merely a mock reproduction made out of thin steel. The example shown here was made out of pine, although you may want to use a different wood.

Cut the mock blade out of steel. Place it diagonally across the table as shown, and mark its position. Cut a groove of sufficient depth in the top (C) so that the blade is flush with the top. Drill pilot holes in the blade and fasten it to the top with wood screws and glue.

The legs (E) are turned from 2 × 2 stock. Drill 1/2"-diameter holes in the tops of the legs and in the table, as shown. Fasten the legs with dowels and glue, cutting off the dowels flush with the top.

Cut grooves the length of the rails (D) as shown in the side detail. Fasten the rails to the table with wood screws and glue, countersinking and filling the holes with wood plugs. Assemble the box by lapping the sides (A) as shown. Attach runners (B) at each side. Slide the box onto the table by fitting the runners into the rail grooves.

MATERIALS LIST

Thin steel strip
1/2"-dia. dowels
Wood screws
Wood glue

CUTTING LIST

KEY	PIECES	SIZE AND DESCRIPTION
A	4	3/4 × 8 × 12 box sides
B	2	1/2 × 1/2 × 12 runners
C	1	1-1/4 × 13-1/2 × 40 top
D	2	1-1/4 × 3 × 40 rails
E	4	1-1/2 × 1-1/2 × 14-1/2 legs

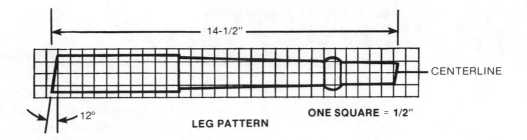

14-1/2"

CENTERLINE

12°

LEG PATTERN

ONE SQUARE = 1/2"

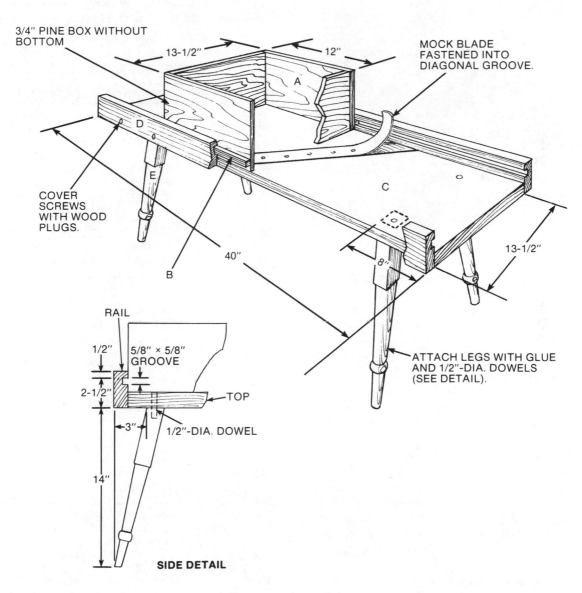

3/4" PINE BOX WITHOUT BOTTOM

13-1/2"

12"

MOCK BLADE FASTENED INTO DIAGONAL GROOVE.

A

D

E

B

COVER SCREWS WITH WOOD PLUGS.

40"

C

8"

13-1/2"

ATTACH LEGS WITH GLUE AND 1/2"-DIA. DOWELS (SEE DETAIL).

RAIL

1/2"

5/8" × 5/8" GROOVE

2-1/2"

TOP

3"

1/2"-DIA. DOWEL

14"

SIDE DETAIL

Sewing Table

frame with nails and glue. Quarter-round strips, fastened with brads and glue, are used to anchor the plywood to the legs.

The back is constructed like the sides with three rails. There are four triangular wooden

This combined chest of drawers and sewing table has the simple charm characteristic of Shaker furniture, along with its functional utility.

The top (H) is made up of three random-width solid planks, edged-glued together at the edges to form a 20″ width, and is nailed and glued to the frame. The framework is made up of 1 × 2s (B, C, D, E), which are joined to the legs (A) with shallow glued mortise-and-tenon joints as shown in Detail 1. An alternate method of joining the front and back rails (B) to the legs is shown in Detail 2. Use two 1″ right-angle braces with screws and glue. Pin the mortise-and-tenon joints with 1/8″ pegs as shown in Detail 3. The stiles (D, E) of the front frame are joined to the rails (B) with glued mortise-and-tenon joints and half lap as shown in the exploded view.

The back (K) and sides (J) are covered with 1/4″ plywood from the inside, fastened to the

CUTTING LIST		
KEY	**PIECES**	**SIZE AND DESCRIPTION**
A	4	1-1/2 × 1-1/2 × 31-1/4 legs
B	5	3/4 × 1-1/2 × 46-1/2 front and back rails
C	6	3/4 × 1-1/2 × 16 side supports
D	1	3/4 × 1-1/2 × 14-3/4 front stile
E	2	3/4 × 1-1/2 × 5-7/8 front stiles
F	22	1/2 × 1/2 × 18-1/4 drawer runners
G	3	3/4 × 1-1/2 × 17 drawer dividers
H	1	3/4 × 21-1/2 × 56-1/2 top (varying width planks)
I	4	1-1/2 × 4 × 4 braces
J	2	1/4 × 15-1/2 × 17 sides (plywood)
K	1	1/4 × 17 × 45 back (plywood)
L1	4	3/4 × 5-3/8 × 10-3/4 small drawer fronts
L2	8	1/2 × 4-7/8 × 16 small drawer sides
L3	4	1/2 × 4-7/8 × 8-1/2 small drawer backs
L4	4	1/8 × 9-1/4 × 16 small drawer bottoms
L5	8	1/2 × 1/2 × 16 small drawer runners
M1	2	3/4 × 8-3/8 × 22-1/2 large drawer fronts
M2	4	1/2 × 7-7/8 × 18 large drawer sides
M3	2	1/2 × 7-7/8 × 20-1/2 large drawer backs
M4	2	1/2 × 18 × 21 large drawer bottoms
M5	4	1/2 × 1/2 × 16 large drawer runners

braces (I) fastened to the rails in each top corner with screws and glue. These braces are notched to fit around the legs.

The drawer runners (F) are simply 1/2″ strips waxed for easy operation. They are attached to the drawer dividers (E, G) with brads and glue. The back drawer dividers (G) are screwed through the plywood back into the back rails.

The drawers are constructed with the simple butt joints shown. The drawer runners (L5, M5) are attached with brads and glue. The edges of the drawer fronts and tabletop are rounded-over after cutting. The three front rails and fronts of the legs have a clear, natural finish for contrast with the rest of the piece.

MATERIALS LIST

1/8″-dia. dowels
1/2″ quarter-round molding
Brads
Finishing nails
Drawer knobs
Wood screws
Wood glue

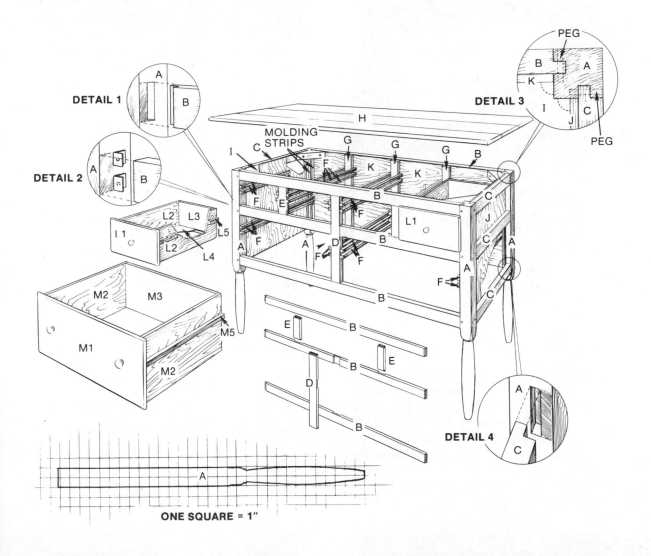

ONE SQUARE = 1″

Bedside Step Table

cut them according to the pattern. Bevel the top edges at a 45° angle to form a miter joint with the top (A). The sides must also be notched to receive the front and rear crosspieces (C, F). Attach the crosspieces squarely to the ends with glue and finishing nails. Set the bottom shelf (E) in place between these pieces, gluing and nailing through both the crosspieces and sides.

MATERIALS LIST

Wood screws
Finishing nails
Triangular wood blocks (2)
1"-dia. hardwood dowels (2)
Wood glue

CUTTING LIST

KEY	PIECES	SIZE AND DESCRIPTION
A	1	3/4 × 11-1/2 × 20 top
B	2	3/4 × 16 × 25-1/2 sides
C	1	3/4 × 2-1/4 × 20 front crosspiece
D	1	3/4 × 15-1/4 × 18-1/2 top shelf
E	1	3/4 × 14-1/2 × 18-1/2 bottom shelf
F	1	3/4 × 9-1/2 × 20 rear crosspiece
G	1	3/4 × 6-1/8 × 18-3/8 drawer front
H	1	3/4 × 6 × 16-3/4 drawer back
I	2	3/4 × 6 × 14-1/2 drawer sides
J	1	1/2 × 14-1/4 × 17-1/2 drawer bottom (plywood)

A forerunner of the standard night table, this bedside step table displays the typical qualities of country furniture. It is simple and serviceable, yet reminiscent of the heritage of the pioneer families as tempered by the needs of frontier living and adapted by colonial craftsmen. Its design makes it a welcome complement to many popular furniture styles.

The table is constructed of 3/4" pine. Edge-glue the boards for the sides (B), then

Next, cut the top, bevel both ends, and secure it in place by gluing and nailing the miter joint. Fasten the top shelf (D) with glue and finishing nails driven through the sides and rear crosspiece.

Assemble the drawer frame around the plywood bottom (J). The bottom is set and glued into dadoes in the front, sides, and back.

For added strength, you can place triangular wood blocks in the front corners for reinforcement; these blocks are fastened to the sides and screwed into the front from inside. The drawer pulls are crafted from 1"-diameter dowels fastened by wood screws through predrilled holes in the front.

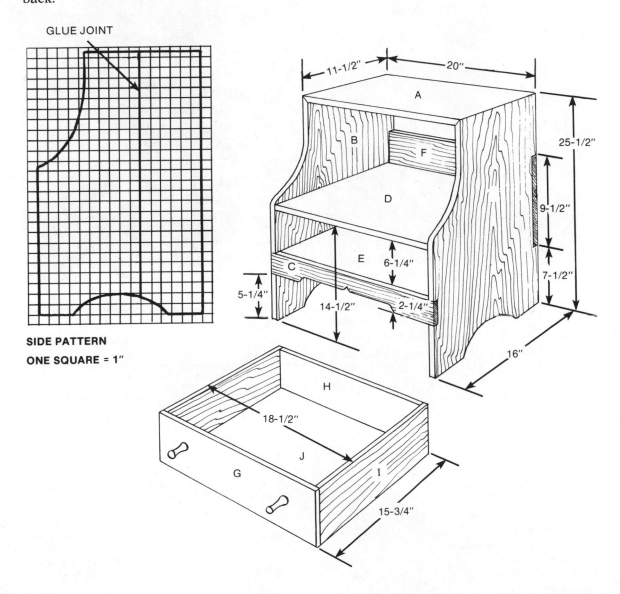

GLUE JOINT

SIDE PATTERN
ONE SQUARE = 1"

Chair Table

When the chair table was originally designed, it combined form with function as a piece of furniture that was a table, chair, and storage chest in a single unit. This oak chair table still serves all three needs and works well in both an Early American or contemporary setting.

Begin by building the top. On a flat surface, arrange the boards (A, B, C, D) to achieve an attractive combination. Joint the edges of the boards to prepare them for gluing. Drill 5/16"-diameter holes 1-1/8" deep in each of the boards to accommodate the dowels. Assemble the top by doweling and edge-gluing, then clamp securely from both sides to prevent bowing.

Assemble the box (H, I, J, K), as shown in the diagram, using the same gluing and doweling techniques. Next, assemble the stiles

(E) and rails (F) with glue and dowels and clamp securely.

CUTTING LIST		
KEY	**PIECES**	**SIZE AND DESCRIPTION**
A	3	3/4 × 5-1/2 × 52 top
B	2	3/4 × 5-1/2 × 48 top
C	2	3/4 × 5-1/2 × 42 top
D	2	3/4 × 5-1/2 × 29 top
E	4	3/4 × 2-1/2 × 29 stiles
F	4	3/4 × 2-1/2 × 12 rails
G	1	3/4 × 2-1/2 × 22-1/2 hinge board
H	2	3/4 × 7 × 22-1/4 box lid
I	4	3/4 × 6-1/2 × 22-1/2 box front and back
J	4	3/4 × 6-1/2 × 15-1/2 box sides
K	2	3/4 × 7-3/4 × 21 box bottom
L	4	3/4 × 3 × 36 cleats

Once all assemblies have dried, lay out the profile of the top with a bar compass and cut out the circular pattern. Similarly, cut the rounded corners of the stiles and cleats (L).

Cut notches in the hinge board (G) to receive two brass hinges. Drill dowel pin holes as before; then glue the hinge board to the assembled box. Attach the box lid, securing

MATERIALS LIST
1"-dia. dowels
5/16"-dia. dowels
3/8"-dia. plugs
No. 10 × 1-1/4" brass wood screws
Brass hinges (2)
Wood glue

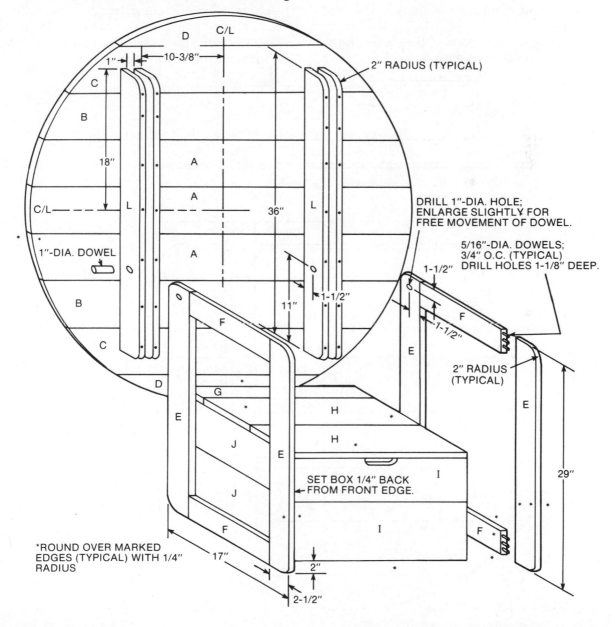

the hinges first to the hinge board. Align the parts carefully.

Counterbore pilot holes in the cleats as shown in the diagram. Next, round over the edges as indicated.

Attach the stiles and rails to the box with No. 10 × 1-1/4" brass wood screws. Set the box back 1/4" from the front of the side frames and mark the positions of the pilot holes.

Lay out the locations of the cleats on the underside of the top. Attach the cleats to the top, fastening them temporarily with two screws.

Set the top on the completed base and check for the proper 1/8" clearances on each of the sides. Attach the cleats permanently with screws and glue; then plug the holes with 3/8"-diameter plugs.

Replace the top on the base; center it accurately; then bore 1"-diameter holes through the cleats and stiles. Enlarge the holes in the frames slightly; then glue 1"-diameter dowels to the cleats to act as pivots.

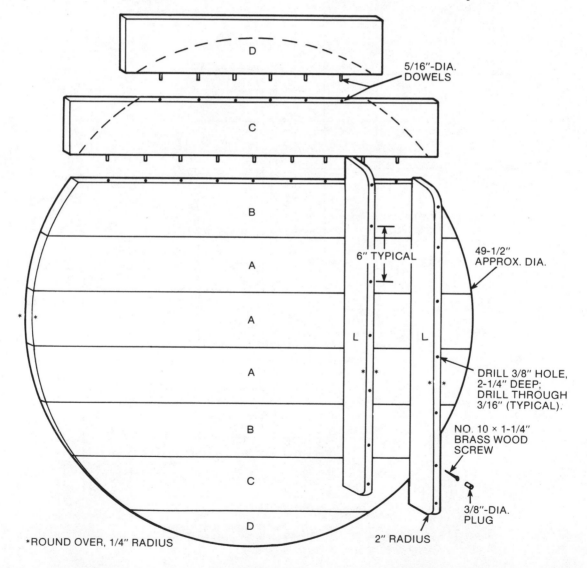

A doweling guide insures accuracy when drilling dowel pin holes. Fluted dowel pins align and reinforce the edge-glued panels.

Mark the positions of all dowel pin holes with boards in face-to-face position to insure proper alignment.

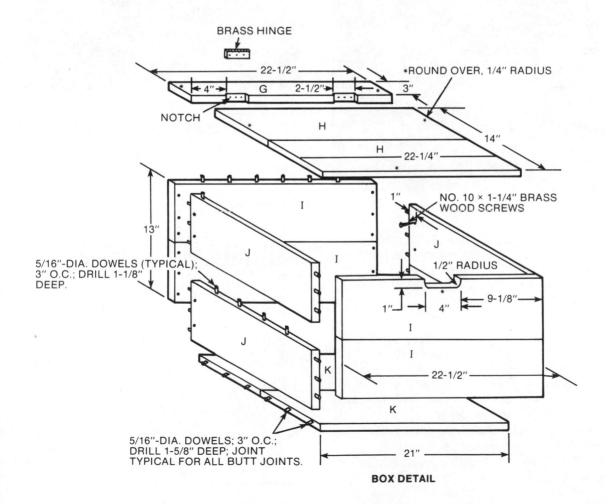

BRASS HINGE

22-1/2"

*ROUND OVER, 1/4" RADIUS

4"   G   2-1/2"   3"

NOTCH

H

H   22-1/4"

14"

I

1"   NO. 10 × 1-1/4" BRASS WOOD SCREWS

13"

J

J

I

1/2" RADIUS

5/16"-DIA. DOWELS (TYPICAL); 3" O.C.; DRILL 1-1/8" DEEP.

1"   4"   9-1/8"

I

J

I

K   22-1/2"

K

5/16"-DIA. DOWELS; 3" O.C.; DRILL 1-5/8" DEEP; JOINT TYPICAL FOR ALL BUTT JOINTS.

21"

BOX DETAIL

Tilt-Top Hutch Table

The snug dimensions of the typical Early American cottage meant that furniture had to earn its place. Often several functions were combined in one unit, so that as the needs of the household altered from hour to hour, the furniture could be altered to serve them. Storage space was always at a premium in such cramped quarters, so compartments were incorporated into many pieces of furniture. This hutch table is a good example of both aspects—it's a triple-function piece, with interior storage, of humble charm. Its height and stability make it an ideal coffee table for any setting with a country flavor. When a bench is required, the two front pegs are removed and the tabletop is

CUTTING LIST

KEY	PIECES	SIZE AND DESCRIPTION
A	2	3/4 × 11-1/4 × 36 removable top
B	2	3/4 × 3-1/2 × 15 pivot cleats
C	1	3/4 × 3-1/2 × 18-1/2 stationary top
D	1	3/4 × 9-1/4 × 18-1/2 lid
E	2	3/4 × 1-1/2 × 11-1/2 side cleats
F	2	3/4 × 13 × 14 sides
G	2	3/4 × 10-1/4 × 18-1/2 front and back panels
H	2	3/4 × 7-1/4 × 24 base platform
I	2	3/4 × 2-1/2 × 24 base front and back
J	2	3/4 × 2-1/2 × 13 base sides

swung up (using the two rear pegs as pivots) to become the bench's back. The top may be completely removed by pulling four pegs, should the need arise for a sturdy step to climb on in order to extend your reach for household chores.

The butt-joint construction appropriate to this piece requires solid stock for all members. Use 1/4"-diameter dowels to glue the boards for the removable top (A), then cut the semicircular ends on a radius of 11-1/2". The pivot cleats (B) are attached with wood screws driven down through the top. Recess the screws and cap them with 1/4"-diameter dowels.

This method is also used to assemble the base. Using 1" graph paper, make full-size patterns of the scrollwork on the base front and back (I) and sides (J). Cut and assemble the base, checking for squareness. The boards for the platform (H) are doweled and edge-glued, then attached with wood screws, and capped with 1/4"-diameter dowels.

This assembly is secured to the rest of the table by wood screws driven up through the platform.

Butterfly hinges are used to attach the lid (D) to the stationary top (C). It's supported on the other three sides by the top edge of the front panel (G) and by two side cleats (E). The removable top unit is secured to the base with 1"-diameter dowels, tapered slightly toward one end for easy insertion and withdrawal.

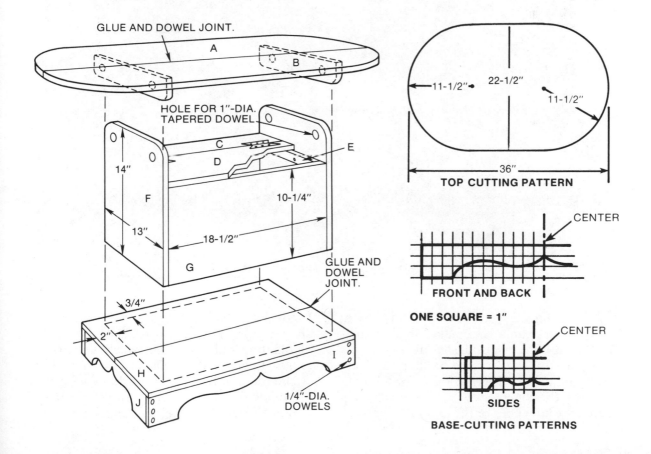

GLUE AND DOWEL JOINT.

A

B

HOLE FOR 1"-DIA. TAPERED DOWEL

C

D

E

14"

F

10-1/4"

13"

18-1/2"

G

GLUE AND DOWEL JOINT.

3/4"

2"

I

H

J

1/4"-DIA. DOWELS

11-1/2"   22-1/2"

11-1/2"

36"

TOP CUTTING PATTERN

CENTER

FRONT AND BACK

ONE SQUARE = 1"

CENTER

SIDES

BASE-CUTTING PATTERNS

Cobbler's Worktable _____

This rugged worktable was built by a Pennsylvania shoemaker in the early 19th century. Certain design details of the piece are unusual or even baffling by modern standards, such as the jog on the left-end cabinet, the lonely strip of wood fastened inside the kneehole, or the log used as a base

for the interchangeable shoe lasts. The plans show it just the way it was originally built, eliminating only the log, which you may choose to eliminate to allow more space.

The top and bottom (A) of the worktable are made of 1-1/4" pine. If you cannot find this in 15" width, dowel and edge-glue two boards together. Plywood may also be used; two pieces can be laminated together to obtain the proper thickness. The back (H), end (I), partitions (J, S), and dividers (G, N) are made of 3/4″ pine or, again, you may use plywood.

Cut the bottom to shape, feathering the edge at the kneehole. Fasten the partitions to the floor, gluing and nailing through the bottom. Fasten the end to the bottom in the same fashion. Attach the dividers, using scrap wood as cleats. Glue and nail the back to the partitions. Glue the front panel (K) in place. Build the frame for the door as shown.

Now set the top in place, again gluing and fastening with 6d finishing nails. Assemble the toolrack frame (B, C, D, E) and tool support (F) around the top as shown, boring holes in the boards to hold awls, knives, etc. Build the drawers butt style as shown; attach wood pulls with screws through the drawer fronts (U1, V1) from inside. A lock may be installed on one of the small drawers, as in the original.

MATERIALS LIST

6d finishing nails
Wood screws
Butt hinges (2)
Drawer pulls (4)
Drawer lock
Doorknob
Floor glides (4)
Door latch
Cleats (4)
Wood filler
Wood glue

CUTTING LIST

KEY	PIECES	SIZE AND DESCRIPTION
A	2	1-1/4 × 15 × 40 top and bottom
B	1	3/4 × 2-1/2 × 13 toolrack frame
C	1	3/4 × 2-1/2 × 40 toolrack frame

CUTTING LIST (continued)

KEY	PIECES	SIZE AND DESCRIPTION
D	1	3/4 × 2-1/2 × 13 toolrack frame
E	1	3/4 × 2-1/2 × 15 toolrack frame
F	1	3/4 × 1-1/4 × 33 tool support
G	1	3/4 × 5 × 14 divider
H	1	1/4 × 22-1/4 × 40 back
I	1	3/4 × 22-1/4 × 14 end
J	1	3/4 × 21 × 9-1/4 partition
K	1	1-1/4 × 22-1/4 × 7-1/4 front panel
L	1	3/4 × 21 × 3-3/4 inner panel
M	1	3/4 × 21 × 1/2 small front panel
N	2	3/4 × 15-1/4 × 14-1/4 dividers
O	1	3/4 × 3/4 × 1-1/2 trim
P	1	1/2 × 1-1/4 × 13-1/4 strip
Q	2	3/4 × 1-1/2 × 9-3/8 door frame
R	2	3/4 × 1-1/2 × 17-1/8 door frame
S	1	3/4 × 21 × 13-1/4 partition
T1	1	1/4 × 19-3/8 × 9-3/8 door backing (plywood)
T2	2	3/4 × 2 × 7-7/8 door frame bottom
T3	2	3/4 × 2 × 19-3/8 door frame
T4	1	1/4 × 4-1/8 × 7-7/8 door panel
T5	1	1/4 × 4-1/8 × 1-1/2 door panel
U1	2	3/4 × 7-1/8 × 15-1/8 drawer fronts
U2	4	3/4 × 7-1/2 × 13-1/4 drawer sides
U3	2	3/4 × 7-1/8 × 13-5/8 drawer backs
U4	2	3/4 × 12-7/8 × 12-1/2 drawer bottoms (plywood)
V1	2	3/4 × 5 × 7-1/8 small drawer fronts
V2	4	3/4 × 5 × 13-1/4 small drawer sides
V3	2	3/4 × 5 × 5-5/8 small drawer backs
V4	2	1/4 × 5-5/8 × 12-1/2 drawer bottoms (plywood)
W1	2	1/2 × 1/2 × 13 brad box sides
W2	2	1/2 × 1/2 × 4-1/2 brad box sides
W3	2	1/2 × 1/2 × 3-1/2 brad box dividers

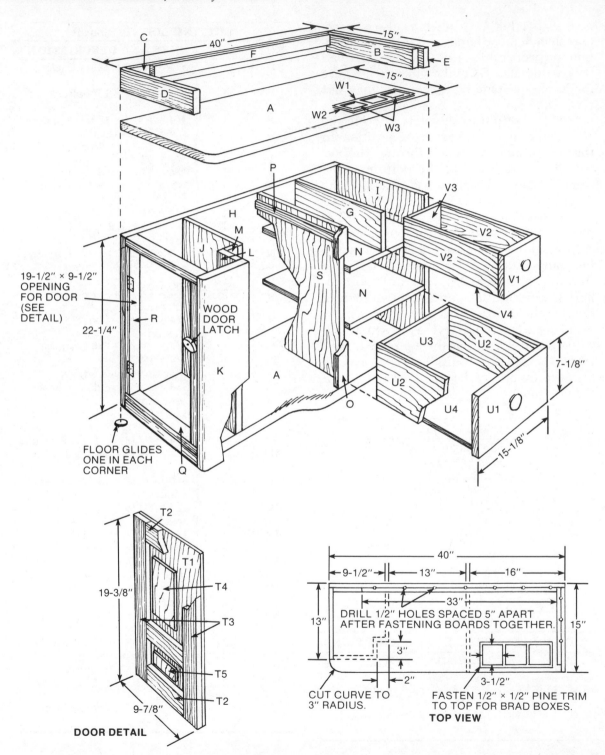

C
40″
F
15″
B
E
D
A
W1
W2
W3
15″

P
I
V3
G
H
V2
M
N
V2
J
L
V1
19-1/2″ × 9-1/2″
OPENING
FOR DOOR
(SEE
DETAIL)
R
S
V4
WOOD
DOOR
LATCH
22-1/4″
N
U3
U2
K
7-1/8″
U2
A
O
U4
U1
FLOOR GLIDES
ONE IN EACH
CORNER
Q
15-1/8″

T2
T1
T4
19-3/8″
T3
T5
T2
9-7/8″
DOOR DETAIL

40″
9-1/2″
13″
16″
33″
13″
DRILL 1/2″ HOLES SPACED 5″ APART
AFTER FASTENING BOARDS TOGETHER.
15″
3″
CUT CURVE TO
3″ RADIUS.
2″
3-1/2″
FASTEN 1/2″ × 1/2″ PINE TRIM
TO TOP FOR BRAD BOXES.
TOP VIEW

Glue the two door panels (T4, T5) to the 1/4" plywood backing (T1) and fasten the doorknob. The door is hung on butt hinges; you may want to obtain antique hinges from a specialty shop. A wood latch holds the door shut.

The present cobbler's worktable is being used as a sewing desk. However, if you want an authentic cobbler's workbench, it can be easily made. The jog is made with two boards (L, M) butted together to support the cutting block on top. This would house the sewing vise, which was often used. The brad box is easily constructed from 1/2" scrap stock (W1, W2, W3) and glued in place.

The kneehole was probably closed when not in use. This would be a good place for the cobbler's seat bench and another parts tray fastened to the front panel. This would explain the use of the strip (P), because there would be one on the tray to keep it lined up with the opening. This part could be leaned against the bench or have a leg in back.

You may wish to duplicate the many characteristic nicks, scratches, and gouges that are borne by the original as a result of its long years of faithful service. Edges and corners should be rounded and sanded smooth. Make sure that all nails are set below the surface and the holes filled with wood filler.

Wagon Seat Table

This little table, which can be used casually in the living room or as a coffee table, obviously takes its name from its shape. Easy to construct, it has plenty of charm and utility. Its four drawers offer hideaways for any number of small items to be kept within easy reach.

The top (A) is preferably a single piece, but if this width is unavailable, it may be composed of several pieces whose total width equals the specified 17-1/2". The curved top edges are cut with a scroll or coping saw.

The legs (H) are 1-1/2" diameter at the top, tapering down to 1" diameter at the bottom. They are set into 1-1/2"-diameter holes drilled at an angle into the cleats (G). The four drawers are of simple box construction with glued and nailed joints.

Assembly of the table begins by fastening the back to the back edge of the top. The recessed-screw method of fastening gives an authentic touch; after inserting the wood screws, plug them with 3/8"-diameter dowels. The end pieces are then fastened to the top and back. They are plug-screwed to the top, but finishing nails may be used for fastening to the back. Glue should be used on all joined edges before putting in the screws or nails. The nails should be countersunk and the holes filled with wood filler.

The drawer spacers are glued and nailed in place from the underside of the top. The ledge is then nailed in place on top of the drawer spacers. These nails are also countersunk and the holes filled. The table is now ready for the addition of the leg assembly. The cleats are screwed to the underside of the top, 4-1/2" from the ends.

MATERIALS LIST
Finishing nails and/or wood screws
Brass or wooden knobs (4)
3/8"-dia. dowels
Wood filler
Wood glue

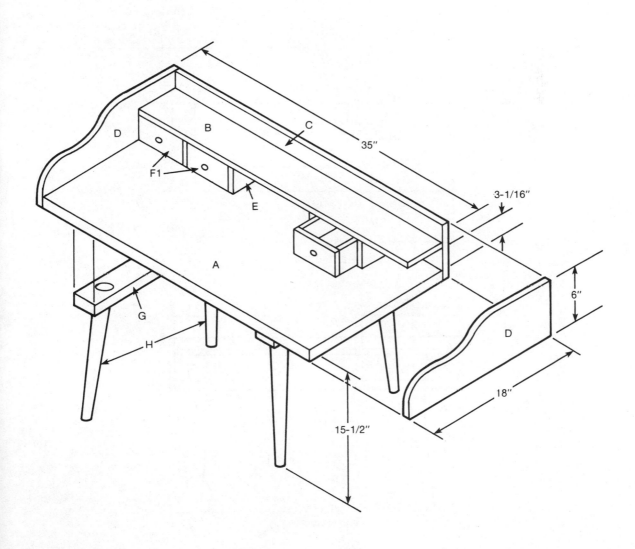

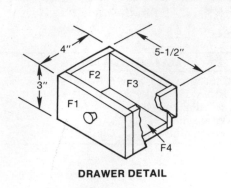

DRAWER DETAIL

CUTTING LIST

KEY	PIECES	SIZE AND DESCRIPTION
A	1	1/2 × 17-1/2 × 34 top
B	1	1/2 × 4 × 34 ledge
C	1	1/2 × 6 × 34 back
D	2	1/2 × 6 × 18 end pieces
E	4	1/2 × 3-1/16 × 4 drawer dividers
F1	4	1/2 × 3 × 5-1/2 drawer fronts
F2	8	1/4 × 3 × 3-1/2 drawer sides (plywood)
F3	4	1/4 × 3 × 5 drawer backs (plywood)
F4	4	1/4 × 3-1/4 × 5 drawer bottoms (plywood)
G	2	1 × 2-1/4 × 16 cleats
H	4	1-1/2 × 13-1/2 legs

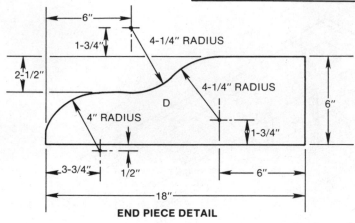

END PIECE DETAIL

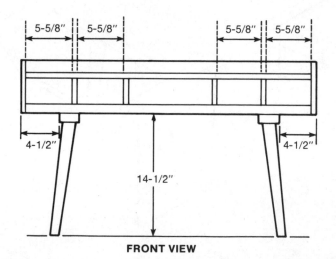

FRONT VIEW

Writing Desk ⎯⎯⎯

This piece is a study in simplicity and orderliness. As a desk designed with organization in mind, you'd have to look far and wide to beat it. The molding strips at the edge of the desktop (B) and writing top (R), and the more subtle molding on the underside of the front (E) help to add a well-finished look.

To build the desk, first turn the legs (C) on a lathe; then groove each of the leg tops twice. The grooves should measure 1/2″ × 1/2″ × 5-1/2″ to allow the sides (A), front (E), and lower back (D) to be glued to them. Precut the front to accommodate the drawers before attaching it to the legs; cut plugs to fill the two leg grooves, which will be exposed when the drawers are open. Install the dividers (F) with nails and wood glue to cleats (G) screwed to the front and back so that the dividers are flush with the interior edges of the drawer openings. Install the drawer runners (H) to the dividers as shown; on the exterior sides of the drawer openings, the runners are mounted on blocks of scrap stock glued and nailed to the side pieces.

Dowel and edge-glue the pieces for the desktop. Cut the center dividers (K) and side trim (I) as shown, and attach them and the upper back (J) to the desktop with nails and wood glue. The dividers and trim are secured to the back with nailed and glued butt joints. Note that the front ends of the trim are notched to accept the molding. Glue and nail the divider shelf (L) halfway up on the dividers. Glue the compartment front (M) to the dividers and shelf. Mount the compartment dividers (N) to the shelf and back with glue, and attach the compartment top (Q) to the back with mortised hinges.

Glue the desktop to the frame; the top shelves (P) to the trim and center dividers; and the dividers (O) to the desktop, back, and shelves. Mount the writing top to the divider shelf with mortised hinges. Butt joint construction is used to build the drawers. Consult your hardware supplier or a locksmith to obtain appropriate locks for the drawers and writing top.

CUTTING LIST

KEY	PIECES	SIZE AND DESCRIPTION
A	2	1/2 × 5-1/2 × 19-1/2 sides
B	2	3/4 × 11-1/4 × 39 desktop
C	4	2 × 2 × 29 legs
D	1	1/2 × 5-1/2 × 36 lower back
E	1	1/2 × 5-1/2 × 36 front
F	2	1/2 × 4-1/2 × 21 dividers
G	4	3/4 × 3/4 × 4-1/2 cleats
H	12	1/2 × 1/2 × 19 drawer runners
I	2	3/4 × 5-1/2 × 22-1/2 side trim
J	1	1/2 × 5-1/2 × 38 upper back
K	2	3/4 × 4-3/4 × 21-1/4 center dividers
L	1	1/2 × 5-1/2 × 15 divider shelf
M	1	1/2 × 2-1/4 × 15 compartment front
N	3	1/2 × 2-1/4 × 3 compartment dividers
O	4	1/2 × 4-3/4 × 6 dividers
P	2	1/2 × 6 × 12 top shelves
Q	1	1/2 × 4-1/8 × 15 compartment top
R	2	3/4 × 16 × 15 writing top
S1	2	3/4 × 3-1/2 × 9 drawer fronts
S2	4	1/2 × 3-1/2 × 19 drawer sides
S3	2	1/2 × 3-1/2 × 8 drawer backs
S4	2	1/2 × 8 × 23-1/2 drawer bottoms

MATERIALS LIST

1/4"-dia. dowels
3/4" half-round molding
1/2" flat molding (for front bottom)
Finishing nails
Wood screws
Hinges
Locks
Wood glue

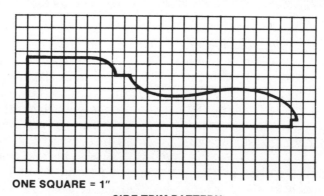

ONE SQUARE = 1"

SIDE TRIM PATTERN

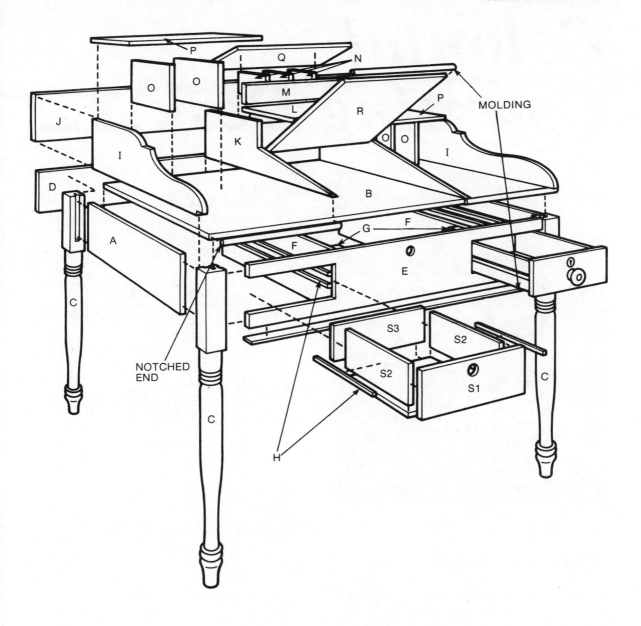

P

Q

N

O   O

M

J   L

R

P

MOLDING

I   K   O   O   I

D   B

F

G   F

A   E

C   NOTCHED END

H

S3

S2

S2   S1

C   C

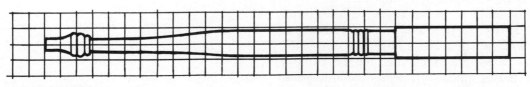

ONE SQUARE = 1"

LEG PATTERN

Colonial Counting Desk

den or, as shown here, as a vanity with flip-top mirror.

All joints in this desk are edge-to-edge butt joints secured with wood screws and glue. All screw holes should be filled with wood filler. The boards for the desktop (A), back

CUTTING LIST		
KEY	**PIECES**	**SIZE AND DESCRIPTION**
A	2	3/4 × 10 × 32 desktop
B	2	3/4 × 10 × 16-3/4 back
C	2	3/4 × 7 × 20 upper sides
D	2	3/4 × 6-1/2 × 16 lower sides
E	4	2 × 2 × 31 legs
F	3	3/4 × 2 × 16 side and center supports
G	2	3/4 × 2 × 28 front and back supports
H	4	1/2 × 7 × 8 box shelves (exterior)
I	1	3/4 × 6 × 19 box top
J	2	3/4 × 10 × 19 hinged lid
K	1	3/4 × 3-1/2 × 18 box front
L	2	3/4 × 9 × 20 box sides
M	1	1/2 × 6 × 16-1/2 box shelf (interior)
N	4	1/4 × 6 × 6 shelf dividers
O	2	3/4 × 5 × 28 drawer front and back
P	2	1/2 × 5 × 20 drawer sides
Q	1	1/4 × 19-1/2 × 27 drawer bottom
R	2	1/2 × 3 × 7 small drawer fronts
S	4	1/2 × 3 × 7-1/2 small drawer sides
T	2	1/2 × 3 × 6 small drawer backs
U	2	1/4 × 6 × 7 small drawer bottoms

Whenever a square-rigged early American merchantman came into port, a longboat was immediately put over the side with a junior officer who would present himself at the shipping firm's counting house to hand over the ship's manifest.

How many transactions these little counting desks participated in will never be known, but their clean lines and simple design made them long-time favorites of busy merchants. Made of pine and walnut stock, this Shaker-style desk can function in the

(B), and hinged lid (J) are all doweled and edge-glued, as required.

Begin assembly with the four legs (E) and five supports (F, G). Then secure the desktop in the legs and one upper drawer support with wood screws and glue. Add the lower sides (D), recessing them between the front and back legs.

Next, fasten the two diagonal box sides (L) to the desktop, allowing 1″ setback in the front and 3/4″ in the back. You can now add the back (B) and the box front (K). Note that the box front will house a lock. Consult a hardware supplier or locksmith to find a suitable type.

Next, screw the four exterior box shelves (H) into place, the top shelves through the backboard and the box sides. Then attach the upper sides (C).

Preassemble the exterior and interior box shelves, including the shelf dividers (N). Slip the entire unit into place within the box, against the back. Attach the hinged lid, making sure the alignment with its base and the lock is correct. Install a lid support to hold the lid/mirror in an open position.

MATERIALS LIST

Wood screws
3/8″-dia. dowels
Butt hinges (2)
Drawer knobs (4)
Lid support
Mirror (optional)
Wood glue

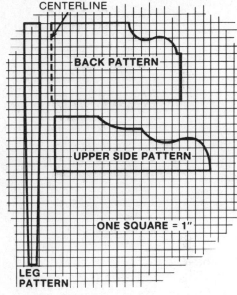

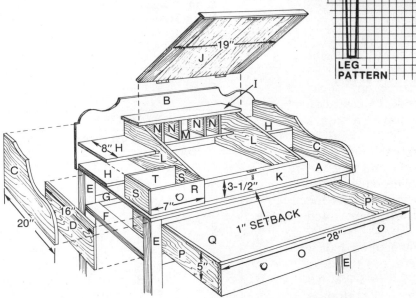

Shaker Desk

Simple and sturdy is one way to describe this Shaker-style desk. But with the addition of the molding, it becomes almost elegant. The bottom part of the desk is essentially an enclosed table; the top is a simple double-shelf construction.

Make the "table" section first, cutting the bottom (C), front (E), back (F), and sides (D) to the given dimensions. The ends of the front, back, and sides are mitered. As the photo and drawing show, the legs are fluted on all sides.

Cut the tops of the legs diagonally in half at a height of 24". Insert them into the desk bottom through 1-1/2" × 1-1/2" × 2-1/8" triangular openings cut into the desk bottom as shown in Detail 1. Finally, fasten them with

wood screws and glue. The corner sides of the openings are set back 3/4" from the edges of the bottom to accommodate the sides.

After the glue sets, attach the sides, front, and back to the leg tops with glue and wood screws driven through the legs into the backs of the pieces. Cut the molding strips, again using miter cuts for the ends of the bottom molding, and attach them to the desk with glue and brads.

Cut the shelf members (G, H, I) to the correct dimensions. The shelf is assembled with nailed butt joints. Attach the shelf molding with glue and brads, and mount the shelf to

MATERIALS LIST

3/4" cove or bead molding
1/2" cove or bead molding
Brads
Wood screws
Finishing nails
Butt hinges (2)
Wood glue

CUTTING LIST

KEY	PIECES	SIZE AND DESCRIPTION
A	2	1-1/2 × 1-1/2 × 31-1/2 back legs
B	2	1-1/2 × 1-1/2 × 28-3/4 front legs
C	1	3/4 × 21 × 21-1/2 bottom
D	2	3/4 × 6-3/4 × 21 sides
E	1	3/4 × 4 × 21-1/2 front
F	1	3/4 × 6-3/4 × 21-1/2 back
G	2	3/4 × 5-1/4 × 20 shelves
H	1	3/4 × 8 × 20 upper back
I	2	3/4 × 5 × 8 upper sides
J	1	3/4 × 15-7/8 × 21-1/2 top

the desk sides and back with finishing nails and glue.

Cut mortises for the hinges and attach the desktop to the shelf. If solid stock is used, it will probably be necessary to edge-glue and dowel together two separate pieces to make the desktop. If plywood is used, apply a veneer over the exposed edges.

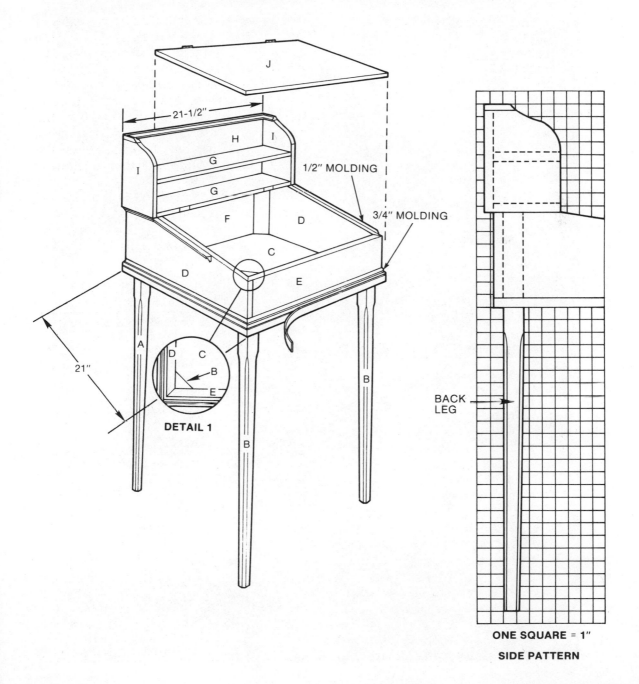

21-1/2"

1/2" MOLDING

3/4" MOLDING

21"

DETAIL 1

BACK LEG

ONE SQUARE = 1"

SIDE PATTERN

Lady's Desk _____

This lady's desk is typical of colonial furniture design.

After turning the legs (A), cut two 1/4″ × 3/8″ × 5″ grooves in the top of each one. Cut the boards for the front and back (B) and sides (C). Cut a 3-5/8″ × 8-5/8″ opening in the front to accommodate the drawer. Assemble the four legs and the frame, using wood glue in the grooves. Clamp each two-legs-and-frame combination.

While the corner joints are drying, make the drawer and drawer supports (G) (with runners) as a separate project. Butt all joints, gluing and nailing. Use the drawer opening in the table framework as a measure, being sure to provide slight play.

There are six drawer runners (H) in all—one nailed to each side of the drawer and two (in the form of a groove) on each drawer support (G). Provide slight play here, also, so that the sliding action of the grooved guides is free.

With the drawer completed, dowel and edge-glue the boards for the top (D). Next, cut the trim pieces (E, F) according to the patterns. Secure the back trim flush with the lower edge of the top, using finishing nails and glue. Attach the side trim to the top and back in the same manner.

Remove all clamps from the framework. Glue and nail the drawer supports in place: first, the right one, against the sides of the front and rear leg tops; next, the left one, with the drawer held in place to assure slight play. Nail through the front and rear underframes at the point of the left support.

The final step in the assembly is to glue the top to the frame. Nail through the top, countersink the heads, and use wood filler in the holes.

MATERIALS LIST

Finishing nails
1/4″-dia. dowels
Drawer pull
Wood filler
Wood glue

CUTTING LIST

KEY	PIECES	SIZE AND DESCRIPTION
A	4	2 × 2 × 28 legs
B	2	1/2 × 5 × 26-7/8 front and back
C	2	1/2 × 5 × 13-1/2 sides
D	2	3/4 × 9 × 32-1/2 top
E	2	3/8 × 4 × 18-3/8 side trim
F	1	3/8 × 9 × 32-1/2 back trim
G	2	1/2 × 4 × 14-1/2 drawer supports
H	6	1/2 × 1 × 13-3/4 drawer runners
I1	1	3/4 × 3-1/2 × 8-1/2 drawer front
I2	2	3/8 × 3 × 13-3/4 drawer sides
I3	1	3/8 × 3 × 7-3/4 drawer back
I4	1	1/4 × 7-3/4 × 13-3/8 drawer bottom

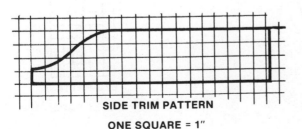

SIDE TRIM PATTERN

ONE SQUARE = 1″

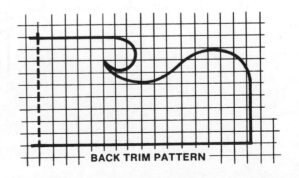

BACK TRIM PATTERN

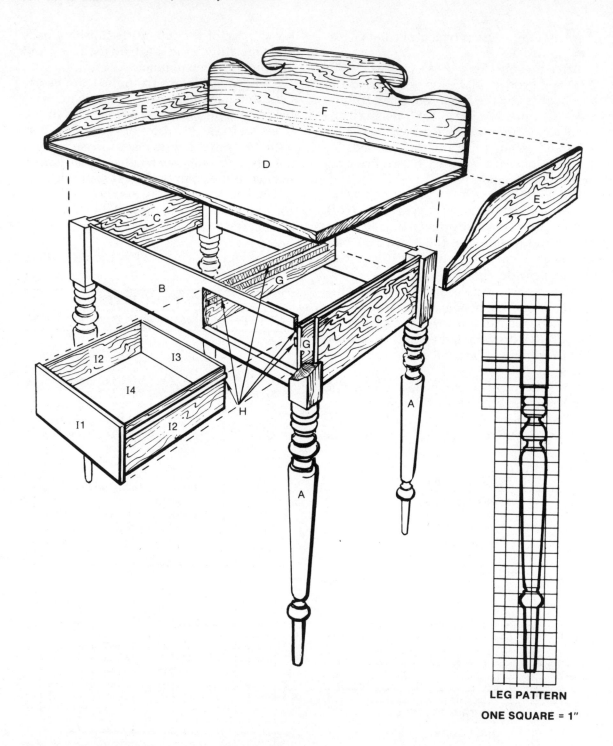

LEG PATTERN

ONE SQUARE = 1″

Child's Desk

Simple, sturdy, and ideally suited to a child's room is the best way to describe this desk. The original dimensions of the piece have been retained within fractions of an inch. It's small, so the use of solid stock is practicable. The original is white pine, but you can select the stock you like best.

Think of the bottom portion of the desk as a table with a drawer, and you'll be able to visualize construction better; the table should be built first. The legs (A) are tapered on the insides only and attached to the lower sides (C) by rabbeting the side panels and gluing them into grooves cut in the legs as shown. Holes should be predrilled in the side panels and legs to accommodate 1/4"-diameter dowels; glue in the dowels for reinforcement.

The front rail (E) is attached to the legs using the same rabbet and groove method. Cut the drawer guides (B) as shown in the detail drawing. Attach the guides, the front trim (F), and the lower back (D) with finishing nails and glue.

Next, the desk bottom (H) is fastened with finishing nails and glue to the legs and sides, thus finishing the table portion. The back of the desk bottom is flush with the back of the piece, but the board's front and side edges protrude 3/8" and are slightly rounded.

Construct the drawer by rabbeting the front (G1), sides (G2), and back (G3) as shown. Cut dadoes 3/8" up from the bottom of these pieces and set the bottom (G4) in place.

The sides (J), back (K), and front (I) of the upper portion of the desk are attached to the desk bottom with 1/4"-diameter dowels and glue. The front corners can be dovetailed together (as seen in the photo) or rabbeted (as seen in the illustration). The desktop (M) is hinged to receive the lid (N), and is attached by 3/8"-diameter dowels around the sides and back.

The upper back is joined to rabbets cut in the back edges of the sides. The lid is beveled on the top and bottom edges to fit the top and to receive the paper stop (O). The paper stop has a rounded top and is fastened to the lid with brads and glue. The pencil tray (L) can be glued to the bottom of the desk. Finally, the hinges are put on to attach the lid.

As far as a finish goes, you'll want to consider using something durable since the piece is intended for use by a child. The original piece has a red stain finish.

MATERIALS LIST

Finishing nails
Brads
1/4"-dia. dowels
3/8"-dia. dowels
Hinges (2)
Drawer pull
Wood glue

CUTTING LIST

KEY	PIECES	SIZE AND DESCRIPTION
A	4	1-3/8 × 1-3/4 × 27-1/2 legs
B	2	1-3/4 × 1-3/4 × 18 drawer guides
C	2	3/4 × 5 × 17 lower sides
D	1	3/4 × 5 × 20-1/4 lower back
E	1	3/4 × 1-1/8 × 20-1/4 front rail
F	2	3/4 × 1-7/16 × 3-7/8 front trim
G1	1	3/4 × 3-7/8 × 16-1/4 drawer front
G2	2	1/2 × 3-7/8 × 17-3/8 drawer sides
G3	1	1/2 × 3-3/4 × 16-1/4 drawer back
G4	1	1/4 × 16-1/4 × 17-3/8 drawer bottom (plywood)
H	1	3/4 × 19-7/8 × 23-1/2 desk bottom
I	1	3/4 × 5 × 22-3/4 desk front
J	2	3/4 × 13 × 19-1/2 upper sides
K	1	3/4 × 13 × 22-3/4 upper back
L	1	1-1/2 × 3 × 21-1/4 pencil tray
M	1	3/4 × 7 × 23-1/2 desktop
N	1	3/4 × 14-1/4 × 23-1/2 desk lid
O	1	3/8 × 1-1/2 × 23-1/2 paper stop

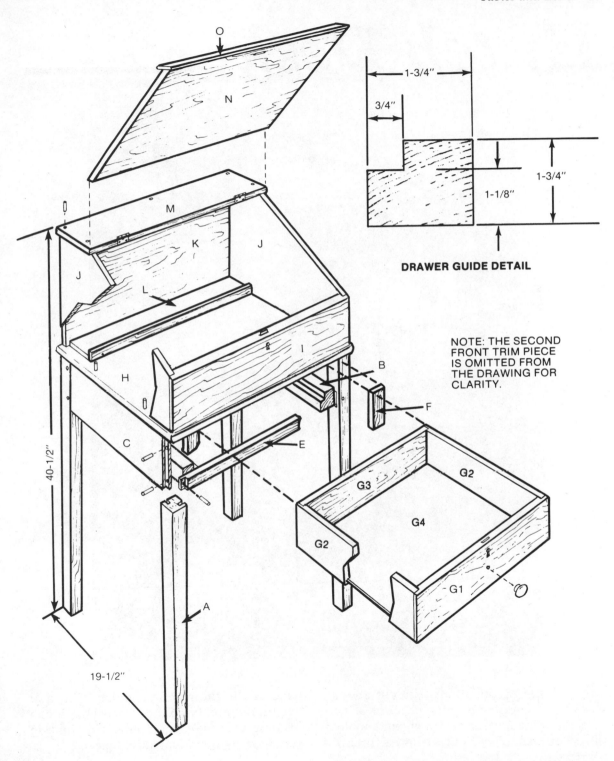

O

N

1-3/4"

3/4"

1-3/4"

1-1/8"

DRAWER GUIDE DETAIL

M

J

K

J

L

J

I

H

C

40-1/2"

A

19-1/2"

B

NOTE: THE SECOND
FRONT TRIM PIECE
IS OMITTED FROM
THE DRAWING FOR
CLARITY.

F

E

G3

G2

G2

G4

G2

G1

Hutch Desk

As desks go, this model is a cut above many country designs because of its straight-line appearance, which suits many different decors. The desk is trim, less than 3' wide at the flip top and under 5' in total height. By modifying the dimensions, it can become an excellent component in a built-in series, or an individual accent piece.

Stock is 3/4″ for the stationary top (A), desktop frame (K, L, M), drawer dividers (R), legs (O), side rails (P), and beveled top (C). Use 1/2″ stock for the drawer pieces (T1-T4), shelves (I), top and bottom rails (D, E), and the cabinet sides (B). Half-inch stock is also used for the desktop panels (N). Quarter-inch stock is used for the desk sides (Q) and back sections (F, J). Scrap stock will do for cleats (H) and drawer runners (S). The flip top and desk sides are paneled; the frame pieces are doweled and edge-glued together, with the inside edges rabbeted 1/4″ deep to accommodate the panels. The panels are also rabbeted 1/4″ deep.

Assemble the desk sides first, minus the front and rear leg halves. Dowel and glue the frame members together; glue in the panels. After the glue sets overnight, mark the locations for the drawer dividers. Notch the front corners of the dividers to fit around the front leg halves and glue the drawer runners to the dividers. After the glue sets, nail the sides to the dividers.

Attach the top, back, and front and rear leg halves with finishing nails and wood glue. Construct the drawers using a rabbet-and-groove joint at the front and dovetailing the back and sides. The bottom is set and glued into 1/4″-deep dadoes cut in the front, back, and sides.

For the cabinet, first glue and nail the uprights to the sides. Attach the cleats to the posts in the same fashion; then join the sides with the beveled top piece and the facing trim. Secure the shelf unit to the desk proper by nailing through the bottoms of the cleats

and lower facing trim. Add the back; then slip the shelves into place.

You can now measure and cut for the flip top to assure a perfect fit with the shelf unit. Attach the top with mortised butt hinges and install a suitable lock. If you intend to use this desk in a contemporary setting, you may wish to substitute other drawer pulls for the button knobs shown.

MATERIALS LIST

Finishing nails
1/4″-dia. dowels
Butt hinges
Lock
Knobs
Wood glue

CUTTING LIST

KEY	PIECES	SIZE AND DESCRIPTION
A	1	3/4 × 22-1/2 × 32-1/2 stationary top
B	2	1/2 × 11-1/2 × 26-1/2 cabinet sides
C	1	3/4 × 12-3/4 × 33-1/2 beveled top
D	1	1/2 × 2-1/2 × 32-1/2 top rail
E	1	1/2 × 1-1/2 × 32-1/2 bottom rail
F	1	1/4 × 29-1/4 × 30 lower back (not shown)
G	4	3/4 × 3/4 × 26-1/2 cabinet uprights
H	6	3/4 × 1 × 9-3/4 shelf cleats
I	3	1/2 × 11-1/4 × 31-1/2 shelves
J	1	1/4 × 26-1/2 × 31-1/2 upper back
K	2	3/4 × 1-1/2 × 22-1/4 desktop stiles
L	2	3/4 × 1-1/2 × 29-1/2 desktop rails
M	1	3/4 × 1-1/2 × 19-1/4 desktop center stile
N	2	1/2 × 14-1/2 × 19-3/4 desktop panels
O	8	3/4 × 2-1/2 × 29-1/4 legs
P	4	3/4 × 2-1/2 × 16-1/2 side rails
Q	2	1/2 × 17 × 21-3/4 desk sides
R	4	3/4 × 21-1/4 × 31 drawer dividers
S	6	3/4 × 1-1/2 × 16-1/2 drawer runners
T1	1	1/2 × 8-3/4 × 26-1/2 drawer fronts
T2	6	1/2 × 8-1/2 × 20 drawer sides
T3	3	1/2 × 8-1/2 × 25-1/2 drawer backs
T4	3	1/4 × 20 × 26 drawer bottoms

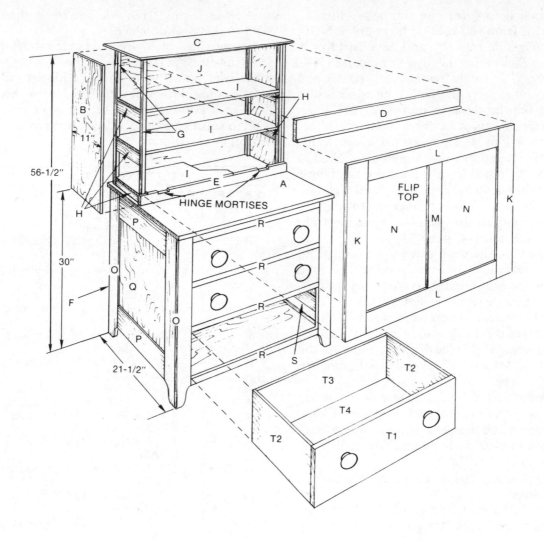

56-1/2"

11"

30"

21-1/2"

C

J

I

B

H

G

I

I

E

A

HINGE MORTISES

H

P

R

P

O

Q

R

O

F

P

R

S

R

D

L

FLIP
TOP

N

K

K

M

N

K

L

T2

T3

T4

T2

T1

Section II
Chairs, Benches, and Beds

Country furniture is supposed to be relaxing. You can rest assured that all of the following projects fill the bill, whether you return to them from the field, shop, or office. Most of them are not too taxing to build, either.

Dimensions given in the cutting list are in finished inches but can be varied to suit your taste. Also, although some projects mention particular wood types, various wood types can be used for any project to suit your individual preferences.

Shaker Chairs ____

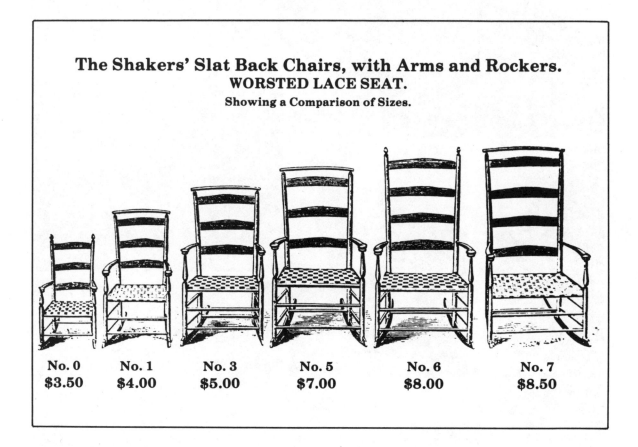

The Shakers' Slat Back Chairs, with Arms and Rockers.
WORSTED LACE SEAT.
Showing a Comparison of Sizes.

No. 0	No. 1	No. 3	No. 5	No. 6	No. 7
$3.50	$4.00	$5.00	$7.00	$8.00	$8.50

Shaker chairs have become very popular with American country-living families, and the reasons are obvious. The chairs are graceful, light in weight, and easy to make using the unique glue and dowel method of assembly developed by the Shaker crafts-men. As seen in this advertisement from an Albany, New York, newspaper (circa 1900), they have been popular since the turn of the century. Of course, their value has gone up *slightly;* about 20 to 25 times.

Elder's Chair

The following method of constructing the elder's chair is also used, with some exceptions, to construct the other Shaker chairs. Any such exceptions are noted in the text. To reproduce this Shaker original, start by making all the turnings from a good grade of birch or maple. The curved slats of the back (A) may present a problem, because these are usually shaped or bent by steaming in a special press. As an alternative, you can cut the slats out of a solid block of wood with a bandsaw to achieve the curved shape. Otherwise, you will have to make them flat.

When all the parts have been cut to size, holes must be drilled for the dowels and rails.

Drill 1/4"-diameter holes in the back slats and back legs (B) as shown in the exploded drawing. Use 3/8"-diameter dowels to fasten the arms (D) and the back leg caps (C) to the back legs. The rails are fastened directly into the legs without the use of dowels. Note that the various rails are different sizes; care is required when drilling the assembly holes.

Next, dry-assemble the chair to be sure everything fits. It may be necessary to sand the ends of the rails slightly if too tight a fit has resulted from absorption of moisture. The chair can now be disassembled for gluing.

Apply glue to the walls of the predrilled holes. Do not apply the glue to the pieces themselves because they may swell rapidly and make it very difficult to assemble the chair. Assemble the two front legs (F) and three front rails (I1, I2) first, making sure that the rail with the largest diameter goes on top. (The rails of the seat all have a slightly larger diameter than the others.) Note that the front rails go into holes that are slightly lower than the holes for the side rails.

To insure tight joints, place the assembly on its side and pound with a hammer and wood block. Now lay the assembly on a flat surface and make sure the legs are parallel. If the legs are not parallel, twist the assembly until they are.

Next, secure the back slats and back rails (H1, H2) to the back legs. Top off the back legs with caps as shown. The side rails (G1, G2) are then attached to the front legs and the preassembled back after the arms have been attached to the legs. Note that the front legs protrude through the arms approximately 1/4". Secure the arms with caps (E).

With the front legs on the floor, pound the back legs with a hammer and wood block to

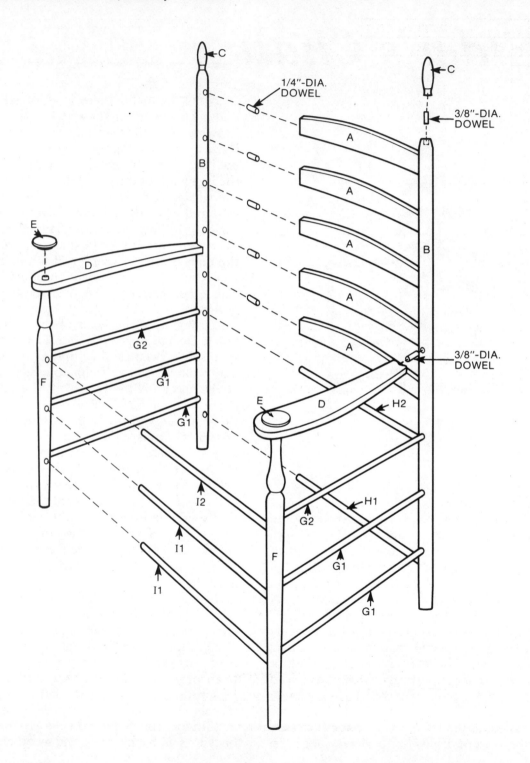

CUTTING LIST

KEY	PIECES	SIZE AND DESCRIPTION
A	5	1/2 × 3-1/4 × 17-5/8 back slats
B	2	1-1/4 × 47 back legs
C	2	1-1/4 × 4-1/2 back leg caps
D	2	5/8 × 3 × 17 arms
E	2	5/8 × 2 arm caps
F	2	1-3/8 × 27 front legs
G1	4	3/4 × 16-3/4 side rails
G2	2	7/8 × 16-3/4 side rails
H1	1	3/4 × 17-5/8 back rail
H2	1	7/8 × 17-5/8 back rail
I1	2	3/4 × 21-7/8 front rails
I2	1	7/8 × 21-7/8 front rail

MATERIALS LIST

1/4"-dia. dowels
3/8"-dia. dowels
120-grit sandpaper
Wood glue

assure a tight fit. Be sure to check the chair for alignment before the glue dries. If all four legs do not rest squarely on the ground, bounce the chair lightly on the leg that appears too long until all four legs are level.

Sand the entire chair with 120-grit sandpaper, then finish as desired. When the finish has dried completely, the seat can be woven as described later in this section.

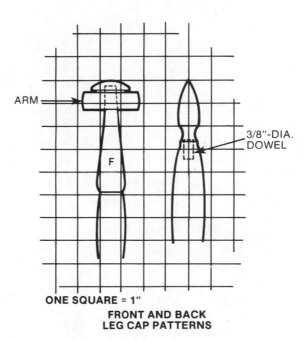

ONE SQUARE = 1"
FRONT AND BACK
LEG CAP PATTERNS

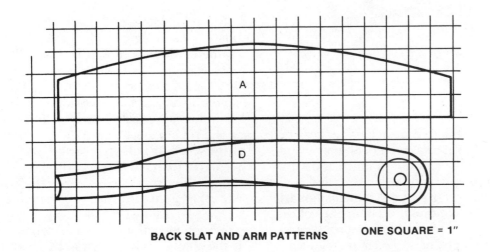

BACK SLAT AND ARM PATTERNS   **ONE SQUARE = 1"**

Armchair Rockers _____

Glue the rockers in place, then drill two holes in each leg at right angles for 5/16"-diameter dowels. For added stability, the dowels should be long enough to go all the way through the legs; saw them off flush and sand off the excess. After staining, the dowels will be practically unnoticeable.

The rocker shown in the illustration features scroll or ladle-type arms (D) as an alternative to the flat style of the elder's chair. Shape the arms according to the pattern. Note that, unlike the flat style, the scroll arms are not secured with caps.

A popular option for the armchair rocker is the shawl back, shown in the photo. The

These distinctive armchair rockers reflect the finest aspects of Shaker craftsmanship. They are built in much the same way as the elder's chair, using 1/4"- and 3/8"-diameter dowels and glue to connect the various pieces. A slot must be cut in each of the legs (B, E) to accommodate the rockers (I), which are shaped as shown in the pattern.

20-1/2"-long cushion rail (J) is perfect for draping items such as shawls, afghans, and blankets. Back leg caps are not used with the shawl back, but 1/4"-diameter dowels are used to secure the cushion rail to the back legs.

Sand down the entire chair with 120-grit sandpaper and finish as desired.

MATERIALS LIST

1/4"-dia. dowels
5/16"-dia. dowels
3/8"-dia. dowels
120-grit sandpaper
Wood glue

CUTTING LIST

KEY	PIECES	SIZE AND DESCRIPTION
A	4	1/2 × 3-1/4 × 17-5/8 back slats
B	2	1-1/4 × 42 back legs
C	2	1-1/4 × 3-1/2 back leg caps
D	2	1-1/4 × 3 × 17 arms
E	2	1-3/8 × 25 front legs
F1	4	3/4 × 16-3/4 side rails
F2	2	7/8 × 16-3/4 side rails
G1	1	3/4 × 17-5/8 back rail
G2	1	7/8 × 17-5/8 back rail
H1	2	3/4 × 21-7/8 front rails
H2	1	7/8 × 21-7/8 front rail
I	2	1/2 × 4-1/2 × 24 rockers
J	1	1/2 × 20-1/2 cushion rail (optional)

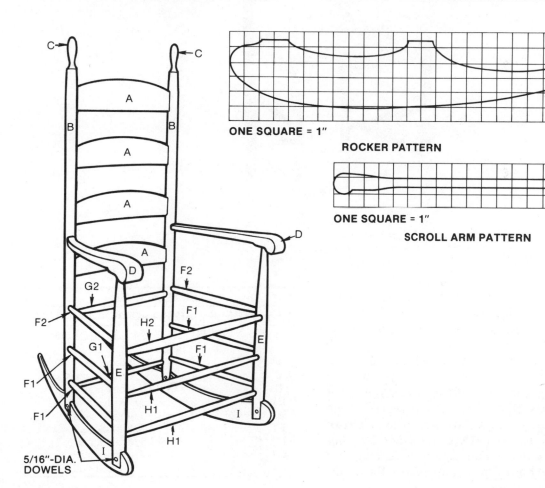

ONE SQUARE = 1"

ROCKER PATTERN

ONE SQUARE = 1"

SCROLL ARM PATTERN

Straight-Back Chair _____

The best known of all the Shaker chairs is the "ladderback" or straight-back chair. The tall back legs, with their delicately rounded finials combine with the smooth curved slats to give it a look of grace and beauty.

Cutting and assembly are the same as for the elder's chair, except that there are no arms and two less slats. Also, the height of the back is only 42", some 9-1/2" smaller than the elder's chair. Again, be sure to sand down the completed chair before finishing.

CUTTING LIST		
KEY	**PIECES**	**SIZE AND DESCRIPTION**
A	3	1/2 × 3-1/4 × 17-5/8 back slats
B	2	1-1/4 × 39 back legs
C	2	1-1/4 × 3 back leg caps
D	2	1-5/8 × 19 front legs
E1	4	3/4 × 16-3/4 side rails
E2	2	7/8 × 16-3/4 side rails
F1	1	3/4 × 17-5/8 back rail
F2	1	7/8 × 17-5/8 back rail
G1	2	3/4 × 21-7/8 front rails
G2	1	7/8 × 21-7/8 front rail

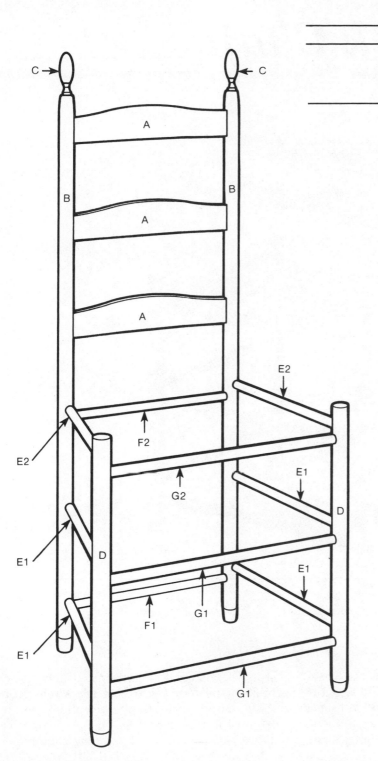

MATERIALS LIST

1/4"-dia. dowels
3/8"-dia. dowels
120-grit sandpaper
Wood glue

Low-Back Chair _____

This chair neatly exemplifies the Shakers' sense of practicality. It was designed with a low, two-slat back so that it could be tucked under the table or hung on the wall after mealtime. Its lightweight, sturdy construction and space-saving size make it perfect for use in the kitchen or dining room, next to the telephone, or in front of a dressing table. The seat height is 17", which is standard for dining chairs.

Note that, because back leg caps and arms are not part of the low-back chair, 3/8"-diameter dowels are not needed. The remainder of the cutting, assembly, and finishing is similar to the elder's chair.

MATERIALS LIST

1/4"-dia. dowels
120-grit sandpaper
Wood glue

CUTTING LIST

KEY	PIECES	SIZE AND DESCRIPTION
A	2	1/2 × 3-1/4 × 16-1/2 back slats
B	2	1-1/4 × 27 back legs
C	2	1-1/4 × 19 front legs
D1	4	3/4 × 16-3/4 side rails
D2	2	7/8 × 16-3/4 side rails
E1	1	3/4 × 17-5/8 back rail
E2	1	7/8 × 17-5/8 back rail
F1	2	3/4 × 21-7/8 front rails
F2	1	7/8 × 21-7/8 front rail

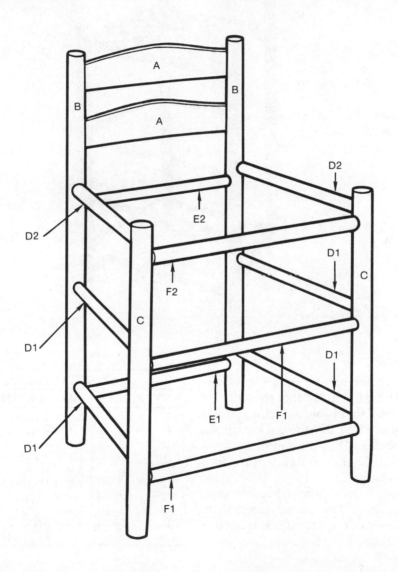

Weaver's Chair _____

The huge Shaker hand looms required chairs with high seats so that the weaver could sit close to his work. The same chairs were also used at shop desks, laundry and ironing tables, and tailor's counters. Today, they are wonderfully suited for use as counter or bar chairs.

The weaver's chair should be made of heavier maple stock for added strength. Note the economy of design; that is, one back slat (A) and no arms.

CUTTING LIST		
KEY	**PIECES**	**SIZE AND DESCRIPTION**
A	1	1/2 × 3-1/4 × 16-1/2 back slat
B	2	1-1/4 × 35-1/2 back legs
C	2	1-1/4 × 3-1/2 back leg caps
D	2	1-1/4 × 28 front legs
E1	4	3/4 × 16-3/4 side rails
E2	2	7/8 × 16-3/4 side rails
F1	2	3/4 × 17-5/8 back rails
F2	1	7/8 × 17-5/8 back rail
G1	3	3/4 × 21-7/8 front rails
G2	1	7/8 × 21-7/8 front rail

MATERIALS LIST

1/4"-dia. dowels
120-grit sandpaper
Wood glue

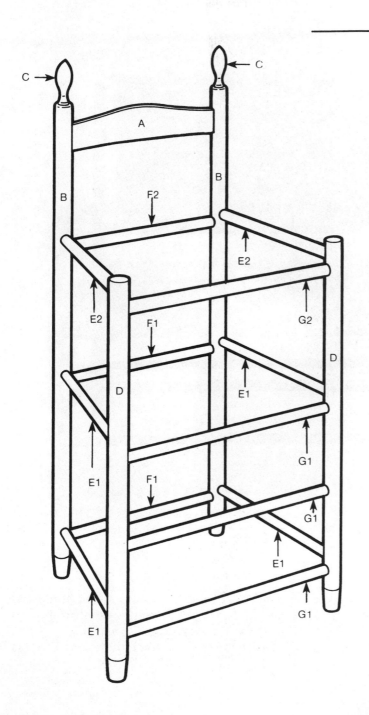

Mt. Lebanon Settee

Described as "the rarest of all Shaker furniture," this settee or double arm-chair was originally made at the end of the 19th century. The scale of the piece is well suited for today's country-styled home; two adults can sit on the settee comfortably.

Only the back posts (A) and back leg caps (C) are tapered to attach directly to the legs;

all other pieces are secured with dowels. For added strength, the arms (D) use 1/4"-diameter dowels; the large-diameter rails (G2, H2, I2) use 1"-diameter dowels; and the small-diameter rails (G1, H1, I1) use 1/2"-diameter dowels.

MATERIALS LIST

1/4"-dia. dowels
1/2"-dia. dowels
1"-dia. dowels
120-grit sandpaper
Wood glue

CUTTING LIST

KEY	PIECES	SIZE AND DESCRIPTION
A	2	1-3/8 × 42-1/2 back posts
B	2	1-3/8 × 35-1/2 back legs
C	2	1-3/8 × 2 back leg caps
D	2	5/8 × 3-1/2 × 18 arms
E	2	5/8 × 2-1/2 arm caps
F	2	1-5/8 × 21-1/2 front legs
G1	4	7/8 × 17-3/4 side rails
G2	2	1-3/8 × 17-3/4 side rails
H1	2	7/8 × 40 back rail
H2	1	1-3/8 × 40 back rail
I1	2	7/8 × 43 front rails
I2	1	1-3/8 × 43 front rail

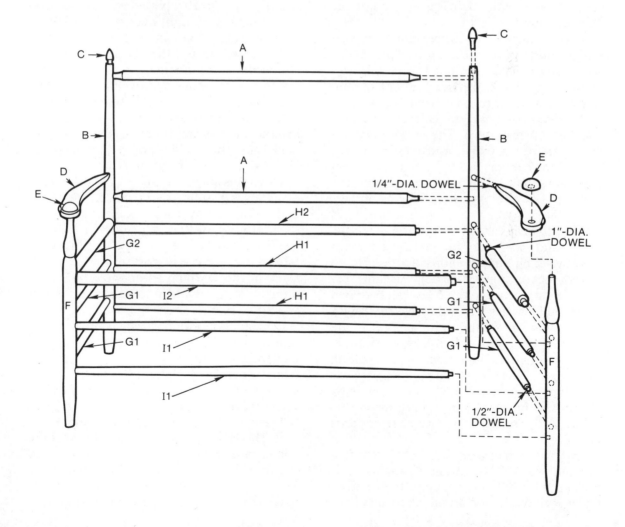

Weaving a Seat with Tape

In just about all the Shaker communities, fabric tape was preferred over fiber rush, wood splint, or cane for seating material because it is so functional. It does not dry out and break, nor does it pinch and snag clothing. It is strong and long lasting, as well as easy to work with. Also, it is very comfortable and quite colorful.

Before starting, it's important that you understand two terms: warp and weft. *Warp* is one length of tape wrapped around the rail from front to back. *Weft* is one length of tape wrapped around the rail from side to side and woven over and under the warp in a checkerboard pattern. The space between the layers of warping is stuffed with a firm 1/2" foam rubber pad. (The Shakers often used horsehair.) This is done not only for comfort, but also to prevent sagging and reduce wear.

Chair tape in various colors and in widths of 1" and 5/8" can be purchased from woodworking supply shops. To determine the correct amount of yardage, use this formula: First, measure the front rail between the posts, in inches. Second, measure straight across from the center of the back rail to the center of the front rail, in inches. Multiply these two figures, then divide the resulting figure by 9. This is the total number of yards of 1" tape required. (For 5/8" tape, divide by 5.3 rather than by 9.) If you are using two colors, order half the total number of yards per color.

The first step in seating the chair is weaving the warp. This entails wrapping tape around the front and back rails to provide a warp both on the top and the bottom of the seat. The procedure is as follows: The end of one coil of tape (doubled over for strength) is tacked to the inner side of the back rail, as close as possible to the left back leg. This doubled-over end must point toward the top of the chair as shown.

With the end firmly tacked in place, the coil of tape is brought over the back rail to the front rail, at right angles to both the front and back rails. It is then brought over the front rail and returned to the back rail, which it goes under and over. *It is essential that the tape not be twisted.* This procedure is continued until the right back leg is reached and there is no space for another warp on the back rail. (There will, however, be spaces at either side on the front rail.)

When this stage is reached, the tape is cut off, allowing about two extra inches. This end is doubled over and securely tacked to the bottom right side of the back rail, where it will overlap the last warp. Before this end is tacked in place it is important that as much slack in the warping as possible be pulled out; the tape should not be stretched but should be firm.

It should be emphasized again that the tape must run at right angles to the front and back rails. Because the side rails are splayed from front to back, there will be a triangular-shaped open area on either side of the seat. These warps will be added at a later stage.

The next step is the actual weaving of the seat. This is begun by securing the end of the coil of tape, which will be the weft. The end (doubled over for strength) is tacked to the inside of the left side rail as close as possible to the left back leg. A foam rubber pad, cut to

When weaving a warp, start by tacking one end of a coil of tape to the inner side of the back rail.

To weave a weft, the tape is brought alternately over and under the warp strips to form a checkerboard pattern.

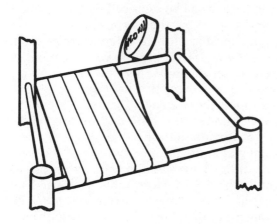

Bring the tape over the back rail to the front rail, over and under the front rail, then back under and over the back rail. Continue this pattern, with the tape always at right angles to the rails.

The corners are filled in by weaving an extra strip of tape parallel to the last warp on either side of the top of the seat.

fill the area of the seat, is now stuffed between the layers of the warping. The free end of the coil of tape is then brought over the first warp strip of the top layer, under the next, over one, under one, etc., until the right back post is reached. The full length of the tape is now pulled through all the top layer of warp strips. The chair is then turned over and the process is repeated on the lower layer of warp strips.

Next, the weft is again woven through the top layer of warp strips, this time starting under the first strip, over the second, etc., so that the result is the start of a checkerboard pattern. The chair is again turned over and the weft is returned through the lower layer of warp strips to form, as on the top layer, the beginning of a checkerboard pattern.

It should be noted that, at the right side of the chair, the end warp of the bottom layer (which has been tacked to the right side of the back rail) will somewhat overlap the second to the last warp on the same side. It is essential that these two be treated as a single warp; that is, the weft must be carried over or under both of them together. Only in this way can a checkerboard pattern be created on the bottom of the seat; in the finished seat, this inconsistency will not be apparent.

This procedure is continued until the weft reaches the front legs. Again, it must be emphasized that the tape must not be twisted. It should be pulled firmly each time it is brought through the warp strips, and the rows should be kept as straight as possible, each one touching the last. The final row on the top of the seat will abut the front legs on the side rails and should curve slightly toward the front rail to keep the warps smooth and flat.

Because at this stage the warps will be tight, a knife should be used for lifting them to permit the weft to pass under them. Now cut the weft so that it will end on the bottom of the chair; then tack it to the left side rail as close as possible to the left front leg. If there is not sufficient room to weave it through to the left side of the chair, as is sometimes the case, it should be tacked to the bottom of the front rail.

The final step in weaving the seat is to fill in the corners with added warps. For this you need two strips of tape of the color used in the warping. Cut these strips to run from the front rail to the back on both the top and the bottom of the seat with 2" or 3" to spare. Now weave them parallel to the last warp on either side of the top of the seat, bring them over the front rail, then weave them in the same fashion on the bottom. The ends, meeting at the back rail, are then tacked in place as inconspicuously as possible on the bottom of the rail.

One (or sometimes two or three, depending on the size and type of the chair) additional warp will be required on either side of the seat to fill out the warping near the front posts. Because of the triangular shape of the areas to be filled in, these warps cannot be carried to the back legs of the chair but should be woven through the wefts until they meet the side rails. Their ends should be tucked under the wefts and secured either by tacking them to the side rails or by carefully gluing them to the bottom of the weft.

Putting in these added warps demands attention and care. The quality of the finished seat depends to a great extent on the workmanship of this final stage. If done with care, the seat will fill out smoothly at the front.

Children's Rocking Chairs

These sturdy and attractive children's rockers will be enjoyed by any little feet that love to rock. They are the right size for youngsters to use and kids appreciate the fact that grown-ups' visits do not make the house SRO when there is one of these around. With the appropriate paint or other finish, one of the two should fit nicely into any setting you have in mind.

Heart Rocker

The heart rocker is constructed from 3/4" plywood. One 4' × 4' piece is all that is needed.

Use the squares to transfer the shape of the side of the rocker to the plywood. Both sides can be cut at one time by tacking two pieces of plywood together.

MATERIALS LIST
No. 6 × 1-1/4" wood screws
No. 6 × 1-1/2" wood screws
5d finishing nails
Edging tape
Screw hole plugs

CUTTING LIST		
KEY	**PIECES**	**SIZE AND DESCRIPTION**
A	1	3/4 × 12-1/2 × 16 back
B	2	3/4 × 20 × 25-1/2 sides
C	1	3/4 × 12-7/8 × 13 seat board
D	2	3/4 × 2 × 12 armrests
E	1	3/4 × 3/4 × 13 rear brace
F	1	3/4 × 1-1/2 × 13-1/2 front brace

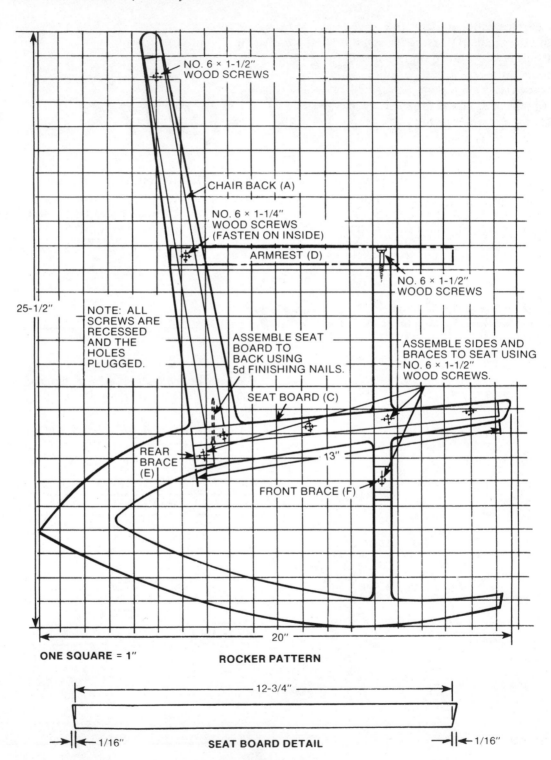

NO. 6 × 1-1/2"
WOOD SCREWS

CHAIR BACK (A)

NO. 6 × 1-1/4"
WOOD SCREWS
(FASTEN ON INSIDE)

ARMREST (D)

NO. 6 × 1-1/2"
WOOD SCREWS

25-1/2"

NOTE: ALL
SCREWS ARE
RECESSED
AND THE
HOLES
PLUGGED.

ASSEMBLE SEAT
BOARD TO
BACK USING
5d FINISHING NAILS.

ASSEMBLE SIDES AND
BRACES TO SEAT USING
NO. 6 × 1-1/2"
WOOD SCREWS.

SEAT BOARD (C)

REAR
BRACE
(E)

13"

FRONT BRACE (F)

20"

ONE SQUARE = 1"

ROCKER PATTERN

12-3/4"

1/16"

SEAT BOARD DETAIL

1/16"

Cut the rocker back (A), seat board (C), and armrests (D) to the illustrated shape. A 4° angle is required on the sides of the seat board and on the ends of the front and rear braces (E, F). A taper cutting jig is needed to cut the sides (B) of the back panel. Note the 4° angle on the bottom edge of the back. If a table saw is used, set the miter gauge at 11-1/2° to the right for the right armrest and 11-1/2° to the left for the left armrest. If a radial saw is used, the head is rotated 11-1/2° to the right and left to make the angle cuts.

Predrill all holes in the sides and armrests for the screws and screw hole plugs before assembly. When screw-fastening into the end grain, hardwood dowels may be used for additional strength.

Edging tape, or flexible wood veneer, makes it easy to cover the exposed plywood edges. The edging is fastened with contact cement. Apply it with hand pressure, then tap it down with a rubber headed mallet to achieve a good bond. Make sure that all of the corners are rounded and sharp edges are sanded smooth.

A 12″ × 12″ knife edge or box-style cushion will add comfort and enhance the beauty of the project.

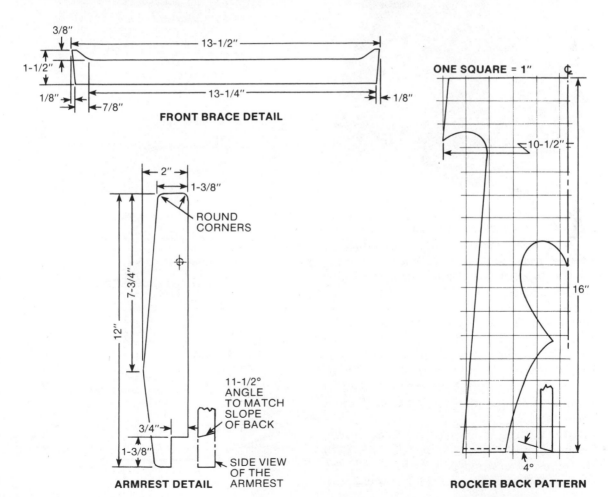

FRONT BRACE DETAIL

ARMREST DETAIL

SIDE VIEW OF THE ARMREST

ROCKER BACK PATTERN

Winged Rocker

CUTTING LIST		
KEY	PIECES	SIZE AND DESCRIPTION
A	2	3/4 × 10-1/2 × 27 sides
B	2	3/4 × 10 × 10-1/2 tails
C	2	3/4 × 4 × 6 cleats
D	1	3/4 × 9-1/2 × 11-1/4 front
E	1	3/4 × 10-1/2 × 11-1/4 seat
F	1	3/4 × 12-3/4 × 16-3/4 back
G	2	3/4 × 1-1/2 × 10-1/2 armrests
H	2	3/4 × 1-1/2 × 3-1/2 armrest supports
I	2	3/4 × 3/4 × 17-1/2 corner wedges (split)
J	1	3/4 × 12 × 12-3/4 tail brace

As with other country furniture pieces, the simple lines of this piece enable it to complement nearly any setting. Depending on the type of wood and finish used, this design can be attractively adapted to any decor.

Construction is as uncomplicated as the lines suggest. Begin by cutting the pieces as described in the cutting list. Cut out the sides (A), armrests (G), and tails (B) to the shapes shown in the graph. Note that the back is notched to accommodate the seat (E) and the cleats (B).

After cutting the rocker edges as shown, begin assembly by edge-gluing the tails (B) to the sides. Use wood screws to attach the cleats (C) to the tails and sides; this will also

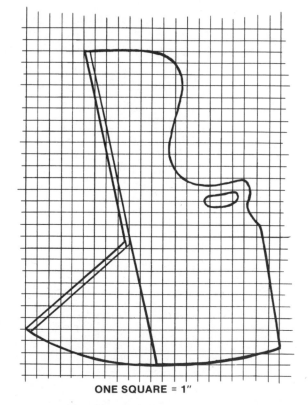

ONE SQUARE = 1"

act to clamp the pieces together until the glue dries.

Attach the rocker front (D) to the sides with wood glue and nails; then set the seat into place on the front and cleats with nails and glue. Attach the back to the sides by gluing and screwing, and fasten the tail brace (J) in the same fashion. Finally, glue the corner wedges (I), armrest supports (H), and armrests in sequence into place.

MATERIALS LIST

Wood screws
Finishing nails
Wood glue

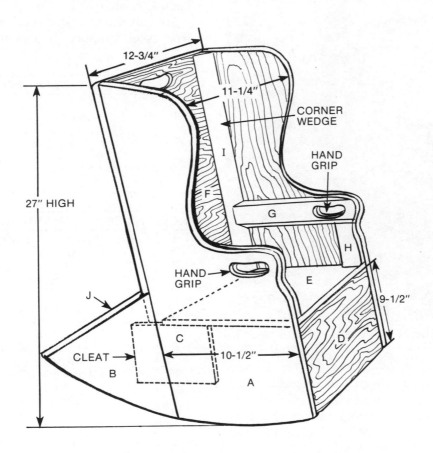

Rugged Chair

along the upper front edge to support the seat. Now you're ready to stand up the two side frame units and attach them across the back as shown.

Cut out the seat side frames (H) and the front seat support (I). Cut a 1/2″ × 1/2″

MATERIALS LIST

3/8″-dia. dowels
1″-dia. dowels
Lag screws
Carriage bolts
Wood glue

CUTTING LIST

KEY	PIECES	SIZE AND DESCRIPTION
A	2	1-1/2 × 11-1/4 × 36 side frames, rear
B	2	1-1/2 × 11-1/4 × 14 side frames, front
C	2	1-1/2 × 11-1/4 × 10 inner armrests
D	2	1-1/2 × 5-1/2 × 18 outer armrests
E	2	1-1/2 × 3-1/2 × 24 side bench supports
F	2	1-1/2 × 3-1/2 × 28 leg bases
G	1	1-1/2 × 3-1/2 × 19-3/8 back bench support
H	2	1-1/2 × 5-1/2 × 22 seat side frames
I	1	1-1/2 × 3-1/2 × 19-3/8 front seat support
J	1	1-1/2 × 3-1/2 × 19-3/8 middle seat support
K	1	1-1/2 × 3-1/2 × 28-1/2 bottom cross support
L	1	1-1/2 × 3-1/2 × 28 back, top member
M	1	1-1/2 × 3-1/2 × 28 back, bottom member
N	2	1-1/2 × 5-1/2 × 18 back, side members

This rugged country chair is assembled primarily with carriage bolts and lag screws so it can be knocked down for easy moving. At its widest point, the chair takes up 30-1/2″; the seat width is 22-1/2″.

To begin, cut out the side frames (A, B) and armrests (C, D) You can glue the inner and outer armrests together any time, but do not attach them to the rest of the chair yet.

Next, cut out the side bench supports (E) and leg bases (F). Assemble the side frames, side bench supports, and leg braces as shown in the drawing. Then cut out the back bench support (G) and cut a 1/2″ × 5/8″ rabbet

rabbet along the upper rear edge of the front seat support to carry the front of the seat. Assemble the sides and front of the seat frame with 3/8"-diameter dowels (not shown) and glue. Drill holes for the lag screws to attach the seat frame to the side

bench supports and for attaching the armrests to the seat frame.

Now fasten the glued-together inner and outer armrests to the seat frame with lag screws coming up from the bottom. The seat frame and armrests can now be put into

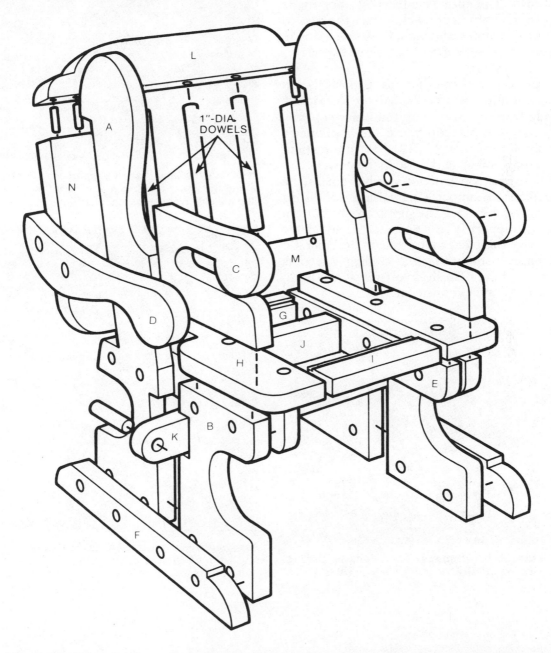

position on top of the side bench frames and fastened down with lag screws. Don't fasten down the seat yet. The rear of the outer armrests are also bolted to the side frames with two lag screws in each arm.

Assemble the back of the chair (L, M, N) as shown. The three center posts are made from 1"-diameter dowels. Attach the back to the side frames with lag screws, being sure to keep the sides vertical (use three lag screws on each side).

Cut out the bottom cross support (K) and slide it into position through the slots in the side frames. After everything else is firmly bolted into position, mark the 1"-diameter holes for the dowels. Drill these in for a tight fit, reassemble, and drive in the dowels.

The final construction step is to cut out the middle seat support (J). Drill holes for the lag screws and attach the support to the bottom cross support. It's not necessary to attach the ends of this piece to the sides of the chair. Do whatever smoothing and sanding is needed; then stain, and finish as you prefer. Add cushions to match your decor.

Now cut the back bench support with a rabbet along the upper front edge for the plywood seat. Tie the side frames together as shown.

Cut the side bench supports and leg bases. Use lag screws to partially assemble the side frames.

Assemble the seat frame unit and cut the plywood seat (don't fasten it down). Add the inner and outer armrests.

The back is put together with 3/8"-diameter dowels at the joints.

Attach the back with lag screws; then add the cross supports under the seat.

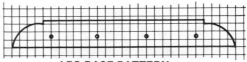

LEG BASE PATTERN

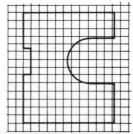

SIDE FRONT FRAME PATTERN

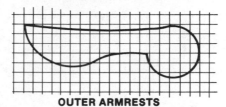

OUTER ARMRESTS

INNER ARMREST PATTERN

ONE SQUARE = 1"

SIDE REAR FRAME PATTERN

BACK TOP PATTERN

Shaker Bench ____

Here's a bench with all the charm, grace, and simplicity that Shaker craftsmanship can provide.

Begin by cutting all parts to the dimensions given in the cutting list. For angled cuts, use the illustration as a guide.

Cut 3/4" × 2-1/4" notches in the center of the legs and 1-1/4" × 2" notches 7" in from the ends of the seat support. The notches in the seat support are cut only 2" deep.

Using a 3-3/4"-diameter template, mark and cut the arches on the bottoms of the legs. Drill holes through the center of the seat support notches. Then cut 1/4" × 1-1/4" × 9-1/2" grooves across the underside of the seat from the back edge, stopping 1/4" short of the front edge.

Place the seat (A) upside down on the floor. Center the seat support (B) on the underside of the seat. The notches and predrilled screw holes of the seat support face upward directly over the leg groove in the underside of the seat.

To make sure that the seat support is properly positioned, place the notch in one of the legs (C) over the notch in the seat support

MATERIALS LIST

Wood screws
Wood glue

CUTTING LIST

KEY	PIECES	SIZE AND DESCRIPTION
A	1	1-1/4 × 9-3/4 × 60 seat
B	1	3/4 × 4 × 54 seat support
C	2	1-1/4 × 9-1/2 × 16 legs
D	1	3/4 × 3 × 60 backrest
E	2	1-1/4 × 3 × 29-7/8 backrest supports

so that both interlock. Then press the leg firmly into the groove. Using a hammer and block of wood, tap the edge of the leg flush with the back edge of the seat. Tap the leg into its groove with the block and hammer. Repeat the operation with the other leg. All this should be done without glue or screws.

Mark the seat support position accurately with a pencil and remove both the seat support and the legs. Glue the top of the seat support, place it in the marked position, and drive screws through the predrilled holes into the underside of the seat.

Glue should then be applied to the notch and upper edges of the legs. With a hammer

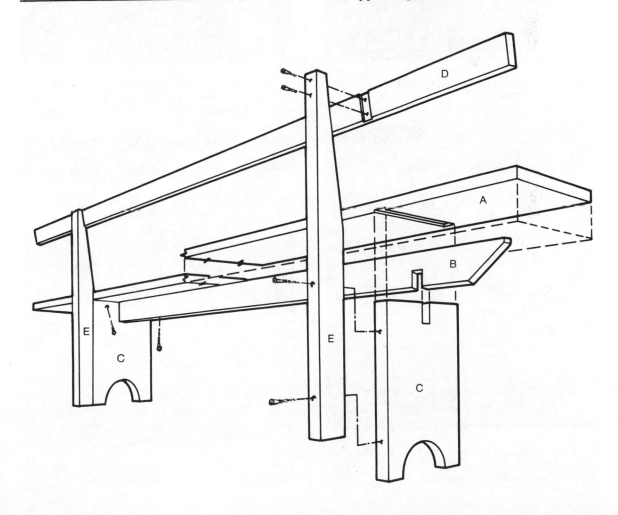

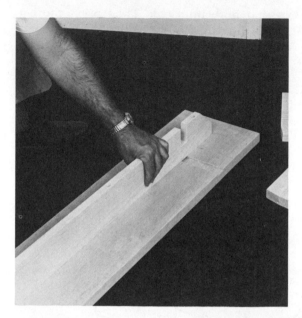

Assembly begins by properly lining up the seat support and seat.

A flush line-up of the backrest supports with the leg bottoms is important. Again a block of wood is used as a straightedge.

Use a hammer and block of wood to tap the edge of the leg flush with the edge of the seat. Repeat the operation with the other leg.

Following this, the screws are driven through the back supports and into the bench legs.

The backrest is joined to the supports, and hole plugs are inserted to finish the assembly.

and block of wood, drive the legs down firmly so that they interlock with the seat support and their upper edges are seated in the grooves. The legs should be fastened with screws in holes drilled diagonally through the sides of the legs.

Turn the bench facedown on the floor. Attach the backrest supports (E) with glue and screws, driving the screws through predrilled holes in the supports into the back edges of the legs. Make sure the bottoms of the supports are flush with those of the legs.

Now put the assembly on its legs. Using glue and recessed screws, attach the backrest (D) to the supports. The supports are inserted into 1/8" × 1-1/4" × 3" grooves at the back of the backrest. The tops of the supports should be flush with the top of the backrest. Glue and tap the hole plugs into the holes in the back supports.

Shaker Bench without Back

This is a simpler, but equally charming, version of the Shaker bench. Without a backrest, the seating area has been slightly expanded. Feel free to raise or lower the height of the seat, depending on where and how you intend to use the bench.

Cut the parts to size according to the dimensions given in the cutting list. Note that the legs (C) are exactly the same as those on the Shaker bench with a back. Cut 3/4" ×

2-1/4" notches in the center of each leg. Then use a 3-3/4"-diameter template to mark off and cut the arches on the bottoms of the legs.

Cut 1-1/4" × 2" notches 7" in from the ends of each seat support (B). Cut two 1/4" × 1-1/4" × 9-1/2" grooves across the underside of the seat (A) as shown in the drawing. Be sure to begin these grooves from the back edge of the seat. Now turn the seat upside down and center the seat support on the underside of the seat. The notches and screw holes (positioned as shown in the illustration) in the seat support should face upward directly over the grooves in the seat.

To make sure that the seat support is properly positioned, place the notch in one of the legs over the notch in the seat support so that both interlock. Then press the leg firmly into the groove. Using a hammer and wood block, tap the edge of the leg flush with the edge of the seat and tap the leg into its groove. Repeat the operation with the other leg. All this should be done without glue or screws.

Mark the seat support position accurately and remove both the seat support and the legs. Apply glue to the top of the seat support, place it in position, and drive screws through the predrilled holes into the underside of the seat.

Glue should then be applied to the notch and upper edges of the legs. With a hammer and wood block, drive the legs down firmly so that they interlock with the seat support; their upper edges should be seated in the notches. Secure the legs with screws drilled diagonally through the sides of the legs.

MATERIALS LIST
Wood screws
Wood glue

CUTTING LIST		
KEY	**PIECES**	**SIZE AND DESCRIPTION**
A	1	1-1/4 × 9-3/4 × 66 seat
B	1	3/4 × 4 × 60 seat support
C	2	1-1/4 × 9-1/2 × 16 legs

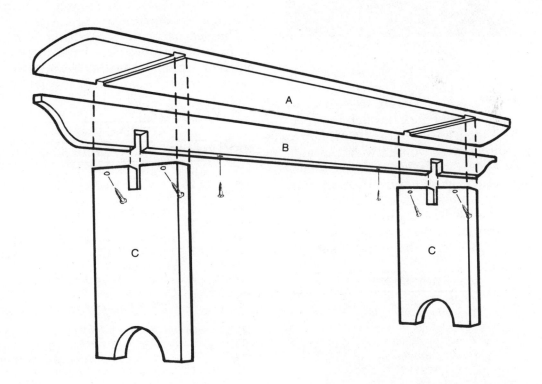

Four-Legged Cobbler's Bench

The sturdy cobbler's bench, once the shoemaker's prime tool, has proved its hardiness and versatility through the years by making the transition from workshop to living room. It has become a welcome addition that blends well with most furnishings for both practical and conversational purposes.

First cut all the pieces to size from pine stock. Exposed edges are roughed and rounded with a rasp, then sanded smooth.

MATERIALS LIST

1"-dia. dowels
Brass screws
Brass tacks
Finishing nails
Foam rubber
Simulated leather
Wood glue

Join legs (D) to the leg supports (E, F) with wood glue and 1"-diameter dowels. Attach them to the underside of the bench top (A) with wood screws. The sides (B) and end (C) are fixed together and mounted to the bench top with ornamental brass screws. The top strip (I) is then attached to the sides with recessed finishing nails and wood glue.

Drawer runners (G) are fastened to the underside of the top with wood screws after the drawer runner guides (H) are attached to them with nails and glue. Drawer assembly is shown in the detail.

The seat is made of 9"-diameter × 1/2" foam rubber and covered with a circular piece of simulated leather secured to the bench top with ornamental brass tacks.

CUTTING LIST

KEY	PIECES	SIZE AND DESCRIPTION
A	1	1-1/4 × 14 × 40 bench top
B	2	3/4 × 4 × 17-3/4 sides
C	1	3/4 × 4 × 14 end
D	4	2 × 2 × 14 legs
E	1	1-1/4 × 6-1/2 × 13 leg support
F	1	1-1/4 × 4 × 14 leg support
G	2	1/2 × 1-1/2 × 12-3/4 drawer runners
H	2	1/2 × 3/4 × 12-3/4 drawer runner guides
I	1	3/4 × 2-3/4 × 14 top strip
J1	1	3/4 × 13 × 4 drawer front
J2	2	3/4 × 12 × 3-3/4 drawer sides
J3	1	3/4 × 13 × 3-3/4 drawer back
J4	1	1/4 × 12 × 12 drawer bottom
J5	2	1/2 × 1/2 × 12-3/4 drawer runners

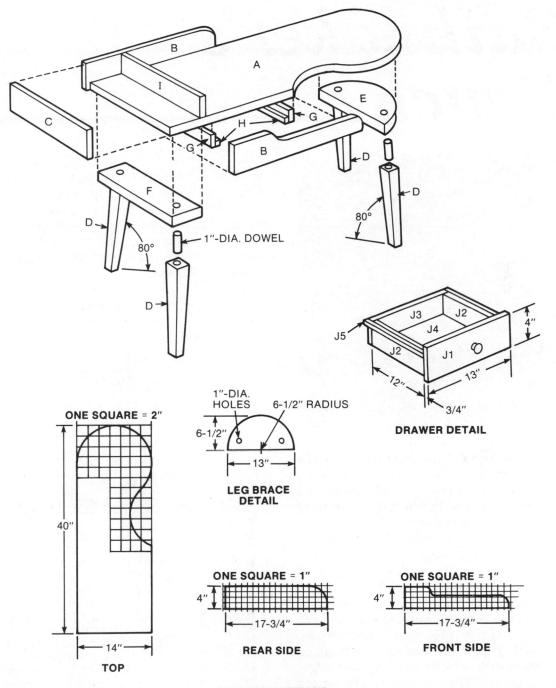

B

A

B

I

C

E

H

G

G

D

D

80°

F

D

1"-DIA. DOWEL

80°

D

DRAWER DETAIL

J3   J2

J4

J5

J2   J1

4"

12"

13"

3/4"

ONE SQUARE = 2"

1"-DIA.
HOLES   6-1/2" RADIUS

6-1/2"

13"

**LEG BRACE
DETAIL**

40"

14"

TOP

ONE SQUARE = 1"

4"

17-3/4"

REAR SIDE

ONE SQUARE = 1"

4"

17-3/4"

FRONT SIDE

CUTTING PATTERNS

Sailmaker's Bench

Cut the pieces to size, and shape the sides (B) and leg bottoms to the contour shown. Fasten the sides to the top with finishing nails and glue. Additional nails, driven through the sides into the legs will provide a good degree of rigidity. Note that the legs are slanted approximately 10° off vertical, as seen in the illustration.

Attach the drawer frame pieces (D, E, G) as shown, using finishing nails and glue. Fit the braces (F) between the legs and fasten them with nails and glue.

L ike the cobbler, the sailmaker also had a customized bench. This sailmaker's bench complements any country decor—its convenient size and height make it just right for use as a coffee table.

The materials used to build the bench will depend, to a large extent, on their availability. In particular, this applies to the 1 × 16 pine boards that are used for the top (A) and legs (C). Stock of this width will not be found at every lumberyard, but many dealers will be able to obtain it for you. As an alternate choice, 3/4" pine plywood can be used, or several boards can be doweled and edge-glued together. The remaining materials are readily available.

MATERIALS LIST

Finishing nails
Screws
Drawer pull
Wood glue

CUTTING LIST

KEY	PIECES	SIZE AND DESCRIPTION
A	1	3/4 × 16 × 48 top
B	2	3/4 × 5 × 48 sides
C	2	3/4 × 16 × 24 legs
D	1	3/4 × 12 × 16 drawer frame
E	1	3/4 × 8 × 12 drawer frame
F	2	3/4 × 4 × 30 leg braces
G	1	3/4 × 8 × 15 drawer frame
H	1	1-1/2 × 3-1/2 × 16 tool rack
I	4	3/4 × 3/4 × 8 top trim
J1	1	3/4 × 7 × 8 drawer front
J2	2	3/4 × 7 × 14 drawer sides
J3	1	3/4 × 7 × 6-1/2 drawer back
J4	1	3/4 × 6-1/2 × 13-1/4 drawer bottom

Now, only the finishing touches remain. Trim the top with 3/4″ stock, as seen in the drawing, and cut a 5″ hole in the top.

Across the end of the top is a length of 2 × 4 into which five equally spaced 3/4″-diameter holes have been drilled. The work-

man used this piece as a tool rack, keeping his unused tools handy by placing them in the holes. After drilling these holes, attach the board to the top with glue and screws. Nail the drawer pieces together, following the sketch, to complete the piece.

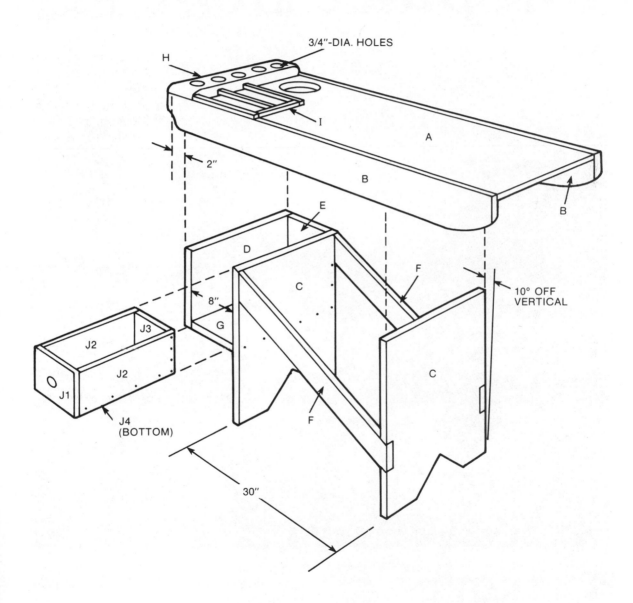

Victorian Fireplace Bench

This pine fireplace bench is a repro- duction of a piece that hasn't been built since Victorian times. Then, benches such as this were used as window seats and daybeds, as well as fireplace benches. It can fit almost anywhere in your home, from foyer to bedroom.

Make a template of the four feet (K). Cut out the shapes and make rabbet cuts where indicated in the drawing. To make the front

(B1, B2) and rear (C1, C2) panels, joint and glue together a 1 × 12 and a 1 × 6 board for each panel. Rip the panels to a 15″ width; then cut the curve on the top of each piece.

Make the four corner uprights (A) simultaneously by stacking them together. The scrolled top design can be cut out with a bandsaw; cut the lower portion on a table saw, being careful not to cut into the curved area. Sand the uprights while still stacked; then separate the stack and rout 1/4″ grooves on each outside face as shown. Later, these grooves will receive bead molding.

The corner uprights also have a routed groove to accept the pillow rails (J). Make a template of this area and transfer its contour onto the uprights. Rout freehand up to the contour line and use a wood chisel to complete the recess.

Glue and dowel three 1 × 6s to form each of the side panels (D). Next, cut the notch and rabbet that allow the panels to lock into the corner uprights. Next, make an end template for shaping the pillow rails. It should fit the routed area that you cut into the uprights with room for inserting the side panels. Cut the stock to length for both rails. Cut a rabbet to accommodate the side panels in the full length of the rails.

Drill holes to accommodate 3/8″-diameter dowels in the pillow rails and side panels. Make a V-shaped jig to hold the rail for boring the dowel holes. Next, join the pillow rails and side panels with glue and dowels.

Bore the remaining dowel holes for assembling the side panels, corner uprights, and front and rear panels. Dry-fit the side panels with the glued pillow rails to the corner uprights in order to clean the routed areas. Finally, glue and clamp these pieces together.

Next, cut two slat support rails (H) to fit inside the front and rear panels. Make sure each rail is parallel; then bore 1/2″-diameter holes spaced to match the mattress slats (I). These holes are bored all the way through the slat support rails and no more than 1/2″ into the rear panels. Attach the slat support rails to the panels with dowels and glue, and secure with clamps.

When dry, assemble the front and rear panels to the assembled side panels with 1/4″-diameter dowels and glue. Square the unit before the glue sets. Cut the five mattress slats and nail them into place. Invert the

MATERIALS LIST

1/4″-dia. dowels
3/8″-dia. dowels
1/2″-dia. dowels
6″ × 15″ × 47″ foam mattress
Finishing nails
120-grit sandpaper
180-grit sandpaper
Wood glue

CUTTING LIST

KEY	PIECES	SIZE AND DESCRIPTION
A	4	3/4 × 7-1/2 × 31 corner uprights
B1	1	3/4 × 11-1/4 × 39 front panel
B2	1	3/4 × 5-1/2 × 39 front panel
C1	1	3/4 × 11-1/4 × 39 rear panel
C2	1	3/4 × 5-1/2 × 39 rear panel
D	6	3/4 × 5-1/2 × 28-1/2 side panels
E	4	3/4 × 4-1/2 × 5-1/2 corner aprons
F	2	3/4 × 4-1/2 × 18 side aprons
G	2	3/4 × 4-1/2 × 39 front and rear aprons
H	2	3/4 × 2-1/2 × 47 slat support rails
I	5	3/4 × 2-1/2 × 15 mattress slats
J	2	1-1/2 × 3-1/2 × 15-1/2 pillow rails
K	4	3 × 3-1/2 × 6-1/4 feet
L	2	1/4 × 1/2 × 18-1/2 bottom trim (corner bead molding)
M	2	1/4 × 1/2 × 17 top trim (corner bead molding)
N	4	1/4 × 1/2 × 5-3/4 bottom trim (corner bead molding)
O	4	1/4 × 1/2 × 4-3/4 top trim (corner bead molding)
P	1	3/8 × 15 × 47 mattress board (plywood)

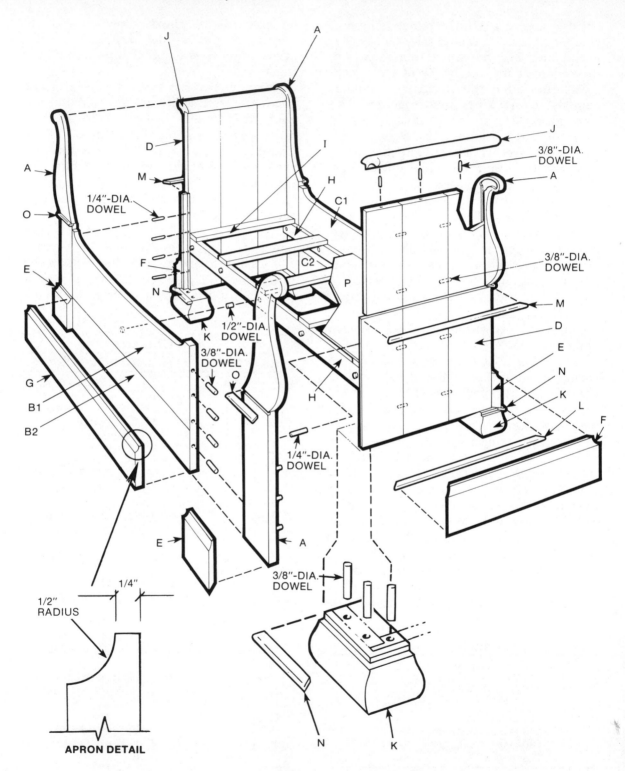

J
A
D
I
A
M
H
C1
1/4"-DIA. DOWEL
O
C2
F
N
P
E
K
1/2"-DIA. DOWEL
G
3/8"-DIA. DOWEL
B1
O
B2
H
Q
E
A
3/8"-DIA. DOWEL
1/4"-DIA. DOWEL
J
3/8"-DIA. DOWEL
A
3/8"-DIA. DOWEL
M
D
E
N
K
L
F

1/4"
1/2" RADIUS

APRON DETAIL

N
K

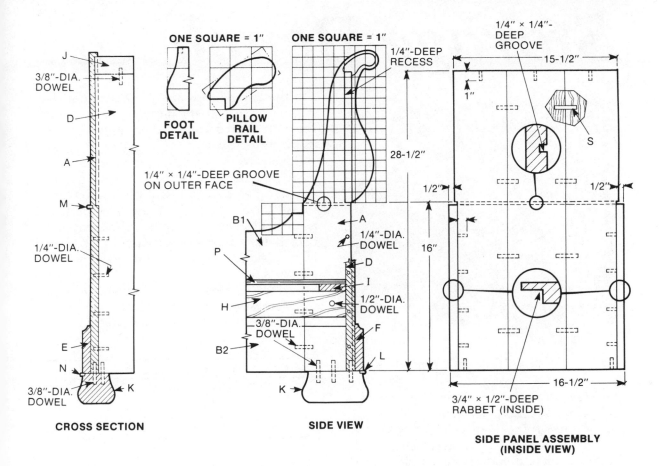

3/8"-DIA. DOWEL

J

D

A

M

1/4"-DIA. DOWEL

E

N

3/8"-DIA. DOWEL

K

CROSS SECTION

ONE SQUARE = 1"

FOOT DETAIL

PILLOW RAIL DETAIL

1/4" × 1/4"-DEEP GROOVE ON OUTER FACE

ONE SQUARE = 1"

1/4"-DEEP RECESS

28-1/2"

B1

P

H

3/8"-DIA. DOWEL

B2

K

A

1/4"-DIA. DOWEL

D

I

1/2"-DIA. DOWEL

F

L

SIDE VIEW

1/4" × 1/4"-DEEP GROOVE

15-1/2"

1"

S

1/2"

1/2"

16"

16-1/2"

3/4" × 1/2"-DEEP RABBET (INSIDE)

SIDE PANEL ASSEMBLY (INSIDE VIEW)

entire unit onto sawhorses, resting it on the slats. The sawhorses should be high enough so that the corner uprights clear the floor.

To make the apron (E, F, G), rout a cove along the top edge of the stock as shown in the detail drawing. Sand the coved stock; then cut the mitered apron pieces to size. Glue the apron to the cabinet.

Cut the corner bead molding (L, M, N, O) to size and round over one edge with a small plane; sand the pieces smooth with 120-grit sandpaper. Cut, miter, and fit the top trim pieces into the corner upright and end panel grooves.

Bore three holes in each foot to accommodate 3/8"-diameter dowels. Two dowels will enter the corner upright and one will tie to the end panel. Locate matching holes with dowel centers, bore, insert the dowels, glue, and fit the feet to the unit. Cut and miter the bottom trim molding pieces to fit the grooves in the feet and across the underside of the panels. Glue the molding into place.

Next, tip the unit upright. Cut the plywood mattress board (P) to size and secure it to the mattress slats with finishing nails. Sand the entire unit with 180-grit paper. Finish as desired.

Storage Bench

Cut the curved tops and the bottom openings of the sides to the dimensions shown in the pattern after tracing the outlines on the assembled pieces.

Edge-glue the back pieces together and attach the back supports (I) as shown with wood screws and glue. Cut the curved bottom of the box front (B) in the same fashion as the sides were cut. Attach the front and back bottom supports (K) with wood screws at the same height as the bottom side supports.

Fasten the sides to the back with recessed wood screws. Drilling the recesses 3/8" wide will permit them to be easily plugged with

This storage bench is a reproduction of a woodbox/fireplace bench. Whether or not you use it for its original purpose, it is both a practical and charming piece that will fit into a hall or dinette, for example, to provide handy storage and additional seating space.

Cut the pieces to the dimensions given in the cutting list. The sides (A1, A2), back (C), and seat (G) are constructed of several pieces of white pine shelving edge-glued and braced together.

Begin construction by edge-gluing the sides together and attaching the seat supports (F) and bottom side supports (J) to them with wood screws. Mount the top edges of the seat supports 15" from the bottom. Mount the top edges of the bottom supports 2-1/4" from the bottom. Besides supporting the seat and box bottom (D) on the assembled piece, the supports will also hold the side pieces together while the glue sets.

MATERIALS LIST
3/8"-dia. dowels
Wood screws
Hinges
Wood glue

CUTTING LIST		
KEY	**PIECES**	**SIZE AND DESCRIPTION**
A1	2	3/4 × 9-3/4 × 39 sides
A2	2	3/4 × 9-3/4 × 25 sides
B	1	3/4 × 15 × 42 box front
C	4	3/4 × 9-3/4 × 42 back
D	1	3/8 × 18 × 42 box bottom (plywood)
E	1	3/4 × 1-1/2 × 42 hinge strip
F	2	3/4 × 1-1/2 × 18 seat supports
G	2	3/4 × 8-3/4 × 42 seat
H	2	3/4 × 3-1/2 × 15 seat supports
I	2	3/4 × 3-1/2 × 33 back supports
J	2	3/4 × 3/4 × 18 bottom side supports
K	2	3/4 × 3/4 × 40 bottom supports
L	2	3/4 × 3/4 × 4 support rests

sections of 3/8"-diameter dowel. Glue the box bottom to its supports and attach the box front to the sides with recessed wood screws. Fasten the front of the bottom to its support with wood screws.

Assemble the seat and seat supports (H) in the same fashion as the sides and back. Attach the hinges to the back edge of the seat and the front edge of the hinge strip (E). Attach the seat assembly to the bench by screwing the corners of the hinge strip to the side supports, with additional screws through the bench back and back edge of the hinge strip. Mark the position of the seat supports on the box front and fasten the support rests (L) with wood screws 3/4" below the inside top of the front.

Plug the recesses in the sides. After a finish is applied, attach any decorative hardware desired.

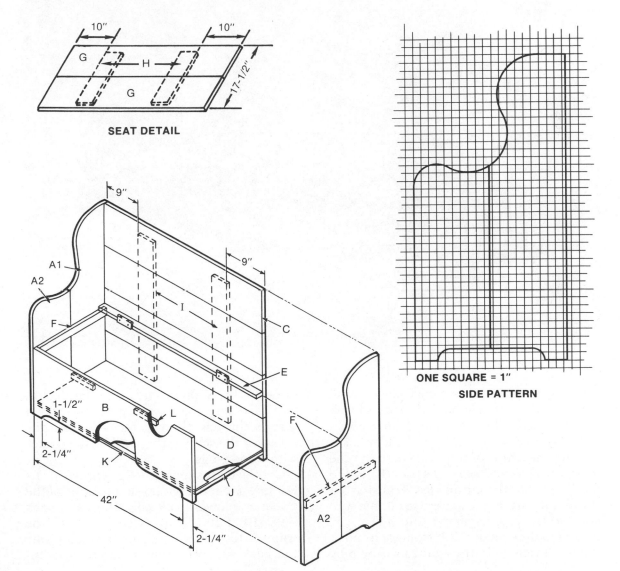

SEAT DETAIL

ONE SQUARE = 1"

SIDE PATTERN

Porch Swing

This porch swing is a cozy place to lull away an afternoon. It's made of oak and designed to be suspended from a porch ceiling or to rest in the optional glider base.

Make the frame of the swing first. Cut the main rails (A) and seat supports (B) to the dimensions in the cutting list. Transfer the contour shown in the pattern to cut the supports to the correct shape. Cut 3/4" × 3/8" dadoes in the center and 3" from each end of the main rails. Join the frame members by inserting the support ends into the dadoes and fastening them with glue and wood screws through the rail faces. Recess the holes for the screws; they will be filled later with wood plugs.

Cut the back supports (C) as shown in Detail 1. Also cut the widths and lengths of the upper and lower back rails (D, E) and back slats (F1, F2). Clamp these pieces to the frame to test for fit; then glue and clamp only the back supports. After the glue sets, remove the clamps and screw the back supports to the side supports with No. 10 × 1-1/4" wood screws.

Using a template made from the illustration of the back slat pattern, cut the back slats to the final shape. With the back rails still positioned in the back supports, assemble and glue the slats to the rails. Align the outer slats flush with the seat supports and space the inner slats evenly. Glue and clamp the slats to the rails, but do not glue the rails to the supports yet.

Cut the armrests (I), front and back ends (J), bottoms (K), and side slats (L) to the given dimensions. Mortise and notch the ends of the bottom and armrest as shown in the photos to accommodate the ends, using the dimensions given in Detail 3. Cut grooves in the armrests and ends for the slats, using the dimensions shown in the same detail. A corresponding groove is also cut into the bottoms for the slats.

Dry-assemble the sides and place them between the main rails to check that they fit snugly. Mark the back slats and the armrests where they meet. The back slats will have to be notched at these locations to permit the sides to be seated tightly against the seat supports. The armrest marks will help get a square fit. Glue and clamp the side members together, making sure to space the slats evenly.

Remove the back slat and rail assembly and drill pilot holes for screws to attach the back supports to the armrests and the ends to the main rails. *Note:* Don't install these screws yet; it is easier to apply a finish to the ends before they are secured in place.

Notch the back slats as previously indicated, and cut the slat supports (G) to rough size. Then place the supports behind the slats and trace the top arc on them; make the lower arc 2-1/2" below the upper one, and cut out the piece. Smooth the lower edge and rout to round it over to a 1/4" radius. Glue

the support to the slats. After the glue dries, sand the edges to a smooth arc. Then round over the sides of the top edge and the inside of the heart shapes in the slats.

Assemble the side, frame, and back components, plugging the screw holes. Cut the filler strips (N) to size and glue them in place. Because the sides and hidden areas of the frame are difficult to reach after the swing is completely assembled, you may want to apply a first finish coat to these areas as you proceed.

MATERIALS LIST

3/8"-dia. plugs
No. 8 × 1" wood screws
No. 10 × 1-1/4" wood screws
3/8"-dia. poly rope
Wood glue

CUTTING LIST

KEY	PIECES	SIZE AND DESCRIPTION
A	2	1-1/8 × 2-1/2 × 53-1/2 main rails
B	3	3/4 × 3-1/2 × 22-1/4 seat supports
C	4	3/4 × 3 × 17-1/2 back supports
D	1	1/2 × 3-1/2 × 47-1/2 back rail
E	1	1/2 × 2-1/2 × 47-1/2 back rail
F1	4	1/2 × 5-1/2 × 20-1/2 back slats
F2	4	1/2 × 5-1/2 × 22 back slats
G	2	1/2 × 7-1/2 × 24 slat supports
H1	6	1/2 × 2-1/2 × 47-1/2 bottom slats
H2	1	1/2 × 2 × 47-1/2 bottom slat
H3	1	1/2 × 3/4 × 46 cleat
I	2	3/4 × 4-1/2 × 24 armrests
J	4	3/4 × 3 × 11 front and back ends
K	2	3/4 × 3 × 21-1/2 bottoms
L	14	1/2 × 2-1/2 × 11 side slats
M	2	3/4 × 3-1/2 × 23-1/2 hanger boards
N	2	1/2 × 3/4 × 1-3/4 filler strips

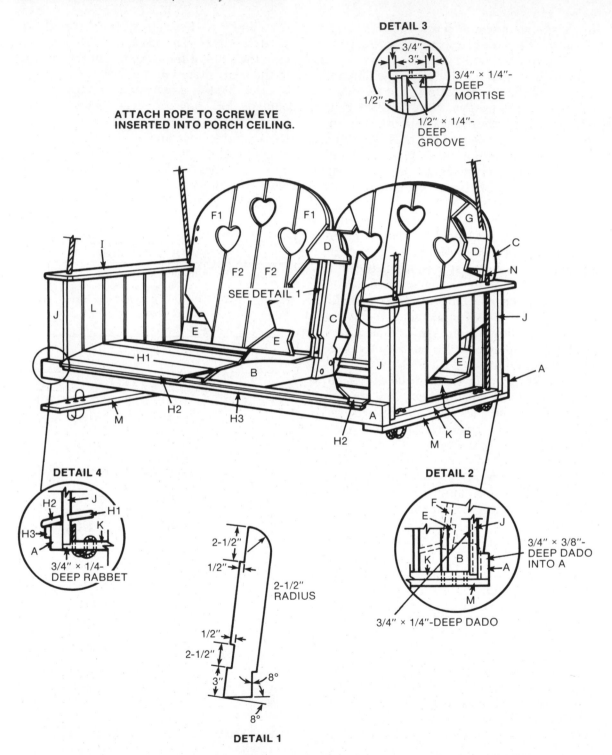

DETAIL 3

3/4"
3"
3/4" × 1/4"- DEEP MORTISE
1/2"
1/2" × 1/4"- DEEP GROOVE

ATTACH ROPE TO SCREW EYE INSERTED INTO PORCH CEILING.

F1   F1
G
D
C
N
F2   F2
D
I
SEE DETAIL 1
C
J   L
J
E
E
E
A
J
B
M
H1
H2   H3
H2
A
M   K   B

DETAIL 4

H2   J
H1
K
H3
A
3/4" × 1/4- DEEP RABBET

DETAIL 2

F
E
J
K   B
A
M
3/4" × 3/8"- DEEP DADO INTO A
3/4" × 1/4"-DEEP DADO

2-1/2"
1/2"
2-1/2" RADIUS
1/2"
2-1/2"
3"   8°
8°

DETAIL 1

ONE SQUARE = 2"

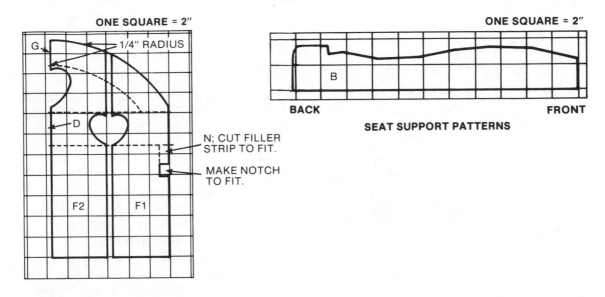

SEAT SUPPORT PATTERNS

G — 1/4" RADIUS

N; CUT FILLER
STRIP TO FIT.

MAKE NOTCH
TO FIT.

D

F2 · F1

BACK SLAT PATTERNS

Grooves are cut into the side frame members for the slats.

Use wood glue to secure slats (L) and ends (J) to the armrests and bottoms.

Cut the bottom slats (H1, H2) and cleat (H3) to size. Align the slats with the side slats for spacing, and attach them to the seat supports with two No. 8 × 1" wood screws per support. Cut the hanger boards (M) to size, and attach them to the undersides of the ends with No. 10 × 1-1/4" wood screws. Drill 3/8"-diameter rope holes through the armrests, bottoms, and hanger boards as indicated in the illustration.

Glider

As an alternative to swinging from a porch ceiling the swing can set in a glider. The body of the glider is the same as the body of the porch swing, and the sides of the glider base are constructed the same way as the swing sides.

Cut parts A, B, C, and D to size. Then make the cuts for the joints and slats (C). Note that the braces (D) rest in the groove cut in the center slat. Test the fit of all parts and assemble the sides with glue and clamps.

When the glue is dry, install two No. 10 × 1-1/4″ wood screws in each of the corner joints. Screw the braces to the top and bottom with one screw per joint.

Next, cut the backbone (E) to shape. Insert it between the braces and secure with three nuts, bolts, and washers per side.

The body is suspended by four ropes that hang from cleats (F). Cut these cleats and drill the necessary rope holes. Then bolt each to the underside of the top and bottom supports.

Cut the leg parts (G1, G2, H1, H2) to size. Make the required tapers and rounded edges as shown in the diagram. Assemble the legs with glue. Drill 1/8″-diameter holes for the rope and install the legs onto the swing with No. 10 × 1-1/4″ screws.

Cut the leg stretchers (J) to size. Screw a stretcher to the underside of the swing end, in place of part M in the porch swing. Then fasten the legs to the stretcher.

Place the swing in position between the glider sides and thread the suspension ropes through the leg holes. Adjust the height of the swing so it does not hit the backbone.

Garage door rollers are installed in the roller blocks (K) above the backbone to keep the swing centered. Casters can also be added.

CUTTING LIST (Optional Glider Base)		
KEY	**PIECES**	**SIZE AND DESCRIPTION**
A	4	3/4 × 3-1/2 × 30-1/2 top and bottom supports
B	4	3/4 × 3-1/2 × 23 ends
C	10	1/2 × 5-1/2 × 23 slats
D	4	1/4 × 2-1/2 × 23 braces
E	1	3/4 × 7-1/4 × 62 backbone
F	4	1-1/2 × 2 × 5 cleats
G1	2	3/4 × 3-1/2 × 22-3/4 front leg braces
G2	2	3/4 × 3-1/2 × 11-3/4 front legs
H1	2	3/4 × 3-1/2 × 20 rear leg braces
H2	2	3/4 × 3-1/2 × 8-1/2 rear legs
I	2	3/4 × 3 × 15-7/8 rub strips
J	2	3/4 × 3-1/2 × 21-7/8 leg stretchers
K	2	3/4 × 2 × 3-3/8 roller blocks

MATERIALS LIST
(Optional Glider Base)

3/8"-dia. plugs
No. 8 × 1" wood screws
No. 10 × 1-1/4" wood screws
5/16" × 3" carriage bolts, nuts, flat, and
  lock washers
1/4" × 2" stove bolts, nuts, and lock washers
1" garage door roller
Casters
Rope
Wood glue

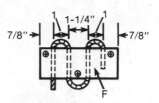

DETAIL 1

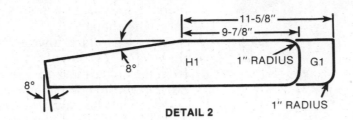

DETAIL 2

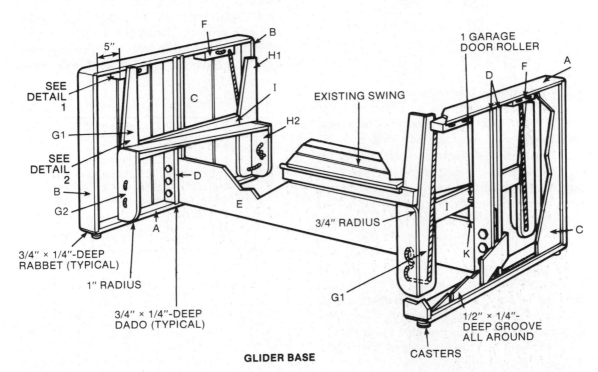

GLIDER BASE

Four-Poster Bed

If you want a heavy bed with four big posts, the one shown here will interest you. The full-size bed frame was designed for a mattress and spring 54" wide and 75" long. A queen-size mattress is 60" wide and 80" long, and a king-size is 76" wide and 80" long. Measure your own mattress to be sure of the dimensions. The frame should be 4" to 5" larger than the mattress so you can easily fit the sheets and blankets when you make the bed.

The carved post tops and designs in the head and footboards should be made with patterns. Draw your patterns on graph paper and transfer them to the wood. Carve the post ends by placing them side by side so that you can compare the shape and size of the designs while carving.

To construct the bed, cut two 10' 4 × 6s so that you have two 4' pieces for the footboard legs (B) and two 6' pieces for the headboard legs (A). On the 6' pieces, mark down 8" from the top for the heads. Make all marks con-

tinuous around the four sides of the piece, using a square. Then mark down 1-3/4" from the first mark for the collar section. From this second point, mark down 12" for the body of the carving. Add another 1-3/4" collar section as shown in the illustration, then make one more mark 5" down from the body mark. These are the points at which you carve and shape.

On the legs, mark down 8" from the top for the head, 1-3/4" down for the collar, 8" down from the collar mark for the body, then another 1-3/4" to complete the carving.

Use a circular saw, drawing knife, rasps, and chisels to carve these areas. Be sure to apply a pattern to the rounded head section, and compare the head carvings often to be sure all four legs match. Set the legs aside until you have cut the 2 × 12s for the head-

MATERIALS LIST

1/2"-dia. dowels
1/2" × 2-1/2" lag bolts
1/2" × 2-1/2" carriage bolts
Nuts and washers
4d finishing nails
Angle irons
Heavy-duty casters
Wood glue

CUTTING LIST

KEY	PIECES	SIZE AND DESCRIPTION
A	2	3-1/2 × 5-1/2 × 72 headboard legs
B	2	3-1/2 × 5-1/2 × 48 footboard legs
C	1	1-1/2 × 46 × 53 headboard
D	2	1-1/2 × 5-1/2 × 78 rails
E	1	1-1/2 × 28-1/2 × 53 footboard
F	2	3/4 × 1-1/2 × 78 slat supports
G	4	3/4 × 3-1/2 × 57 bed slats

board (C) and footboard (E). After you have cut them, you can determine the right length for the leg mortises.

Cut seven 2 × 12s to 53″ lengths. Glue and dowel the edges of the 2 × 12s together for the headboard and footboard. Glue the 2 × 12s in pairs; then double up two pairs to make the headboard four 2 × 12s wide. Note that the end grain in the boards has an arc: alternate the end grain—one arc up, the next down—to minimize warping. Use pipe clamps to hold the pieces together until the glue is set.

Apply your patterns to cut the head and footboards to the desired shape. Cut the notch at the bottom of the paired 2 × 12s

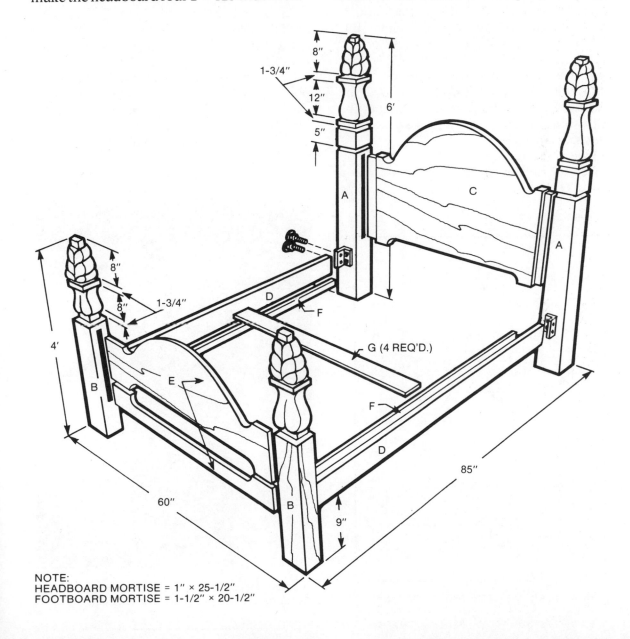

NOTE:
HEADBOARD MORTISE = 1″ × 25-1/2″
FOOTBOARD MORTISE = 1-1/2″ × 20-1/2″

that form the footboard; then use that notch as a pattern to mark the last 2 × 6. Cut out the notch in the top of the 2 × 6 and glue it to the bottom of the footboard to make the design shown in the photo.

When you have cut the headboard and footboard arcs, mark in 2″ from each end where a 53″ width remains. Cut tenons at this point. Leave a tenon that is 1″ thick and 2″ wide. Measure the length of the tenons; this will be the length of the leg mortises.

The mortises should be marked 1″ wide at the exact center of the legs (on the 4″ side). Bore out most of the wood stock. Drill the mortises 2″ deep. Use a chisel to cut out the remaining wood stock and to square and true the mortises.

Insert the tenons into the mortises and check for fit; slight trimming may be necessary. Then glue the tenons and use pipe clamps to hold the legs and boards together until the glue sets.

Cut two 2 × 6s, 78″ long, for the rails (D). Attach the rails to the legs so the bottoms are 9″ above the floor. Use 1/2″ × 2-1/2″ lag bolts to attach the 5″ angle irons to the legs. Use 1/2″ × 2-1/2″ carriage bolts to attach the rails to the angle irons. Nail 1 × 2 strips, 78″ long, to the bottom inside edge of the rails to hold the bed slats.

Cut the bed slats (G) from the 1 × 4s so they fit snugly between the rails.

The four-poster bed is very heavy. To be able to move it, attach heavy-duty casters to the bottoms of the legs. Get the widest casters you can find; then bore holes into the center of the leg bottoms and insert the caster stems.

ONE SQUARE = 4″

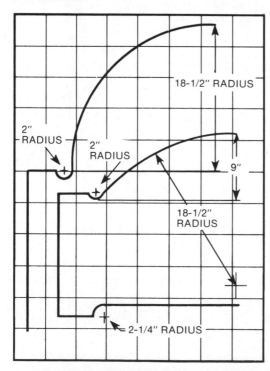

HEADBOARD AND FOOTBOARD PATTERNS

A hand-carved design on post tops and in the headboard can make your bed unique.

A drawing knife is used to shape the heads of the four posts. Final carving is done with chisels.

Grooves are first kerfed using a circular saw; then the wood stock is removed with a chisel.

Use a circular saw on collars below the head. Collars are 1-3/4" wide and shaped with rasps.

A wood rasp is used for final shaping, smoothing. The last step is sanding the edges.

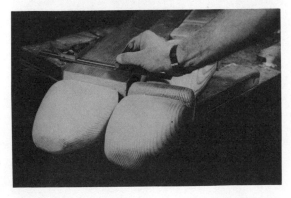

Place the posts side-by-side and carve them together.

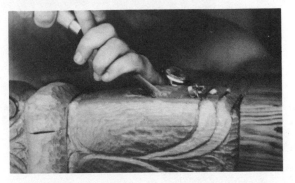

Carving time depends on the intricacy of the pattern you choose. Use an electric carving tool to speed up the carving operation.

Baby Cradles——

As attractive and convenient today as they were in earlier times, these cradles make great conversation pieces even without a bubbling baby nesting inside. If your interest in cradles is more practical than decorative, make sure you can obtain a suitable mattress before building the cradle. Also, be sure not to leave babies unattended in these cradles.

Colonial Hooded Cradle ——

This reproduction of a colonial pine cradle is destined to become a country furniture heirloom. It accepts standard cradle bedding and rocks gently on safe, wide rockers. All edges are rounded over to soften its lines, and for additional safety.

Begin by cutting all the components to their overall widths and lengths. Cut all the cradle end pieces first—the rest of the construction depends on their dimensions.

Starting with the bottom end piece (B1), cut the board at a 7-1/2° angle. Place parts B2 and B3 together as they will be in the completed cradle, mark the ends to indicate mating edges, and cut the 7-1/2° angles.

Drill matching dowel holes in the edges; then join the boards with glue and dowels. Clamp until dry.

Assemble the cradle's remaining end (C1, C2), sides (A1, A2), and bottom (F) in the same way, being careful to note on each side the outer faces of the boards.

Once the assemblies have dried, rip beveled edges into the cradle's end, sides, and bottom, as shown in the diagram. Remember that the cradle's sides are mirror images of each other. The beveled edges face in opposite directions.

Next, cut the angles for the roof on the top end piece (B3) of the cradle. Make certain the outer edges match the sides.

Once these basic assemblies are complete, enlarge the patterns shown in the diagrams. Lay out a grid of 2" squares on a sheet of paper and draw the patterns to correspond with the diagrams. Then, using carbon paper, transfer the designs to the respective cradle parts.

Cut out the rockers (D) and the sides. Clamp each group together, cutting the multiple pieces at one time. This helps keep them identical.

Next, lay out and drill the holes for the screws in each part. Because wood plugs will be used to cover all of these screw heads,

each hole needs to be recessed with a 3/8" bit to a depth of 3/8".

Before assembly, use a 1/4" rounding-over bit, with pilot, in a router on the exposed edges of the rockers, stretchers (E), and fascia (J).

Begin assembly by attaching the ends to the cradle's bottom, then add the sides. Use glue along with wood screws for added strength.

Attach the roof sides (G) and top (H), first to the fascia board, then to the end. The edges of the roof top will protrude slightly. This will be leveled during sanding.

Assemble the rocker and stretchers to one another. Then carefully center the cradle on its base and fasten it securely with wood screws, countersunk to be flush with the cradle's bottom. Do not glue the cradle to the base, since you may want to disassemble the unit for simpler transportation or storage.

Glue the 3/8"-diameter wood plugs in place and round over the cradle's remaining exposed edges.

MATERIALS LIST

1/4"-dia. dowels
3/8"-dia. plugs
Wood screws
Wood glue

CUTTING LIST

KEY	PIECES	SIZE AND DESCRIPTION
A1	2	3/4 × 7-1/2 × 36 bottom side piece
A2	2	3/4 × 7-1/2 × 36 center side piece
A3	2	3/4 × 4 × 11-1/4 top side piece
B1	1	3/4 × 7-1/2 × 19 bottom end piece
B2	1	3/4 × 7-1/2 × 21 center end piece
B3	1	3/4 × 7-1/2 × 24 top end piece
C1	1	3/4 × 7-1/2 × 19 bottom end piece
C2	1	3/4 × 7-1/2 × 21 top end piece
D	2	3/4 × 8 × 36 rockers
E	2	3/4 × 4 × 28 stretchers
F	1	3/4 × 8-5/8 × 34-1/2 bottom
G	2	3/4 × 9-1/4 × 12 roof sides
H	1	3/4 × 8 × 12 roof top
J	1	3/4 × 6-1/2 × 24 fascia

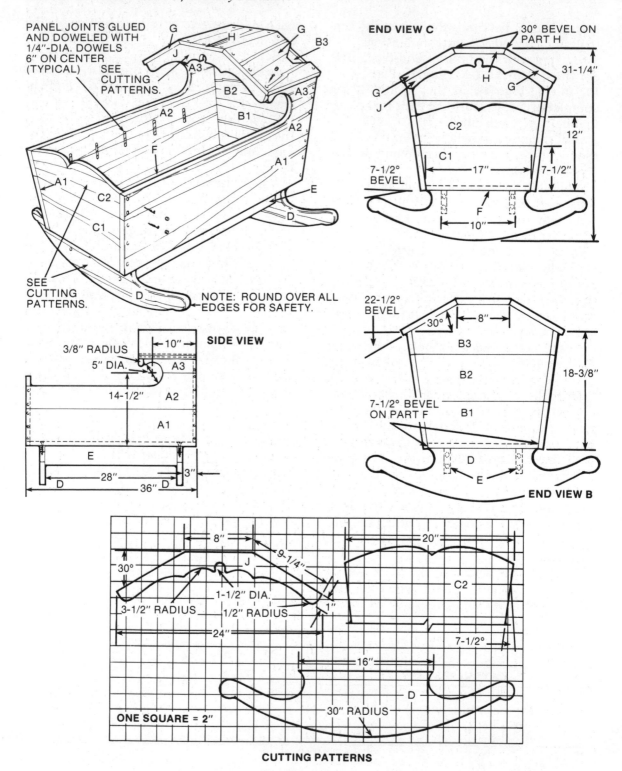

PANEL JOINTS GLUED AND DOWELED WITH 1/4"-DIA. DOWELS 6" ON CENTER (TYPICAL) SEE CUTTING PATTERNS.

G
H
G
J
B3
A3
B2
A2
B1
A2
A1
F
A1
C2
C1
E
D
D

SEE CUTTING PATTERNS.

NOTE: ROUND OVER ALL EDGES FOR SAFETY.

END VIEW C

30° BEVEL ON PART H

31-1/4"

G
J
H
G
C2
C1
12"
17"
7-1/2"

7-1/2° BEVEL

F

10"

SIDE VIEW

3/8" RADIUS
5" DIA.
10"
A3
14-1/2"
A2
A1
E
28"
3"
D
36"
D

22-1/2° BEVEL
30°
8"
B3
B2
18-3/8"
7-1/2° BEVEL ON PART F
B1
D
E

END VIEW B

CUTTING PATTERNS

8"
9-1/4"
30°
J
20"
C2
1-1/2" DIA.
3-1/2" RADIUS
1/2" RADIUS
1"
7-1/2°
24"
16"
D
ONE SQUARE = 2"
30" RADIUS

Drill holes into adjoining boards with a doweling jig.

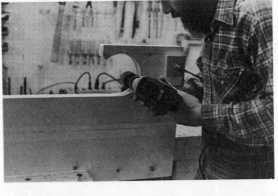

Sand the edges of both sides together. Use a drum sander inserted into a drill for the inside contours.

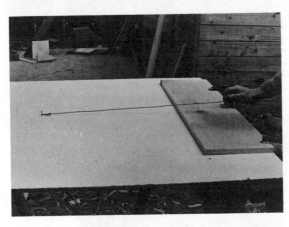

Draw the 30" radius for the bottom of the rocker using the pencil and string method as shown.

After cradle assembly, round over the edges of the hood with a rounding-over bit and pilot bearing chucked into a router.

Rocking Cradle _____

If you build this rocking cradle, you can be sure that it will last for years and will be handed down from one baby to the next. The cradle and frame are easily disassembled for storage.

To start the project, cut each of the pieces as detailed in the drawing. Then rabbet the inside edges of the head and footboards (B). Duplicate the flowers on a sheet of paper and trace the design, using carbon paper,

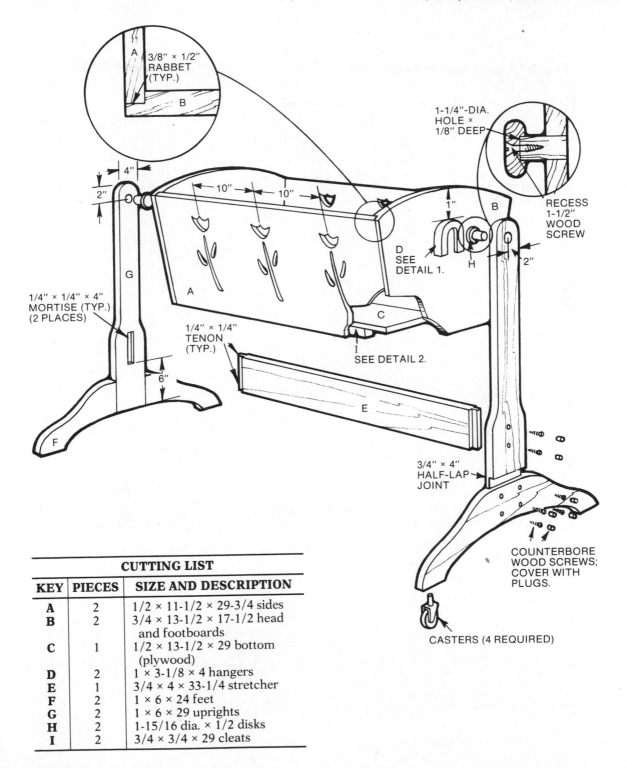

A
3/8" × 1/2"
RABBET
(TYP.)

B

1-1/4"-DIA.
HOLE ×
1/8" DEEP

RECESS
1-1/2"
WOOD
SCREW

4"

2"

10"

10"

1"

B

D
SEE
DETAIL 1.

H

2"

G

1/4" × 1/4" × 4"
MORTISE (TYP.)
(2 PLACES)

1/4" × 1/4"
TENON
(TYP.)

A

C

I
SEE DETAIL 2.

6"

E

F

3/4" × 4"
HALF-LAP
JOINT

COUNTERBORE
WOOD SCREWS;
COVER WITH
PLUGS.

CASTERS (4 REQUIRED)

CUTTING LIST		
KEY	**PIECES**	**SIZE AND DESCRIPTION**
A	2	1/2 × 11-1/2 × 29-3/4 sides
B	2	3/4 × 13-1/2 × 17-1/2 head and footboards
C	1	1/2 × 13-1/2 × 29 bottom (plywood)
D	2	1 × 3-1/8 × 4 hangers
E	1	3/4 × 4 × 33-1/4 stretcher
F	2	1 × 6 × 24 feet
G	2	1 × 6 × 29 uprights
H	2	1-15/16 dia. × 1/2 disks
I	2	3/4 × 3/4 × 29 cleats

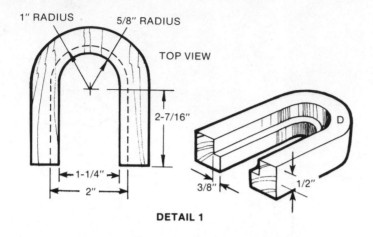

1" RADIUS

5/8" RADIUS

TOP VIEW

2-7/16"

1-1/4"

2"

3/8"

1/2"

D

DETAIL 1

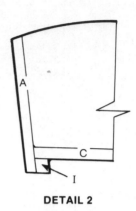

A

C

I

DETAIL 2

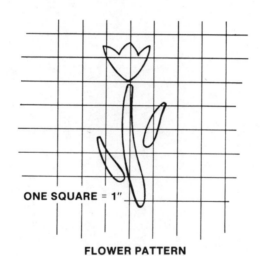

ONE SQUARE = 1"

FLOWER PATTERN

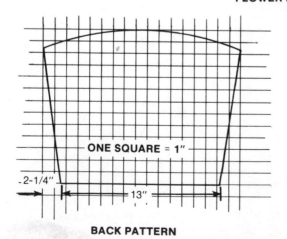

ONE SQUARE = 1"

-2-1/4"

13"

BACK PATTERN

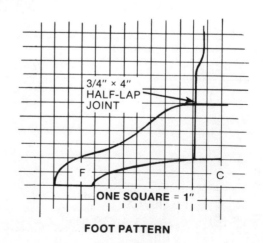

3/4" × 4"
HALF-LAP
JOINT

F

C

ONE SQUARE = 1"

FOOT PATTERN

MATERIALS LIST

1-1/4"-dia. dowels
3/8"-dia. plugs
Casters
Wood screws
Wood glue

---

onto the sides of the cradle (A). Make sure the designs are centered and equally spaced. Cut them out and sand the inside edges smooth.

Fit and glue the cradle's sides into the head and footboard rabbets. Predrill the screw holes, then secure the sides with counterbored wood screws and plugs.

Attach the cleats (I) with wood screws and custom-fit the bottom (C).

Cut the U-shaped hangers (D) and rabbet the inside (one surface only). The visible sur-faces are rounded over. Attach the hanger to the head and footboard with recessed wood screws.

Rabbet the ends of the stretcher (E) and the uprights (G). Also, mortise the uprights where the stretcher is to be inserted.

Cut out the design for the feet (F) and dado the area where the upright is to be located. Then drill the holes for the 1-1/4"-diameter dowels and attach them with glue. The disks (H) are fastened to the dowels with wood screws.

Secure the uprights to the feet and round all of the exterior edges of the upright assembly, stretcher, and cradle. If you want the unit to come apart easily, attach the stretcher with wood screws and do not glue.

Drill holes for the casters and sand the completed project.

Section III
Cabinets and Storage Units

Country-style or not, every home can use additional organized storage space. The cabinets and storage units in this section are ideal country pieces, but many of them will look just as good in any number of different settings.

Feel free to vary the actual finished dimensions given in the cutting lists to construct your project so that it most suits the setting you intend for it. The choice of wood for each project is up to you, although as a guide some projects mention types that work especially well with the design.

Dry Sinks —————————

Early American homes made do with the dry sink—a washstand for bowl and water pitcher, and storage cabinet for related objects. Today, dry sinks are eagerly sought by collectors, because they fit in with modern settings.

Dry sinks have been the most popular pieces of country furniture. To give you some idea of the styles, six designs have been selected: four reproductions and, for the purist, two authentic designs.

Two-Door Dry Sink ———————

This reproduction is modeled after sinks still seen in New England. The design simplifies construction so that even the person of limited skills and few tools can do a praise-worthy job.

Begin by cutting the sides (A) and top (B) from 1 × 10 pine stock. Cut the stock to length plus 1". Dowel and edge-glue the boards to the right width. Clamp the boards firmly and set the parts aside to dry.

Next, cut out the face frame stiles and rails (C, D, E). Locate and drill 3/8"-diameter dowel holes where the pieces will be joined. Join the face frame stiles and rails with dowels and glue. Use a carpenter's square to check the alignment of the frame and clamp the pieces tightly while they dry.

Cut the sides and top to their proper dimensions. To cut the ends square, clamp a straight board to them as a saw guide. Next, rout a 3/8" × 3/8" rabbet in the back edges of each.

Attach the face frame to the sides. Use glue and 1-5/8" drywall screws, countersunk through the face frame into the front edges of the sides. Attach the bottom shelf cleats (F, G) to the sides and the back of the face frame with 1-1/4" drywall screws. The bottoms of the cleats should be mounted 1" from the bottom of the sides. Check squareness as you proceed. Fasten the top to the sides and face frame with screws. Position the screws so they will be concealed by the splashboard pieces later. Attach the bottom (V) to the cleats with glue and screws.

Cut the base sides (H) to the dimensions given; then cut the base front (I) to length plus 1/8". Make patterns from the drawings on 1" grid paper, and transfer them with carbon paper to the wood for cutting.

Join the base pieces with glue and countersunk wood screws. After the glue dries, sand the front base flush with the sides; then attach the base cleats (J, K) inside the base parts. The tops of the cleats should be 1/2" lower than the top of the base parts. Set the cabinet on the base assembly and join them with 1-1/4" drywall screws.

Cut the splashboard parts (L, M, N, O) to their overall size. Bevel the bottom edge of the front (M) 15° and miter the front ends of the splashboard sides (L) 15° on a table saw. Transfer the patterns from the drawings to the splashboard front and sides, then cut out with a saber saw. Sand the contours.

Assemble the splashboard with countersunk 1-5/8" drywall screws. Sand the ends flush with the sides. Now, attach the splashboard assembly to the cabinet with glue and dowels. Place weights on top to ensure a tight bond.

Cut the door stiles (P) and rails (Q). Locate and drill dowel holes for the door frames; then glue and lightly clamp them together. Check to make sure that the assembly is square.

Cut the door panels (R) and bevel the panel fronts 15° all around.

Rout a 3/8" × 3/8" rabbet in the door stiles and rails (P, Q) as shown in the diagram. Set the panels inside the rabbets and secure with the door cleats (S, T), which are made from mitered screen door molding and tacked to the door frame with brads.

Cut the plywood back (U) to size and attach it to the sides and top with 2d nails. Finally, cut the half shelf (W) to size and set it

MATERIALS LIST

3/8"-dia. dowels
1-1/4" drywall screws
1-5/8" drywall screws
No. 8 × 1-1/4" wood screws
No. 8 × 1-1/2" wood screws
2d nails
5/8" wire brads
Shelf supports (4)
Hinges (4)
Doorknobs (2)
Bullet catches (2)
Wood glue

CUTTING LIST

KEY	PIECES	SIZE AND DESCRIPTION
A	2	3/4 × 16-3/4 × 33 sides
B	1	3/4 × 18-1/2 × 37-3/4 top
C	2	3/4 × 2-1/8 × 33 frame stiles
D	1	3/4 × 2-1/8 × 32 top frame rail
E	1	3/4 × 2-5/8 × 32 bottom frame rail
F	2	3/4 × 1/2 × 16-1/4 bottom shelf cleats
G	1	3/4 × 1/2 × 33 bottom shelf cleat
H	2	3/4 × 3-1/2 × 17-1/2 base sides
I	1	3/4 × 3-1/2 × 37-3/4 base front
J	2	3/4 × 1/2 × 17-1/2 side base cleats
K	1	3/4 × 1/2 × 34-3/4 front base cleat
L	2	3/4 × 5-1/2 × 17-3/4 splashboard sides
M	1	3/4 × 3-1/2 × 36-1/4 splashboard front
N	1	3/4 × 5-1/2 × 34-3/4 splashboard back
O	1	3/4 × 5-1/2 × 37-3/4 splashboard shelf
P	4	3/4 × 2-5/8 × 28-1/8 door stiles
Q	4	3/4 × 2-5/8 × 10-3/4 door rails
R	2	3/4 × 11-1/2 × 23-5/8 door panels
S	4	1/8 × 3/4 × 12-1/4 door cleats
T	4	1/8 × 3/4 × 24-3/8 door cleats
U	1	1/4 × 33-3/8 × 35-1/2 back (plywood)
V	1	3/4 × 16-3/8 × 34-3/4 bottom shelf (plywood)
W	1	3/4 × 11-1/2 × 34-3/4 half shelf

aside. Drill 1/4" holes for each of the plastic shelf supports that will support the half shelf.

Make matching wood plugs for all the countersunk screw holes with a 3/8" plug cutter. Glue the plugs in place. After the glue

dries, sand the plugs flush with the cabinet's surface.

After the finish is completed, mount the doors, knobs, and bullet catches and set the half shelf to complete the project.

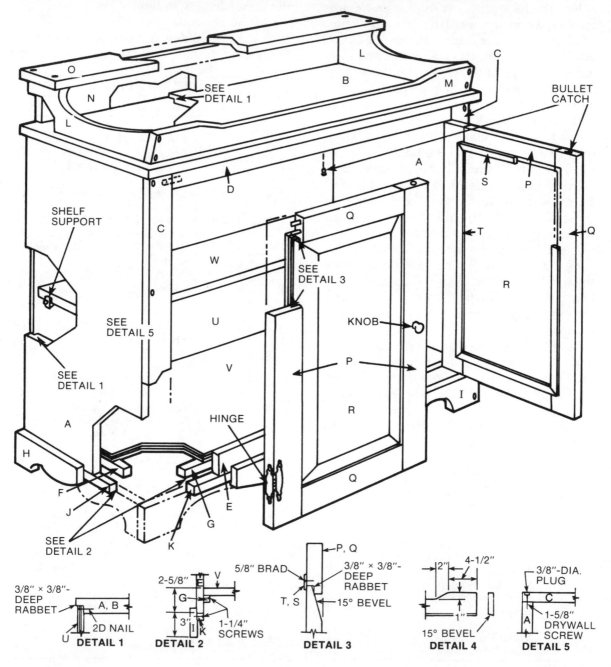

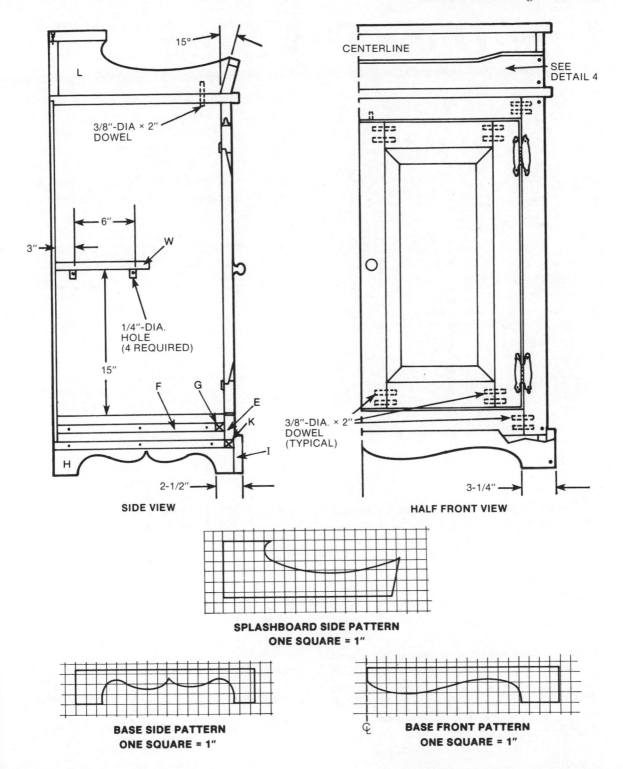

15°

L

3/8"-DIA × 2"
DOWEL

6"

3"

W

1/4"-DIA.
HOLE
(4 REQUIRED)

15"

F   G

E

K

H

I

2-1/2"

SIDE VIEW

CENTERLINE

SEE
DETAIL 4

3/8"-DIA. × 2"
DOWEL
(TYPICAL)

3-1/4"

HALF FRONT VIEW

SPLASHBOARD SIDE PATTERN
ONE SQUARE = 1"

BASE SIDE PATTERN
ONE SQUARE = 1"

BASE FRONT PATTERN
ONE SQUARE = 1"

144

One-Door Dry Sink

The front pieces (I, J, K) are assembled next. Cut a 3-1/4" × 5-1/4" opening in each of the front sides (I). The opening is centered on the pieces, with the bottom of the opening 5-1/2" from the top of the piece. Cut two 3/4" × 3/4" × 1/4" mortises, 1/4" apart, directly beneath the opening and centered on it on the inside of each piece. Next, drill 3/8"-

KEY	PIECES	SIZE AND DESCRIPTION
A	1	3/4 × 4 × 34 tray front
B	2	3/4 × 5 × 16 tray sides
C	1	3/4 × 6 × 32-1/2 tray back
D	1	3/4 × 6 × 34 tray top
E	3	3/4 × 15 × 32-1/2 shelves (plywood)
F	4	3/4 × 6-1/2 × 33 end pieces
G	2	3/4 × 2 × 29 center pieces
H1	6	3/4 × 3/4 × 15 shelf cleats
H2	2	3/4 × 3/4 × 2 drawer runner cleats
I	2	3/4 × 7-1/2 × 33 front sides
J	1	3/4 × 4-1/2 × 19 top front rail
K	1	3/4 × 2 × 19 bottom front rail
L	1	1/2 × 18-1/2 × 24-7/8 door back (plywood)
M	2	1/4 × 3 × 24-7/8 door stiles (plywood)
N	1	1/4 × 3 × 12-1/2 door bottom rail (plywood)
O	1	1/4 × 5 × 12-1/2 door head rail (plywood)
P	1	1/4 × 30 × 34 cabinet back (plywood)
Q	4	3/4 × 3/4 × 15-1/4 drawer runners
R1	2	3/4 × 4 × 6 false drawer fronts
R2	2	1/2 × 3 × 4 drawer fronts (plywood)
R3	4	1/2 × 3 × 14-3/8 drawer sides (plywood)
R4	2	1/2 × 3 × 4 drawer backs (plywood)
R5	2	1/2 × 4 × 13-3/8 drawer bottoms (plywood)

CUTTING LIST

Construction of this one-door dry sink is as simple as country living.

Start by cutting all the pieces to the dimensions given in the cutting list. The sides are constructed first. Join the side center piece (G) with the two end pieces (F) by drilling two centered 3/8"-diameter holes into the facing sides of each piece. The holes are drilled 1/2" deep, at 3" and 26" from the tops of the pieces. The pieces are then edge-glued and doweled together, and the shelf cleats (H1) are joined to the sides with wood screws at 3/4", 13-1/2", and 26-3/4" distances from the top. Besides holding the shelves on the assembled sink, the cleats will act as clamps to hold the side pieces together while the glue dries.

MATERIALS LIST

3/8"-dia. dowels
Wood screws
Roundhead screws
Butterfly hinges
Door latch or catch
Drawer pulls
Wood glue

diameter dowel holes in both ends of the top and bottom rails (J, K), and in the facing sides of the front. Dowel and edge-glue together all the front pieces.

Attach the top and bottom shelves (E) to the sides with wood screws recessed into the side 3/8". The recesses will later be plugged with short dowel sections, so drill them 3/8" wide. Next, attach the cabinet back (P), flush with the sides and top shelf. Drive wood screws through the back into the sides and shelf, checking for square as you proceed. The screws need not be recessed.

Attach the drawer runner cleats (H2) to the cabinet back with wood screws and glue 1-1/4" in from the sides and 5-1/2" down from the bottom of the top shelf. Attach the

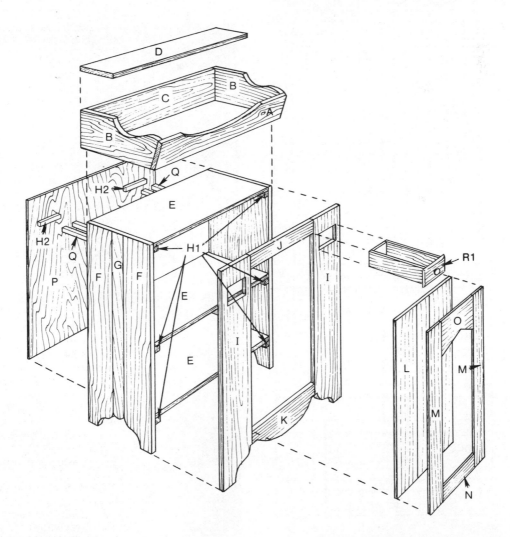

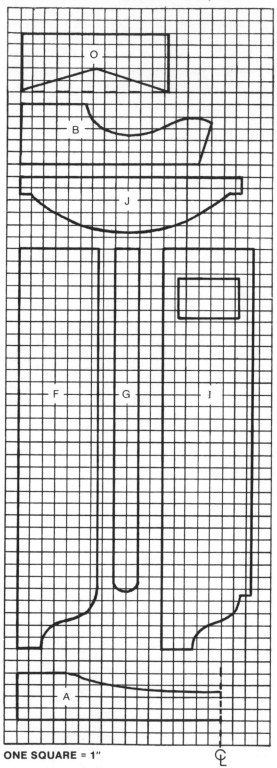

ONE SQUARE = 1"

middle shelf to the remaining shelf cleats with wood screws and glue.

Glue the drawer runners (Q) into the mortises cut into the cabinet front, and attach the front to the sides and top shelf with recessed wood screws, again checking for square as you proceed. These recesses will also be 3/8"-diameter × 3/8" deep. Glue and clamp the drawer runners to the back cleats until the glue sets.

Cut the tray pieces according to the diagram; then assemble the tray by recess-screwing the sides (B) to the back (C), and the

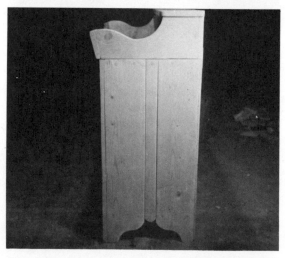

front (A) and top (D) to the tray sides. Again, the recesses are 3/8"-diameter × 3/8" deep. Attach the tray to the cabinet with glued dowels.

Next, assemble the door. Dadoes 1/8" are cut lengthwise through the door back (L) to simulate the appearance of split board construction. After cutting the head rail (O) as shown in the illustration, the stiles and rails (M, N, O) are attached with wood screws driven through the door back. Screw the hardware onto the door and hang the door.

Construct the drawers with butt joints as shown. Attach the false drawer fronts (R1) to the drawer fronts (R2) with wood screws and drill a hole through the center of both pieces to accommodate the drawer pulls. Slide the drawers onto the drawer runners and run roundhead screws and washers between the guides and into the drawer bottoms. Plug the screw holes and apply the desired finish.

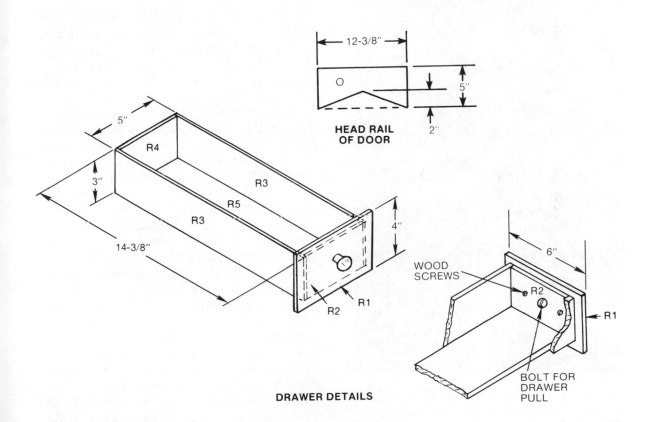

Dry Sink with Wall Cabinet

Dishes and other treasures can be displayed in this dry sink with wall cabinet. Both are made of oak and oak-veneer plywood and have plenty of storage space. Use the back shelf for displaying decorative items, and the drawers for silverware and other necessities. The lower cabinet has a half shelf for items that do not stack easily. The grooved shelf in the upper cabinet allows dishes to be displayed upright. By lining the sink basin with water-resistant material, you will have a handy place to keep houseplants.

To construct the dry sink, cut the pieces to the dimensions in the cutting list. Rout the appropriate edges on the sink back (A), sides (B), and shelf (C) as shown in the illustration. The pieces will be assembled with recessed wood screws and wood plugs.

Rabbet the inside back edges of the sides (Q) and dado their bottoms as shown in the illustrations. With wood screws and glue, assemble the sides flush to the back edge of the bottom (M) and the top braces (S) as shown in the cross section. Be sure to square the cabinet. Cut the stiles (I) and rails (F, G, J) to ensure a tight joint; assemble them with dowels and wood glue. Join them to the front edges of the sides with dowels and wood glue. Rout the half-shelf supports (P) as shown in the illustration, and assemble them to the cabinet with recessed and plugged wood screws. Glue the half shelf (N) to the supports. Glue a strip of oak (O) onto the front of the shelf if plywood is used.

Mount the back brace (R) to the back after the drawer runner hardware has been selected. Cut the front and side trim (K, L) contours according to the grid diagrams. Miter the corners and attach them to the cabinet as illustrated.

The doors are constructed from solid oak, with the exterior face edges of the insert door fronts (U1) shaped with a router and 1/4" roman ogee bit after they have been cut to size. The abutting edges of all of the door pieces are dadoed 1/2" deep × 1/8" wide, because the pieces will be joined with glued splines. Glue the side pieces (U3) to the door front first, after they have been cut and routed. When the glue has set, measure the door for the exact length of the end pieces (U2), and cut and assemble them to the door in the same manner. When the doors are completed, rout the exterior face edges. Detail illustration B-B shows the end result of the door construction in cross section.

Construction and assembly of the drawers is similarly straight forward. After cutting the component pieces to size and routing the exterior face edges of the drawer fronts (V1) with the 1/4" roman ogee bit, further cuts are needed to accommodate the joints. Cut 1/4" × 3/4" rabbets on the inside back edges of the drawer sides (V3) to seat the drawer backs (V4). A 1/4" × 1/8" dado is run along the inside of the drawer sides and ends for the drawer bottoms. Assemble three sides of the drawer with counterbored 1-1/2" wood screws and glue. Insert the drawer bottom and attach the final side in the same fashion as the others. Make sure that the drawers are constructed square.

Recess the screws for the drawer pull and mount the drawer front onto the drawer frame. Attach with several counterbored wood screws. Do not use glue.

Mortise the doors for the mounting hinges. The depth should be the thickness of a folded hinge. Also, attach a magnetic latch for each door.

Mount the drawer runner hardware following the directions provided by the manufacturer.

Finally, attach the back panel with 2d common nails.

To construct the overhead wall cabinet, transfer the design onto the sides (D). Rout the outside edges. A dado or V-groove is made on the shelf (G) for supporting the dishes upright. Rabbet the inside backs of the sides, bottom, and top sections. When assembled, square the corners of the rabbeted sections with a wood chisel. Then rout the top (C) and assemble the basic frame with counterbored wood screws and glue. Attach oak plugs to the bottom. Clamp on a flat surface, square, and allow the glue to dry.

Fasten the rail from the top with screws. Mount the side braces (F) with wood screws from inside of the cabinet and cover the holes with oak plugs. Add the top trim pieces (A, B) after having routed the edge and join them with miters.

Assemble the door frame (I1, I2) with glue and counterbored wood screws or 3/8"-diameter dowels. Plug the recesses. Rout the outside and inside showing edges of both frames, making sure to allow room for a rabbet cut on the inside. Then use a rabbeting bit with a pilot guide to make the inside rabbet for the plastic panel. Square each rabbeted corner with a wood chisel. Before mounting the glass (I3) with retaining buttons, finish the cabinet to match the dry sink. The back (H) can be stained or cut from an existing oak wall panel.

Also, mortise the door hinges the thickness of a folded hinge and use a magnetic latch for each door. Add two knobs and this wall hutch will be ready to complement the dry sink. Mount it to a wall with four wood screws attached along the top of the inside panel. If the unit does not fit flat against the wall, locate two screws in both lower corners.

MATERIALS LIST (Dry Sink)

3/8"-dia. plugs
No. 8 × 1-1/4" wood screws
No. 8 × 1-1/2" wood screws
No. 8 × 2" wood screws
2d common nails
Door hinge
Doorknob
Door pull
Magnetic door latch
Drawer runner hardware
Wood glue

CUTTING LIST (Dry Sink)

KEY	PIECES	SIZE AND DESCRIPTION
A	1	3/4 × 10 × 36 sink back
B	2	3/4 × 6-3/4 × 19-1/2 sink sides
C	1	3/4 × 4-1/4 × 36 sink shelf
D	1	3/4 × 3-1/8 × 37-3/4 sink front
E	1	3/4 × 19-1/8 × 36 sink bottom (plywood)
F	1	3/4 × 1 × 33 front rail
G	1	3/4 × 1-1/2 × 33 front rail
H	1	3/4 × 1-1/2 × 4 rail brace
I	2	3/4 × 1-1/2 × 27-1/4 stiles
J	1	3/4 × 2 × 33 bottom rail
K	1	3/4 × 3-1/2 × 37-1/2 front trim
L	2	3/4 × 3-1/2 × 18-3/4 side trim
M	1	3/4 × 17-1/8 × 35 bottom (plywood)
N	1	3/4 × 8 × 34-1/2 half shelf (plywood)
O	1	1/8 × 3/4 × 34-1/2 shelf edge
P	2	3/4 × 2 × 8 shelf supports
Q	2	3/4 × 17-1/4 × 27-1/4 sides (plywood)
R	1	3/4 × 3 × 34-1/2 back brace (plywood)
S	2	3/4 × 3 × 34-1/2 top braces
T	1	1/8 × 27-1/4 × 35-1/4 back
U1	2	3/4 × 14 × 15-3/4 door fronts
U2	4	3/4 × 2 × 14 door frame
U3	4	3/4 × 2 × 19-3/4 door frame
V1	2	3/4 × 4-1/2 × 17-1/8 drawer fronts
V2	2	3/4 × 3-1/2 × 14 drawer supports
V3	4	3/4 × 3-1/2 × 15 drawer sides
V4	2	3/4 × 3-1/2 × 14-1/2 drawer backs
V5	2	1/8 × 14 × 14-1/2 drawer bottoms

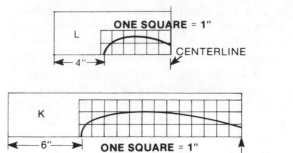

FRONT AND SIDE TRIM PATTERNS

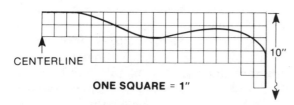

SINK BACK PATTERN

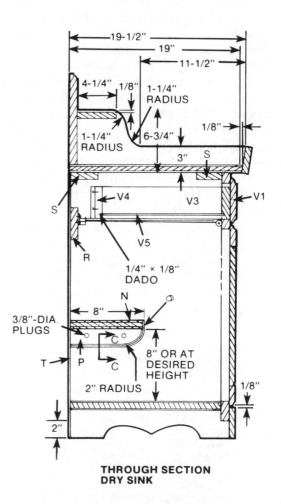

THROUGH SECTION DRY SINK

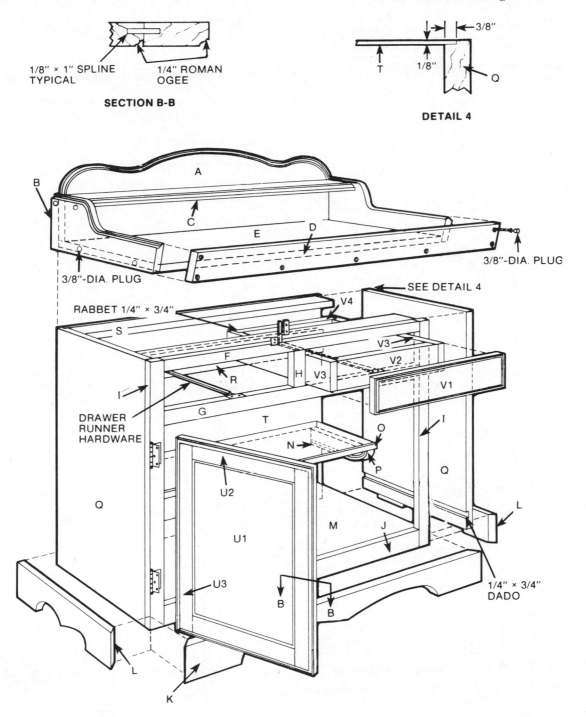

1/8" × 1" SPLINE
TYPICAL

1/4" ROMAN
OGEE

SECTION B-B

3/8"

T

1/8"

Q

DETAIL 4

A

B

C

E

D

3/8"-DIA. PLUG

3/8"-DIA. PLUG

SEE DETAIL 4

V4

RABBET 1/4" × 3/4"

S

V3

F

V3

V2

H

R

V1

I

DRAWER
RUNNER
HARDWARE

G

T

O

N

I

P

Q

U2

Q

U1

M

J

L

U3

L

1/4" × 3/4"
DADO

B

B

K

DRY SINK CABINET

CUTTING LIST (Wall Cabinet)

KEY	PIECES	SIZE AND DESCRIPTION
A	1	1 × 2 × 40 top trim
B	2	1 × 2 × 10-1/4 top trim
C	1	1 × 9-1/4 × 38 top
D	2	1 × 7-3/4 × 20-1/2 sides
E	1	1 × 1-1/2 × 34 rail
F	2	1 × 1 × 12-1/4 side braces
G	1	1 × 7-3/4 × 34-1/2 shelf
H	1	1/4 × 14-3/4 × 35 back
I1	4	1 × 2 × 14-1/4 door frames
I2	4	1 × 2 × 13-9/16 door frames
I3	2	3/16 × 10-5/8 × 13-15/16 glass

MATERIALS LIST (Wall Cabinet)

3/8"-dia. dowels
Door hinges
Doorknobs
Magnetic door latches
3/16" × 10-5/8" × 13-15/16" glass
Glass retaining buttons
Wood screws
2d common nails
Wood glue

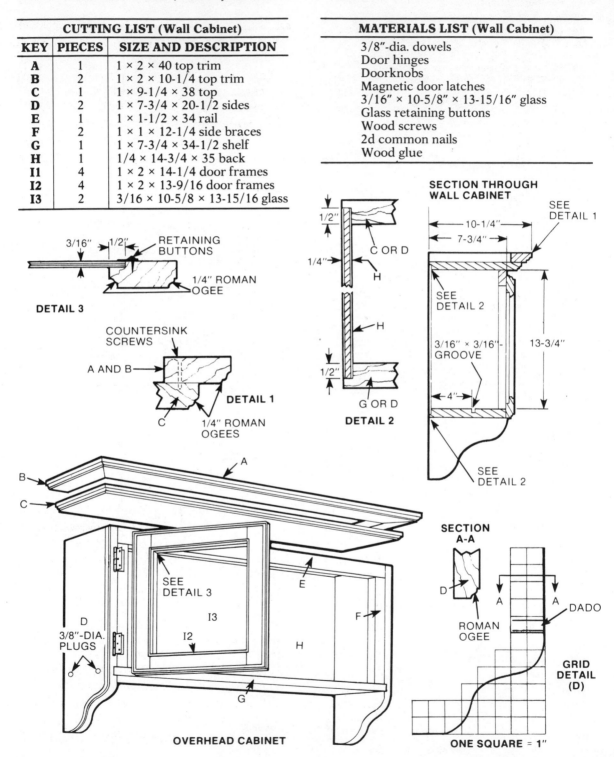

DETAIL 3

DETAIL 1

DETAIL 2

SECTION THROUGH WALL CABINET

OVERHEAD CABINET

SECTION A-A

GRID DETAIL (D)

ONE SQUARE = 1"

Dry Sink with Attached Overhead Cupboard

	MATERIALS LIST
	Recessed screws
	Dowel plugs
	Finishing nails
	Planter box or tray
	Wood glue

CUTTING LIST

KEY	PIECES	SIZE AND DESCRIPTION
A	1	1/2 × 40 × 68 back
B	2	3/4 × 18 × 68 sides
C	1	3/4 × 9 × 40 top
D	2	3/4 × 9 × 40 drawer supports
E	2	3/4 × 4 × 12 door uprights
F	1	3/4 × 8-1/4 × 12 cabinet divider
G1	3	3/4 × 14-1/2 × 40 shelves
G2	1	3/4 × 13 × 40 sink top
H	8	3/4 × 1-1/2 × 14-1/2 cleats
I	1	3/4 × 1-1/2 × 40 stretcher
J	2	3/4 × 4 × 29 front panels
K1	2	1/4 × 17-1/4 × 24 lower door panels
K2	4	1/2 × 3 × 24 stiles
K3	2	1/2 × 6 × 11-1/4 top rails
K4	2	1/2 × 3 × 11-1/4 bottom rails
L	1	3/4 × 6 × 41-1/2 sink front
M1	2	1/4 × 12 × 16 upper door panels
M2	4	1/2 × 3 × 12 stiles
M3	2	1/2 × 5 × 5 top rails
M4	2	1/2 × 3 × 5 bottom rails
N	2	3/4 × 5 × 9 drawer dividers
O1	3	3/4 × 4-7/8 × 12-1/2 drawer fronts
O2	6	1/2 × 4-7/8 × 8-1/4 drawer sides
O3	3	1/2 × 4-7/8 × 11-1/2 drawer backs
O4	3	1/2 × 7-3/4 × 11-1/2 drawer bottoms

This country dry sink combines an overhead storage cabinet with the basic lower unit. The sides (B) are wide 1″ boards, but if they can't be purchased in your lumberyard, edge-glue and dowel narrow pieces together. Then cut to shape, following the pattern.

Cut the remaining pieces to size and join the sides with the shelves (G2) and sink top (G1), top (C), drawer supports (D), and back (A). These are secured with finishing nails through the sides, all joints glued. Insert drawer dividers (N), then attach the sink front (L) with glue and recessed screws covered with dowel plugs. Make the sink front with an angled cut so that it can be positioned as shown.

Doors are made of stiles (K2) and rails (K3) glued and attached with brads to 1/4" veneer plywood (K1). Rout the inside edges before fastening them to the panel. After cutting the front panels (J) to size, chamfer their outer edges as shown. Attach them to the sides by gluing and nailing.

The cabinet back may be 1/2" plywood, in which case the visible grain will be vertical instead of horizontal. Showing the grain at this exposed central section—and above the top shelf—accentuates the beauty but calls for a second veneer plywood piece applied over the back with the visible grain placed horizontally. Attach it with glue only.

A metal or plastic planter box of appropriate size is then installed.

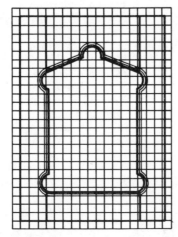

ONE SQUARE = 1"

DOOR PATTERN

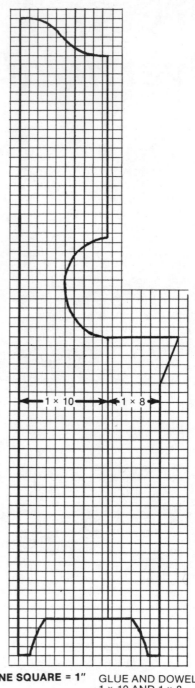

← 1 × 10 → ← 1 × 8 →

ONE SQUARE = 1"   GLUE AND DOWEL
1 × 10 AND 1 × 8

SIDE PATTERN

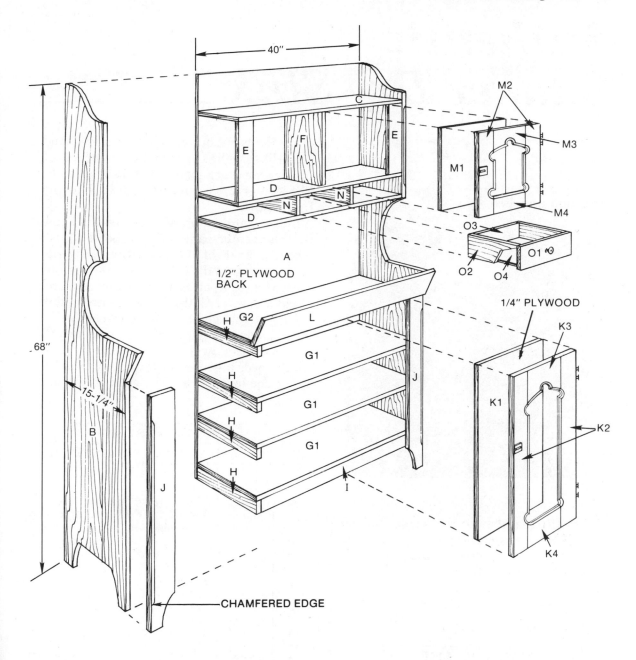

40"

68"

15-1/4"

B

J

A
1/2" PLYWOOD
BACK

C

E

F

E

D

N

N

D

G2

H

L

G1

H

G1

H

G1

H

J

I

CHAMFERED EDGE

M2

M1

M3

M4

O3

O2

O1

O4

1/4" PLYWOOD

K3

K1

K2

K4

Authentic Shaker Dry Sink

The first authentic dry sinks had no *sinks*—a basin and pitcher served the purpose. Metal sinks didn't come into use for this piece of country furniture until the turn of the 19th century.

The method of building this dry sink, as outlined in the drawing, is quite simple. Most of the joints are butted, but the back (A) and sides (F), as well as most of the frame (B, C) of the dry sink, are joined with rabbet joints. The center crosspiece is dadoed into the frame sides.

Close examination of the door will show that the center panel (M) is rabbeted flush with the back of the door. Cut 1/4"-wide rabbets around the inside edges of the door members (K, L) after they are doweled and glued together. All the joints of the dry sink are nailed and glued for extra strength.

Depending on the stock you're using, you may wish to dowel and edge-glue three or four boards together for the back instead of using one large piece. The cutting list calls

MATERIALS LIST

Finishing nails
1/4"-dia. dowels
Butt hinges (2)
Doorknob
Door latch
Wood glue

CUTTING LIST

KEY	PIECES	SIZE AND DESCRIPTION
A	1	3/8 × 36-3/4 × 42 back (plywood)
B	2	3/4 × 2-1/2 × 36 frame sides
C	3	3/4 × 2-1/2 × 15-1/8 frame crosspieces
D	4	3/4 × 1-1/2 × 17-1/8 cleats
E	2	3/4 × 1-1/2 × 36 top shelf supports
F	2	3/4 × 17-1/2 × 40 sides
G	3	1/2 × 17-1/8 × 36 shelves
H	2	3/4 × 7-11/16 × 24-1/2 front panels
I	1	3/4 × 1-1/2 × 37-1/2 front facing
J	2	3/4 × 5-1/2 × 6 corner shelves
K	2	3/4 × 3-1/2 × 24-3/8 door frame
L	2	3/4 × 3-1/2 × 15-1/8 door frame
M	1	1/4 × 15-5/8 × 17-7/8 door center panel

for 3/8″ plywood, which can simply be cut to the correct dimensions.

The use of wood laminate strips to cover the edges of the sides and back is optional. Obviously, they will be needed only if plywood is used for those pieces. Although the original is pine with a yellow stain, you can finish the piece as desired.

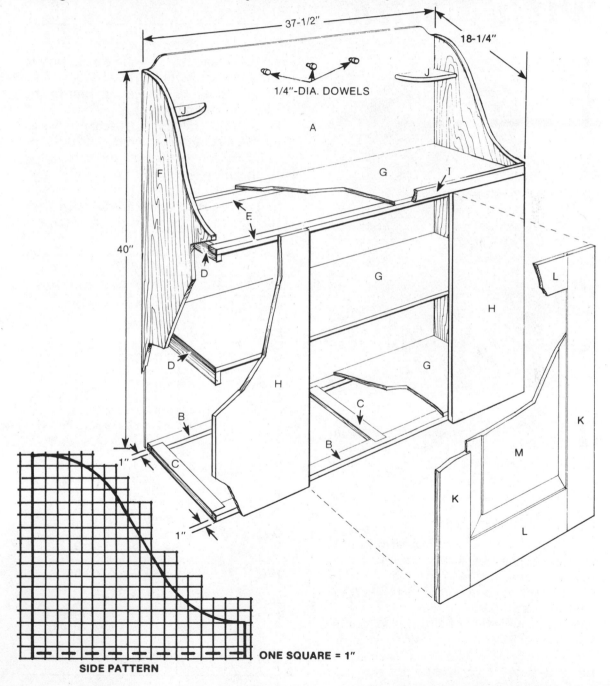

37-1/2″

18-1/4″

1/4″-DIA. DOWELS

40″

1″

1″

SIDE PATTERN

ONE SQUARE = 1″

Shaker Dry Sink with "Sink"

This dry sink is an especially interesting piece because the original contained what was probably one of the first iron sinks. Cast in a Shaker foundry about 1850 with a drain in one end that emptied into a bucket in the cupboard, it is, however, a feature you'll probably want to forego in your reproduction. With a practical substitute in mind, these plans show details for a recessed sink that can be copper- or tin-lined for use as a planter or to accommodate the traditional crockery basin.

First, assemble the sides (B), back (A), cupboard shelf (P), and cleats (M) to form the base of the dry sink. Note that each side is made of two 1 × 12 boards doweled and

edge-glued together. (It will be necessary to trim each side to achieve the 21-1/2" width.) Next, attach the two pieces of front facing (K) and the crosspiece (L).

Prepare the sink (H, N, O) separately and slip it into place after attaching both the wide (G) and narrow (I) surface strips. Next, secure the horizontal trim (J) and the 1/4" scoop molding under it.

Nail cleats to the sides in the open shelf section—two for the full-width shelf (D) and

CUTTING LIST		
KEY	**PIECES**	**SIZE AND DESCRIPTION**
A	1	1/4 × 33-1/2 × 45 back (plywood)
B	4	3/4 × 11-1/4 × 45 sides
C	1	3/4 × 10-1/4 × 35 top
D	1	3/4 × 9 × 33-1/2 shelf
E	1	3/4 × 9 × 16-1/4 shelf
F	1	3/4 × 9 × 12-3/4 divider
G	1	3/4 × 6 × 12-1/4 surface strip
H	2	3/4 × 5 × 10-3/4 sink sides
I	1	3/4 × 2 × 12-1/4 surface strip
J	1	3/4 × 5-1/2 × 35 horizontal trim
K	2	3/4 × 5 × 30-1/2 front facing
L	1	1/2 × 1/2 × 25 crosspiece
M	2	3/4 × 1 × 21-1/4 cleats
N	1	1/4 × 11-1/2 × 23-1/2 sink bottom
O	1	3/4 × 5 × 23-1/2 sink back
P	1	3/4 × 21-1/4 × 33-1/2 cupboard shelf
Q1	2	3/4 × 3 × 24 door stiles
Q2	2	3/4 × 3 × 19 rails
Q3	1	3/4 × 1-1/2 × 18 strip
Q4	2	1/4 × 9-1/4 × 18-1/2 panels
R	2	3/4 × 1-3/4 × 13-1/2 front facing
S	1	3/4 × 1 × 34 horizontal trim
T	4	3/4 × 1 × 9 cleats

two for the short shelf (E). Install the full-width shelf, then the shelf divider (F), followed by the short shelf. Secure the top (C), front facing (R), and horizontal trim (S) with wood glue and finishing nails.

The detail drawing shows how the door frame (Q1, Q2) is rabbeted and inset with the panels (Q4) and quarter-round molding that acts as a stop strip. Note that a center strip (Q3) has been added, creating a strong vertical effect. Hang the door with mortise hinges.

MATERIALS LIST
1/4" scoop molding
Quarter-round molding
Mortise hinges (2)
Doorknob
Door latch
Finishing nails
Wood glue

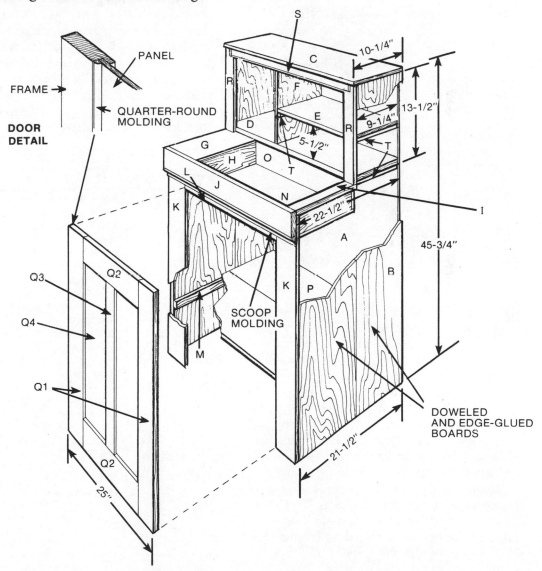

PANEL

FRAME →

QUARTER-ROUND MOLDING

DOOR DETAIL

S

C

R

F

E

R

D

T

9-1/4"

5-1/2"

13-1/2"

10-1/4"

G H O T

L

J

K

N

I

22-1/2"

A

B

45-3/4"

K P

M

SCOOP MOLDING

Q3

Q2

Q4

Q1

Q2

25"

21-1/2"

DOWELED AND EDGE-GLUED BOARDS

Country Cupboard

the two inside shelves (K) and the top (A) and bottom (C) backpieces; use 1/4" stock for the door panels (H3) and the optional midsection back panel. Scrap stock will do for the small drawers, but for the faces use 1-1/4" stock beveled as shown in the detail drawing or a combination of 1/2" base and 3/4" beveled face.

Dadoes and grooves are used as shown for the drawer-shelf network, with all other

I n the 1700s and early 1800s, settlers in Pennsylvania favored this style of cupboard for both the kitchen and bath, the enclosed lower half concealing jugs of reserve water and the waist-level top displaying the traditional pitcher and basin. A decorative back panel in this version covers the usual see-through separation between the top and the small beveled drawers. But either version makes the water bench, as it is also known, a conversation piece.

Woods such as cherry, beech, ash, or pine make an accurate reproduction. Use 1-1/4" stock for the sides (B), drawer-shelf network (D, E, F, G), bench top (J), door frames (H1, H2), and door uprights. Use 3/4" stock for

CUTTING LIST		
KEY	**PIECES**	**SIZE AND DESCRIPTION**
A	1	3/4 × 12-1/2 × 39 top back
B	2	1-1/4 × 16-3/4 × 52 sides
C	1	3/4 × 27-1/2 × 39 bottom back
D	2	1-1/4 × 12-1/2 × 40 top shelves
E	2	1-1/4 × 6 × 12-1/4 shelf dividers
F	2	1-1/4 × 3-1/4 × 24 door uprights
G	1	1-1/4 × 3-1/4 × 20 center upright
H1	4	1-1/4 × 3-1/4 × 20 door side frames
H2	4	1-1/4 × 3-1/4 × 8-1/2 top/bottom frames
H3	2	1/4 × 9 × 14 door panels
I1	3	1-1/4 × 5 × 12 drawer fronts
I2	6	3/4 × 5 × 11 drawer sides
I3	3	3/4 × 5 × 10-1/2 drawer backs
I4	3	3/4 × 12 × 12-1/4 drawer bottoms
J	1	1-1/4 × 17-1/4 × 41-1/2 bench top
K	2	3/4 × 16 × 39 shelves
L	6	1 × 2 × 16 cleats

joints being glued and nailed butt joints. For the sides, dowel and edge-glue two boards or cut a single board, shaping the two cutout areas of each side and rounded corner. Attach the three sets of cleats (L) to each side, add the bottom back, the notched bench top (J), and the two inner shelves (K). The notches on each side of the bench top measure 1-1/4" deep × 16-3/4" long to accommodate the sides.

MATERIALS LIST

Door and drawer pulls
Spring or magnetic catches

This done, fasten a connecting cleat to the underside of the bench top, set back 1-1/4" from the front edge. Now, secure the three door uprights (F, G) to the sides, shelves, and cleat, later building the doors to the exact fit of the openings.

Attach the top panel and shelf network next. At this point, you can elect to leave the midsection open—or decorate and install the midsection back panel. Our model shows a wallpaper-covered sheet of 1/4" plywood, overlapped and tacked into place.

Finish off with door and drawer pulls, and spring or magnetic catches for the doors.

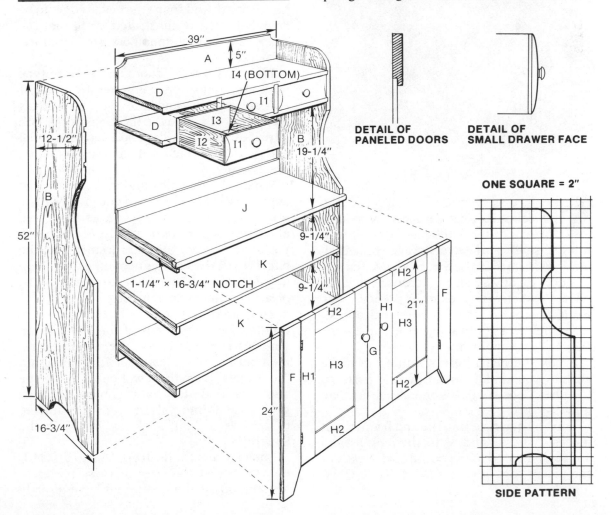

DETAIL OF PANELED DOORS

DETAIL OF SMALL DRAWER FACE

ONE SQUARE = 2"

SIDE PATTERN

Oak Icebox

This icebox is designed, naturally enough, for use in the kitchen—where it is at home visually and extra storage space is always welcome. Crafted in solid oak, the box features readily available hardware that duplicates exactly the look of its predecessors. Both sides of the unit are fitted with adjustable shelves so storage space can be arranged to suit your needs.

Study the plans before cutting to make certain you understand how the parts go together. Construction is actually easier than it looks.

Start by constructing the end frames. Cut pieces D, G, K, and V to the lengths and widths indicated in the cutting list. Next, cut the pieces for the doors (M, N, O, P, Q, W, and X).

Lay the boards on your workbench and position the stiles and rails to achieve the most pleasing grain arrangement. Make light match marks with a pencil so you can quickly return the parts to the same arrangement later. Also, mark all the same surfaces, that is, put a light X on the back surface of all the stiles and rails.

With the frames laid out on the workbench, mark and shape the inside edges to be rounded over, as illustrated. Note that the shape stops on all members 3/4" from the corners.

The stiles for the doors on the prototype were cut with stopped grooves. However, if you lack the tools and know-how for making stopped grooves, make through grooves on all pieces. You can fill the holes created at the ends with small pieces of oak after the doors are assembled.

When all the stiles and rails have been appropriately edge-shaped and grooved, use the matchmarks to reassemble the panel and door sections temporarily. At this point, you can take accurate measurements for the panels to fit the various openings. Again, use a system of matchmarks to ensure the most pleasing grain arrangement.

You can also make accurate dowel location marks at the joints at this time. When you cut the panels for the openings, remember to lay the panels so that the grain "continues" from the lower panel to the one above it. If desired, you can route small grooves at 3" intervals through the paneling to achieve a "slat" look, as shown in the illustration.

Cut all pieces for the front frame (E, F, H, I) to size. Adjust the sizes of these pieces to accommodate the doors you have already cut. Lay out the pieces in the same manner as the doors.

Using the surface marks made during the previous dry assembly, bore all members to receive dowels. The dowels should be no heavier than 3/8" in diameter. Bore all holes in all parts for both of the end panels.

Insert the dowels into the holes in the first stile with wood glue. Apply glue to the joining surfaces and dowels and, starting with the top rail, slip the rails onto the dowels. Insert the appropriate plywood panels into the grooves without glue. Apply glue to the other ends of the rails and to dowels and insert the dowels into the rail ends.

Glue the joining surfaces of the second stile and slip the stile onto the dowels. Use bar clamps to close all joints tightly. Use wood scraps between the clamp jaws and wood to avoid marring the oak. Also, watch for bowing as the clamps are tightened. If the setup has that tendency, turn the frame convex-side up and position weights to force the frame flat. Allow the frames to dry overnight.

Next day, bore holes in the edges of the stiles that will butt the back of the front frame stiles. Insert dowel centers and transfer the centerpoints to the backs of the front frame stiles. The holes in the back of the front frame stiles should be bored a maximum of 1/2" deep.

Once these holes have been bored, the front oak frame can be assembled with dowels and clamps. Again, allow the setup to dry overnight.

Before finally assembling the carcass, lay out and cut all dadoes and grooves in the end sections and in the front frame. There are several important points to keep in mind when doing this step: Dadoes and grooves in the solid oak are 3/8" deep—except in the

CUTTING LIST		
KEY	**PIECES**	**SIZE AND DESCRIPTION**
A	1	13/16 × 19-3/8 × 42 top
B	2	1-3/16 × 1 × 19-1/8 moldings
C	1	1-3/16 × 1 × 41 molding
D	4	13/16 × 2-5/8 × 44-1/2 end stiles
E	2	13/16 × 3 × 41-7/8 front stiles
F	1	13/16 × 3-1/4 × 31-1/4 front center stile
G	4	13/16 × 2-5/8 × 12-7/8 end rails
H	2	13/16 × 2-5/8 × 33 top and bottom front rails
I	1	13/16 × 2-3/4 × 13 center rail
J	2	13/16 × 6-1/2 × 33 bottom false front and finishing rails
K	2	13/16 × 6-1/2 × 12-7/8 end rails
L	2	1-1/8 × 3 × 8-1/4 plinths
M	2	13/16 × 2-5/8 × 31-3/4 door stiles
N	2	13/16 × 2-5/8 × 12 right-hand door top, bottom rails
O	1	13/16 × 2 × 12 right-hand door center rail
P	4	13/16 × 2-5/8 × 14-3/4 door stiles
Q	4	13/16 × 2-5/8 × 8-1/4 door rails
R	1	3/4 × 18-1/8 × 34-1/8 center divider (birch plywood)
S	1	3/4 × 17-1/4 × 18-1/8 center shelf (birch plywood)
T	1	3/4 × 18-1/8 × 37-3/4 bottom shelf (birch plywood)
U	1	1/4 × 37-3/4 × 34-1/2 back (oak plywood)
V	4	1/4 × 13-5/8 × 16-1/8 end panels (oak plywood)
W	2	1/4 × 8-3/4 × 10 left door panels (oak plywood)
X	2	1/4 × 12-3/4 × 12-1/2 right-hand door panels (oak plywood)

MATERIALS LIST
3/8"-dia. dowels
21-3/4" shelf standards
1-1/4" brads
5/8" brads
Hardware
Wood glue

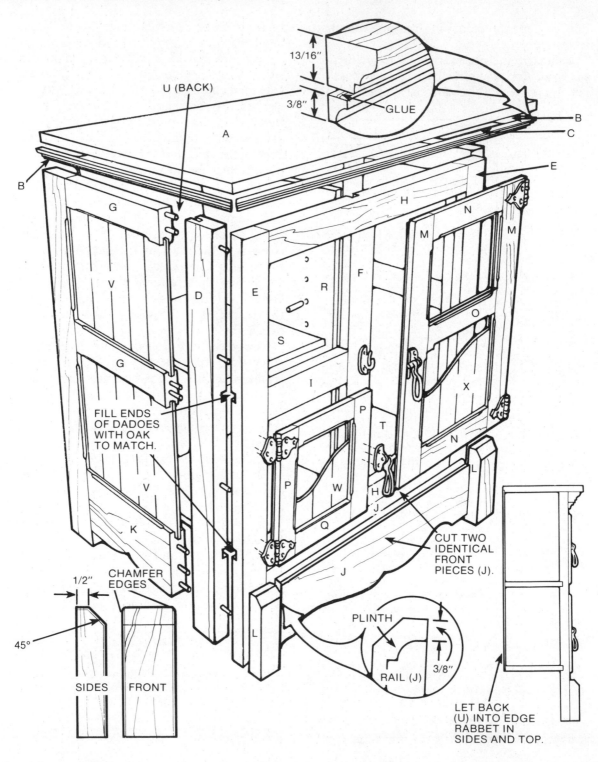

13/16"

3/8"

GLUE

U (BACK)

A

B

C

B

E

G

H

N

M

V

M

D

E

F

M

R

N

S

O

I

X

FILL ENDS OF DADOES WITH OAK TO MATCH.

P

T

H

L

V

P

W

J

K

Q

CUT TWO IDENTICAL FRONT PIECES (J).

J

L

1/2"

CHAMFER EDGES

45°

PLINTH

3/8"

SIDES

FRONT

RAIL (J)

LET BACK (U) INTO EDGE RABBET IN SIDES AND TOP.

stiles and rails of the end sections, where they are only 1/4" deep .

The horizontal grooves at the back of the front frame should be located so that the fixed shelves will be just a hair higher than the rails in front of them. This makes it a snap to clean dirt or dust from the cabinet. If the rails are higher than the shelves behind them, the dirt is trapped inside.

Assemble the first end panel to the front frame and, without stopping, add the bottom shelf (T), center divider (R), and center shelf (S). Without hesitating, add the second end panel and temporarily get a couple of long bar clamps across the front frame. Check the front for square and use the measurements to make certain the back is square. Install the 1/4" plywood back (U) using glue and small nails. Check frequently with a large square to make certain the cabinet remains square as you progress. Any time that you find something out of square, immediately force it into square and use either clamps, braces, or both to hold it that way.

Cut, shape, and install the top (A) as shown in the drawing. Then enlist the aid of a helper to heft the carcass up onto your workbench, upside down (see photo). Slip a couple of 2 × 3s between the top and your workbench as you do, so that you will have room for clamps later. Complete the clamping operation as shown in the photos. If you lack an adequate number of clamps, use ropes and temporary tacked-on braces.

Let the unit sit for at least 24 hours.

If you position your clamps carefully, you can save time by adding the moldings (B, C), just below the top, at this time. The pieces are installed with 45° miter joints at the outside corners.

Cut all pieces of molding to fit; then install the parts. Position the larger molding and glue and clamp the pieces securely overnight. Next day, bore undersize lead holes through them and secure the molding into

the top from beneath with well-set 1-1/4" brads. Repeat for the smaller molding; affix with glue and clamps only and allow to dry. Then bore lead holes and add 5/8" brads. Use a fine nailset to set these as well.

Once the cabinet construction is completed, you can assemble the doors as you did the side panels. Use the openings to determine the actual sizes and construct them in the same fashion as the end panel sections.

When the doors are assembled, lay them out on the cabinet to locate holes for the hardware screws. Bore pilot holes for all screws and attach the hardware. Attach the false front (J) and plinths (L) as indicated. With the cabinet completely assembled, cut the plywood shelves to fit their respective compartments.

Carefully inspect the assembled cabinet for flaws, errors, or rough spots that need additional sanding.

Remove all hardware and you can proceed with the finishing.

When all end panel stiles and rails are cut to length, assemble the ends—dry and without dowels—to check for fit. Both end panels should be exactly the same width and length. Then make matchmarks on rails and stiles to indicate all dowel locations.

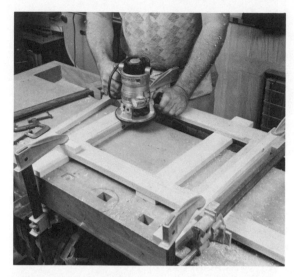

Using a rounding-over bit, rout the inside only on all stiles and rails. Relocate the clamps (at least two) as necessary to provide clearance for router shoe. Stops clamped at both ends of the router run are positioned so the last 3/4" (i.e., the corners) will not be shaped.

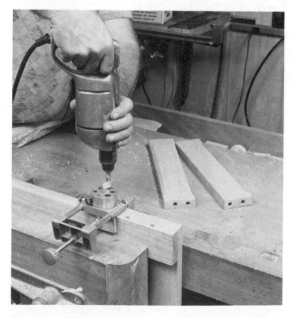

Disassemble the end panels and bore the holes for the dowels. To achieve accurate hole drilling, use a doweling jig such as the one shown and a brad point bit.

After all stiles and rails are edge-shaped and drilled for dowels, plow the grooves to receive the plywood panels. The groove width should be slightly more than 1/4" to assure a free fit.

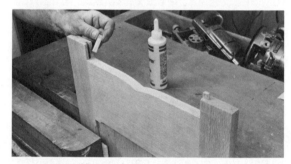

Next, assemble the two end panels using glue and dowels. After assembly, exposed portions of the grooves should be filled with pieces of oak.

Securely clamp the cabinet-front stile and a guide rail for the end panel to slide against. Insert dowel centers and carefully push the end panel forward to transfer the dowel hole locations; then bore the dowel holes in the front stiles so the joint can be made.

It is easiest to assemble the unit upside down on the workbench as shown.

Because of the longer vertical run, the shelves in the right compartment rest on shelf clips inserted into let-in pilaster standards.

Because smaller openings on cabinet left dictated not more than one shelf each, the dowel-and-hole method for shelf support is used.

The skirt at front is cut 3/8" narrower than the false front behind it (see drawing); this creates an edge reveal below the case's bottom rail.

Step-Back Hutch

The construction of this step-back hutch has been simplified. The dentil and vine trim have been eliminated, but the proportion and simple Federal style of the piece remain.

The step-back hutch uses 3/4″ pine for most components. Due to the size of the sides (B), partition (K), and shelves (H, L), it will be necessary to glue up several boards

for each of these pieces. Glue all edges, clamp, and allow the glue to dry overnight. In the meantime, cut the other parts to size.

Bore 1/4″-diameter holes in the rails (D, G, J) and stiles (F, P) as shown in the drawing. Bore each hole 1″ deep. Apply glue and insert the dowels, then assemble the upper and lower face frames. Clamp, then measure diagonally in each direction to assure square assemblies.

Assemble the hutch cabinet with the back side down. Measure and mark locations for the shelves (H, L) on each side (B). Then glue and nail the top (M) to the sides and clamp. Repeat the process by attaching the bottom (C) and the fixed shelf (H) to the side's lower portion. Use glue and finishing nails to assemble, countersinking the heads. Check for squareness by measuring diagonally.

Next, glue and nail the lower face frame to the cabinet. Fit, glue, and nail the partition (K) in position. Follow by attaching the upper face frame in the same manner. When the glue has dried on these components, turn the cabinet facedown. Be careful to protect the cabinet's front when doing this.

Cut the back (A) to size, then glue and nail it into position so it fits snugly between the sides. Flip the box again and miter cove molding (T, U) to length as specified in the cutting list. Glue and nail the molding to the top rail and sides as shown. Cut half-round molding (R, S) to fit on the partition's front and exposed sides. Glue and nail it in place; sink all nails and fill the recess with wood putty.

Stand the hutch erect. Locate and bore holes for shelf clips as shown in the side detail. Bore the holes, 1/2″ deep. Install the

The opened lower cabinet reveals plenty of space for storing your dishes.

clips and shelves. (Cleats made out of wood scraps may also be used.)

Simulate paneling on the bottom doors (Q1) by applying lattice (Q2, Q3) to the doors. Carefully cut the lattice pieces to form tight, square corners. Glue and clamp or use brads to attach the lattice.

With a 1/4" bit and dowel jig, bore 1"-deep holes for dowels in the top door frame pieces (N1, N2) as per the drawing. Apply glue, insert the dowels, clamp, and measure diagonally to square. When the glue has dried, rout a rabbet along the inside to accommo-

date the glass inserts (E1) and bead molding (E2, E3).

Cut the glass to fit, then place it in each door. Push in a few glazers or 3/4" brads to secure the glass. Then miter the bead molding to size and install with brads.

Finally, mortise the top and bottom doors and cabinets to accommodate 2-1/2" brass butt hinges. Attach the doorknobs, also.

MATERIALS LIST

Shelf clips or cleats
2-1/2" brass butt hinges (8)
1/4"-dia. dowels
Wood screws
Finishing nails
Doorknobs (4)
Roller catches and strikes
Wood glue

CUTTING LIST

KEY	PIECES	SIZE AND DESCRIPTION
A	1	1/2 × 45 × 86 back (plywood)
B	2	3/4 × 23-1/2 × 86 sides
C	1	3/4 × 45 × 23 bottom (plywood)
D	1	3/4 × 7-1/4 × 46-1/2 base rail
E1	2	1/8 × 15-3/4 × 37-1/8 upper door inserts (glass)
E2	4	3/8 × 3/8 × 15-7/8 bead molding
E3	4	3/8 × 3/8 × 37-1/4 bead molding
F	2	3/4 × 3-1/2 × 28-1/2 lower stiles
G	1	3/4 × 3-1/2 × 39-1/2 middle rail
H	1	3/4 × 45 × 22-3/4 fixed shelf
J	1	3/4 × 5-1/2 × 39-1/2 top rail
K	1	3/4 × 24 × 46-1/2 partition
L	3	3/4 × 16 × 44-1/2 adjustable shelves
M	1	3/4 × 16-3/4 × 45 top (plywood)
N1	4	3/4 × 2-1/4 × 19-5/8 top doors, horizontals
N2	4	3/4 × 2-1/4 × 41 top doors, verticals
P	2	3/4 × 3-1/2 × 49-1/2 upper stiles
Q1	2	3/4 × 19-5/8 × 25 bottom doors
Q2	4	1/4 × 2-1/4 × 15-1/8 lattice
Q3	4	1/4 × 2-1/4 × 25 lattice
R	2	3/4 × 7-3/4 half-round molding
S	1	3/4 × 49 half-round molding
T	1	3-1/4 × 50-3/4 cove molding
U	2	3-1/2 × 20 cove molding

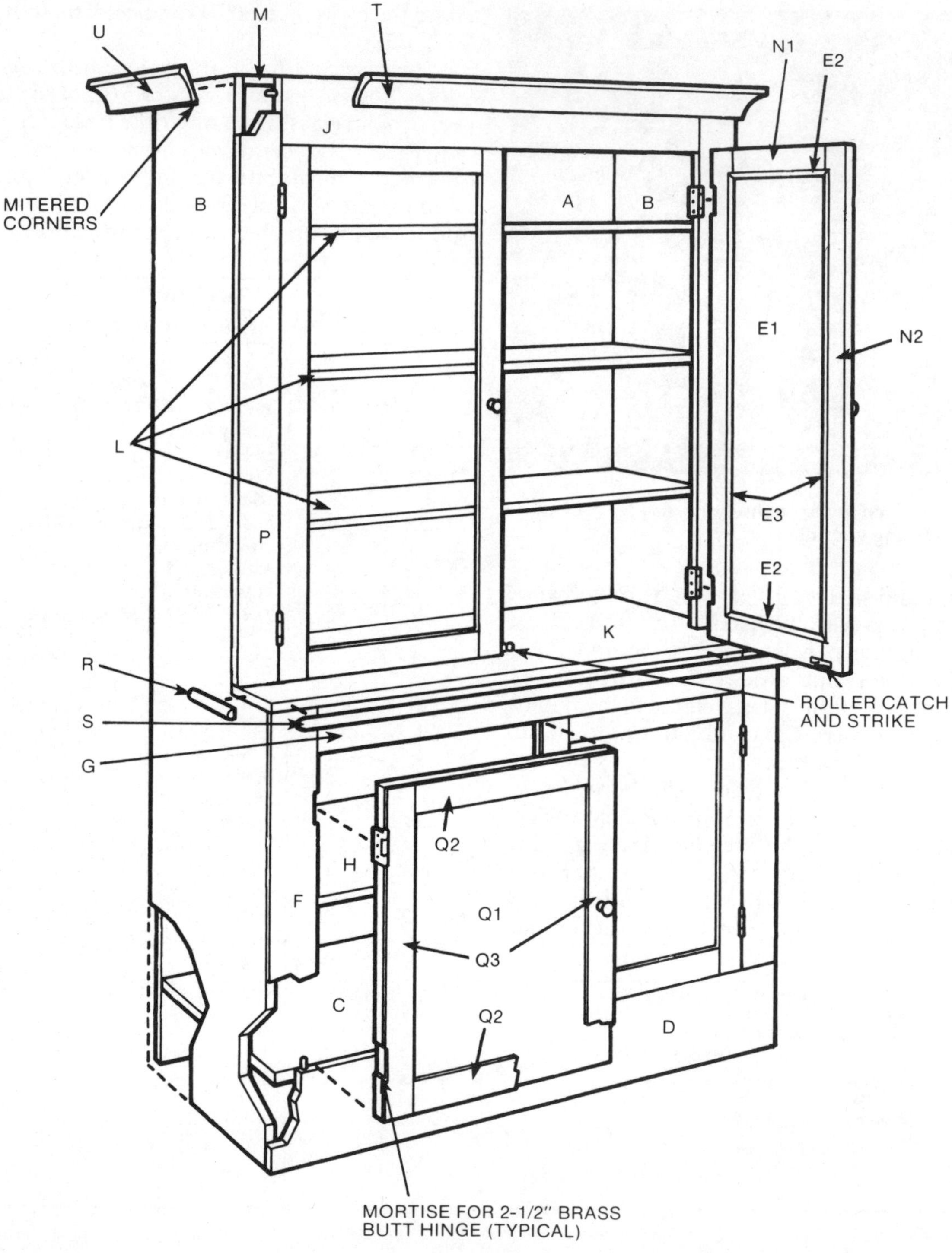
U
M
T
N1
E2
MITERED CORNERS
B
J
A
B
E1
N2
L
E3
P
E2
K
R
S
G
ROLLER CATCH AND STRIKE
Q2
H
F
Q1
Q3
C
Q2
D
MORTISE FOR 2-1/2" BRASS BUTT HINGE (TYPICAL)

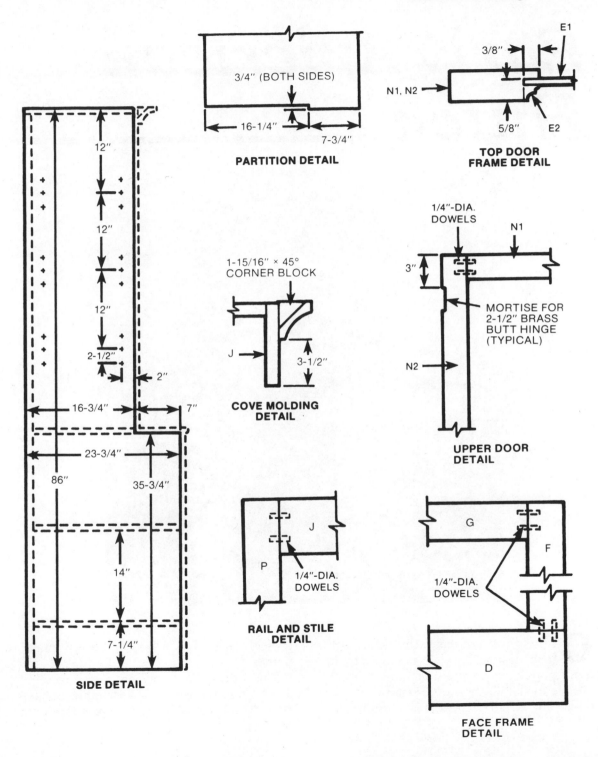

PARTITION DETAIL

3/4" (BOTH SIDES)

16-1/4"

7-3/4"

TOP DOOR FRAME DETAIL

E1

3/8"

N1, N2

5/8"

E2

SIDE DETAIL

12"

12"

12"

2-1/2"

2"

16-3/4"

7"

23-3/4"

86"

35-3/4"

14"

7-1/4"

COVE MOLDING DETAIL

1-15/16" × 45° CORNER BLOCK

J

3-1/2"

UPPER DOOR DETAIL

1/4"-DIA. DOWELS

N1

3"

MORTISE FOR 2-1/2" BRASS BUTT HINGE (TYPICAL)

N2

RAIL AND STILE DETAIL

J

P

1/4"-DIA. DOWELS

FACE FRAME DETAIL

G

F

1/4"-DIA. DOWELS

D

Early American Hutch

Of the dozens of early American furniture designs, no piece seems to be more popular than the unassuming hutch. Simple in detail, the hutch is a favorite of do-it-yourselfers because it is a fast-moving project, as well as a fine addition for any home.

This one is an imposing piece (roughly 3' × 6'), so exercise care in selecting stock—stick to a clear ash, cherry, or something warm like spiced maple. Avoid rich or knotty woods.

Construction is a duplication process, the top being a slimmer version of the base cabinet. The base extends only 12" from the wall and the cabinet over it only 8", providing a 4" setback at counter height.

Construct two separate cabinets. Size and cut the four sides (B, M), (note the cutaway on the base cabinet), the two tops (A, L), the two backs (C, N), and the lower shelf (O) for the base cabinet. Next, cut the three pieces of facing trim (E, F) for the top cabinet and the four pieces of trim (P, Q) for the base cabinet. Assemble the boxes with finishing nails and wood glue. Nail through the sides into the bottom shelf. Attach the four shelves in the top cabinet and the middle shelf in the base cabinet again, nailing through the sides. Attach the seven pieces of facing trim and, finally, the three lengths of 3/4" cove molding beneath the upper cabinet top.

Join the upper cabinet to the base cabinet with cleats as shown in the sketch. The cleats are screwed and glued to the sides and back of the top cabinet. The cabinet is then fastened to the top shelf of the lower cabinet with screws driven through the cleats into the shelf.

You will note that the door frames use rabbet joints throughout. Rabbets are also used for the frame edges where the two doors meet (see Detail 2), assuring a snug closure. The rabbet cuts serve as lips into which the doors' plywood panels are also set. Chip molding acts as a retainer strip for holding the panels in place.

Concealed spring catches, mortised hinges, and decorative pulls make up the hardware.

MATERIALS LIST

3/4" cove molding
Finishing nails
Chip molding
Hinges
Doorknobs
Wood screws
Wood glue

CUTTING LIST

KEY	PIECES	SIZE AND DESCRIPTION
A	1	3/4 × 10 × 39 hutch top
B	2	3/4 × 7-1/4 × 41-1/4 upper cabinet sides
C	1	3/4 × 33-1/2 × 41-1/4 upper cabinet back (plywood)
D	4	3/4 × 6-1/2 × 33-1/2 upper shelves
E	2	3/4 × 2-1/2 × 41-1/4 upper cabinet side trim
F	1	3/4 × 3/4 × 30 upper cabinet head trim (not shown)
G	4	3/4 × 2-1/2 × 10 upper door rails
H	4	3/4 × 2-1/2 × 40-1/4 upper door stiles
I	2	1/4 × 10-1/2 × 39-3/4 upper door panels
J	2	3/4 × 3/4 × 6-1/4 side cleats
K	1	3/4 × 3/4 × 33-1/2 back cleat
L	1	3/4 × 12-3/4 × 36-1/2 lower cabinet top
M	2	3/4 × 11-1/4 × 30-3/4 lower cabinet sides
N	1	3/4 × 31-1/2 × 33-1/2 lower cabinet back (plywood, not shown)
O	2	3/4 × 10-1/2 × 33-1/2 lower shelves
P	2	3/4 × 2-1/2 × 30 lower cabinet trim
Q	2	3/4 × 2-1/2 × 30-3/4 lower cabinet trim
R	4	3/4 × 2-1/2 × 10 lower door rails
S	4	3/4 × 2-1/2 × 26-1/2 lower door stiles
T	2	1/4 × 10-1/2 × 22 lower door panels

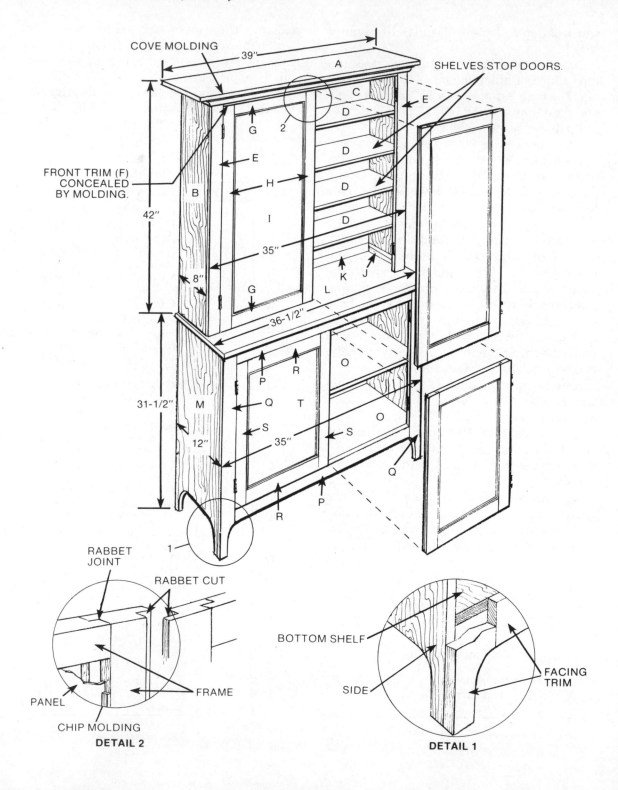

COVE MOLDING

SHELVES STOP DOORS.

39"

A

C

D

D

D

D

E

G

2

E

FRONT TRIM (F)
CONCEALED
BY MOLDING.

B

42"

H

I

35"

8"

K

J

G

L

36-1/2"

P

R

O

31-1/2"

M

Q

T

S

O

S

12"

35"

Q

R

P

1

RABBET
JOINT

RABBET CUT

PANEL

FRAME

CHIP MOLDING

DETAIL 2

BOTTOM SHELF

SIDE

FACING
TRIM

DETAIL 1

Classic Corner Cupboard

The original corner cupboard on which this adaptation is based was made in Indiana in about 1820 by Thomas Lincoln, a relative of President Abraham Lincoln.

The cabinet falls somewhere in the middle range of Lincoln's work—not his best, but certainly not done in haste. Apparently, the raised panel doors were fitted after the shelves were fixed. At that point it was necessary for Lincoln to cut horizontal dadoes in the back of each door so they cleared the shelves.

Lincoln made his corner cupboard from cherry and poplar. For economy this adaptation uses pine and plywood.

Begin by laying out the top, shelf and bottom (A), sides (B, D), back (G), and the three shelves (E) on plywood.

Lay out your work so the good face is the one that will show. Draw on the poor side to minimize chipping and tearing as you cut out the components with a circular saw. Cut the required angles in such a way that your final dimensions remain true.

Next, mark the back (G) and sides (B, D) to locate the top, shelf, and bottom (A) pieces for nailing.

Then attach the pieces to the sides. Use cleats to temporarily hold them in place during assembly.

Glue and nail (6d finishing nails) the back (G) in place. Carefully square the assembly. Before the glue sets up, remove the cleats.

Temporarily nail the removed cleats to the cabinet bottom to prevent wood splintering when sliding the assembly on the shop floor during construction.

Next, cut the side fascia (C), base (H), rail (P), and fascia (O) to size.

Per the diagram, rip the 67-1/2° angle onto the edge of the fascia. Rip or plane the board's edges to establish the angle of this joint and carefully plane or sand until the edges of the fascia and the side (D) meet perfectly at the proper angle.

Locate positions for the dowel pins on the side fascia (C), base (H), rail (P), and fascia (O). Then, using a dowel jig, bore 1/4" holes 1-1/8" deep to accept 2" dowel pins. Apply glue to the dowels and assemble the entire facing to the cabinet. The glue will fill the extra 1/8" in the dowel holes. Clamp and measure diagonally until both dimensions match. This assures a square frame. Now, glue on the bead molding (Q). When the glue dries, sand the frame with medium-grit paper.

Next, make a wood gauge that will locate holes for the shelf clips. Use the gauge to bore holes through the side pieces.

CUTTING LIST

KEY	PIECES	SIZE AND DESCRIPTION
A	3	3/4" × 18-3/4 × 49-1/2 top, shelf, and bottom (plywood)
B	2	1/2 × 22 × 87 sides (plywood)
C	2	3/4 × 6-3/4 × 87 side fascia
D	2	3/4 × 5-3/8 × 87 sides (plywood)
E	3	3/4 × 18-3/4 × 49-1/4 shelves (plywood)
F	2	3/4 × 14-7/8 × 24-7/8 door panels
G	1	1/2 × 19-1/2 × 87 back (plywood)
H	1	3/4 × 7-1/4 × 30 base
J	4	1/4 × 2-1/2 × 25 lattice
K	4	1/4 × 2-1/2 × 9-7/8 lattice
L	1	3-1/4 × 45-1/2 cove molding
M	73	1/4 × 3/4 × 1-1/2 dentil
N	2	3-1/4 × 6-1/2 cove molding
O	1	3/4 × 7-1/4 × 30 fascia
P	1	3/4 × 1-1/2 × 30 rail
Q	3	3/4 × 42-1/2 bead molding

MATERIALS LIST

Wood knobs
1/4"-dia. dowels
Hinges
Shelf support clips
Roller catches
6d finishing nails
4d finishing nails
Wood glue

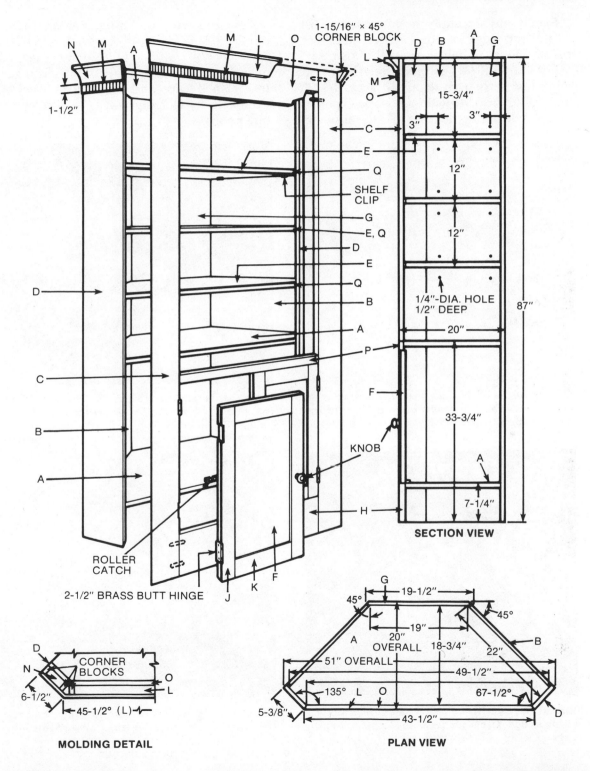

1-15/16" × 45°
CORNER BLOCK

N   M   A   M   L   O

1-1/2"

D
B
A
G

L
M
O

15-3/4"

3"   3"

C

E

Q

SHELF
CLIP

12"

G

E, Q

12"

D

E

Q

1/4"-DIA. HOLE
1/2" DEEP

B

A

20"

D

C

P

B

F

A

33-3/4"

87"

KNOB

A

7-1/4"

H

SECTION VIEW

ROLLER
CATCH

2-1/2" BRASS BUTT HINGE

J   K   F

D

N

CORNER
BLOCKS

O

L

6-1/2"

45-1/2° (L)

MOLDING DETAIL

G

45°   19-1/2"

45°

A   19"

B

20"
OVERALL   18-3/4"

22"

51" OVERALL

49-1/2"

135°   L   O   67-1/2°

5-3/8"   43-1/2"   D

PLAN VIEW

Finally, cut and apply the cove molding (L) to the top edge of the cabinet face. Use corner blocks to help support the cove.

For the dentil (M), a fluted screen bead and miter box were used to cut 72 pieces 1-1/2" long. Glue the 3/4"-wide screen bead pieces side by side under the cove, as in the drawing.

Next, measure and cut the cabinet door panels (F) from 3/4" thick pine; attach 2-1/4" × 1/4" lattice (J, K) with glue and nails. Mortise the doors and install all hinges. Insert shelf clips and roller door catches. Complete by locating and boring holes for pull knobs.

Determine the 67-1/2° angle with a protractor for the cabinet shelf, top and bottom (A). Cut out pieces with a circular saw.

Mark the back (G) and sides (B, D) to locate the top, shelf, and bottom (A) pieces for nailing.

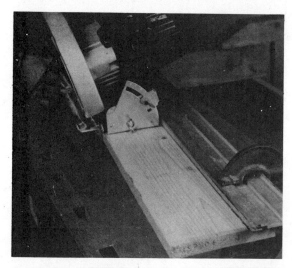

Cut the bevels with a circular saw guided along a straightedge. Use a planer blade to get a smooth edge.

Attach the top, shelf, and bottom (A) to the back (G) and then the sides (B) with glue and finishing nails.

Use a scrap cutoff piece to provide the precise angle for nailing the back (G) to sides (B). Glue all parts before nailing.

Bevel and then test-fit the side fascia (C) and showing side (D) where they join together.

Smooth any gaps that show when the side fascia (C) and the showing side (D) are joined.

Use a miter box, marked for the dentil (M) height, to cut 72 equal length pieces of fluted screen bead.

Country-Style Corner Cupboard

This simple cabinet is a piece that found much favor, both in colonial times and through the 1800s, with its practical use for awkward corner space. In today's country home, it is an attractive accent piece as well. *Note:* When completed, this cupboard stands just over 4′ tall. For a taller unit, simply extend the measurements to suit your room.

Construction is simple and straight forward. Begin by cutting the shelves (B) to the dimensions in the cutting list. Cut the sides (D) to the proper dimensions. The back edges of the sides are cut straight, but the front edges are cut at 45° angles as seen in the illustration. Mark the locations for the shelves on the sides and attach the sides to the shelves, by gluing and nailing through the sides. Join the sides with a nailed butt joint. Cut the front pieces (E), the trim (C), and the top (A). The outside edges of the front pieces and trim molding are also cut at 45° angles. Nail the front pieces and trim to the sides and top and bottom shelves. Cut the base trim (G) and top (A), and attach them to the cabinet.

MATERIALS LIST
Finishing nails
Butt hinges
Knob
1″ cove molding
Wooden door catch
Wood glue

CUTTING LIST

KEY	PIECES	SIZE AND DESCRIPTION
A	1	3/4 × 19 × 19 × 30 top
B	5	3/4 × 16-3/4 × 16-3/4 × 26 shelves
C	1	3/4 × 2-1/2 × 14 front trim
D	2	1/4 × 16-3/4 × 50 sides
E	2	3/4 × 6 × 46-1/2 front
F	1	3/4 × 14 × 46-1/2 door
G	1	3/4 × 3-1/2 × 26 base trim

Double-check the measurements for the door against the actual opening. The door should be 1/8″ narrower and 1/8″ shorter than the opening. The door (F) is hung with butt hinges.

This is a good beginner's piece because there are few curved or angled cuts, and it is an ideal piece for plywood because the only edges normally exposed to view are the top and sides of the base trim piece.

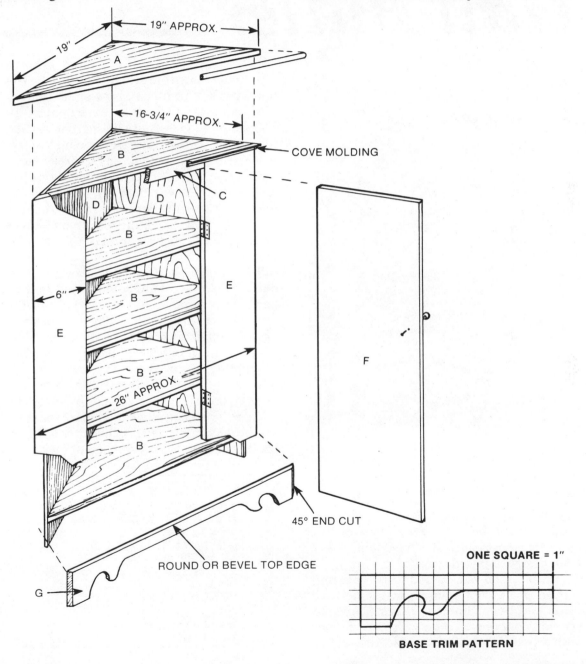

19″ APPROX.

19″

A

16-3/4″ APPROX.

COVE MOLDING

B

C

D

D

D

B

E

6″

B

E

B

26″ APPROX.

B

F

45° END CUT

ROUND OR BEVEL TOP EDGE

G

ONE SQUARE = 1″

BASE TRIM PATTERN

Victorian Hall Butler

Enhance your entry foyer with this Victorian hall butler. Made of richly figured oak, the overall effect is one of fine cabinetry, yet relatively simple joinery has been designed into the piece.

The recessed backboard features a mirror, an opalescent stained-glass panel, and brass and porcelain coat hooks. The chest section contains a roomy drawer topped with a two-tier shelf. Alongside, the seat lid

lifts for access to foul-weather footwear. The bottom is lined with an easy-to-make aluminum pan that will contain any water runoff.

Opalescent glass, not transparent, is used for the decorative stained glass panel. This is because clear stained glass requires rear illumination in order to be properly visible, whereas opalescent glass can be seen more easily because it reflects the light striking it from the front. Since the glass panel backs up to a wall, no transmitted light will be present.

While assembling a stained-glass panel requires relatively simple soldering of the lead came butt joints, successfully cutting the glass is another matter. Since opalescent glass is relatively costly, the overall project could get fairly expensive, particularly while attempting to cut the curved sections. To reduce the cost, consider buying a precut glass kit or have the panel made by an expert.

There is an alternative procedure for making the decorative panel, which utilizes liquid leading and glass stains in lieu of authentic

MATERIALS LIST
1"-dia. porcelain knobs (2)
18 ga. × 19" × 39-1/2" aluminum
Locking lid stay
Coat hooks (3)
35" × 38" cloth
1" × 16-1/2" × 36-1/2" foam
Brads
Wood screws
Finishing nails
Wood filler
Wood glue

KEY	PIECES	SIZE AND DESCRIPTION
CUTTING LIST		
A	1	13/16 × 3-1/2 × 54 top rail
B	3	13/16 × 2-1/2 × 54 rails
C	1	13/16 × 2-1/2 × 38-1/2 rail
D	3	13/16 × 2-1/2 × 78 stiles
E	2	13/16 × 2-1/2 × 64-1/2 stiles
F	1	13/16 × 10-3/8 × 13-3/4 arches
G	1	13/16 × 10-3/8 × 34-1/4 arches
H	2	13/16 × 3-1/4 × 78 side strips
I	2	1/2 × 1/2 × 78 glue strips
J	1	1-1/16 × 3-5/16 × 54 cornice
K	1	1-1/16 × 2-1/4 × 54 cornice
L	3	1/4 × 10-1/4 × 32-1/4 panels (plywood)
M	1	1/4 × 9-3/4 × 13-3/4 panel (plywood)
N	3	1/4 × 9-3/4 × 10-1/4 panel (plywood)
O	1	1/8 × 13-5/8 × 43-1/8 mirror
P	1	1/8 × 9-1/8 × 31-1/8 plastic insert or stained glass
Q	4	3/8 × 3/4 × 17 mirror retaining snaps
R	6	mirror retaining clips
S	1	3/4 × 16-3/4 × 53-1/8 chest back (plywood)
T1	1	3/4 × 15 × 53-1/8 chest bottom (plywood)
T2	1	3/4 × 1-1/2 × 53-1/8 chest bottom facing (oak)
U	1	3/4 × 2-5/8 × 52-1/2 cleat (plywood)
V	1	13/16 × 17-1/4 × 28-3/4 compartment

KEY	PIECES	SIZE AND DESCRIPTION
CUTTING LIST (continued)		
W	1	13/16 × 17-1/4 × 25-3/8 compartment
X	1	13/16 × 11-3/4 × 16-7/8 compartment
Y	1	13/16 × 15-3/4 × 17-1/4 compartment shelf
Z	1	13/16 × 16-3/4 × 17-1/4 chest side
AA	1	13/16 × 15-1/2 × 36-7/8 chest lid
BB	2	13/16 × 2-1/2 × 36-1/4 frame rails
CC	2	13/16 × 2-1/2 × 13-3/8 frame stiles
DD	1	13/16 × 2 × 36 cleat
EE	1	13/16 × 2 × 14-1/2 cleat
FF	1	13/16 × 1-5/8 × 37-1/8 lid back
GG	1	1/4 × 9-1/8 × 32 panel (plywood)
HH	1	1-1/2 × 1-1/2 × 36-1/4 cleat
II	1	13/16 × 3-1/4 × 55-5/8 skirt
JJ	2	13/16 × 3-1/4 × 15-1/16 skirt
KK	1	1-1/2 × 36 piano hinge
LL	1	13/16 × 13-1/4 × 15-1/8 drawer front
MM	2	1/2 × 12 × 15 drawer sides
NN	2	1/2 × 12 × 14-1/8 drawer ends
OO	1	1/2 × 13-1/4 × 14-1/8 drawer bottom (plywood)
PP	2	1/2 × 1/2 × 12 glue block
QQ	1	3/4 × 1-1/4 × 8 backstop
RR1	1	1/2 × 1-5/8 × 6-1/2 backstop
RR2	1	1-1/8 × 1-1/8 × 4 stopblock

leaded stained glass. This is described later in the project.

The backboard framing (A, B, C, D, E) is made with end and middle half lap joints. Rip the frame stock to size; then cut the pieces to the required lengths. Lay the pieces in their respective positions on the floor, measuring carefully so they will be accurately spaced. Mark the intersections for the lap joints. Identify each piece for easy reassembly later.

A radial arm saw equipped with a dado head will make the quickest work of cutting the half laps. Of course, you can do an equally good job with a table saw or with a router and a straight-cutting mortising bit. Whichever tool you use, adjust the depth of cut to exactly one-half the thickness of the stock. Make repeated passes to clear out the waste. When all the pieces have been notched, make a dry assembly to check for proper fit before gluing.

Start the assembly by laying down the two stiles (D) that abut the stained-glass section. Insert the second and third rails (B) (count-

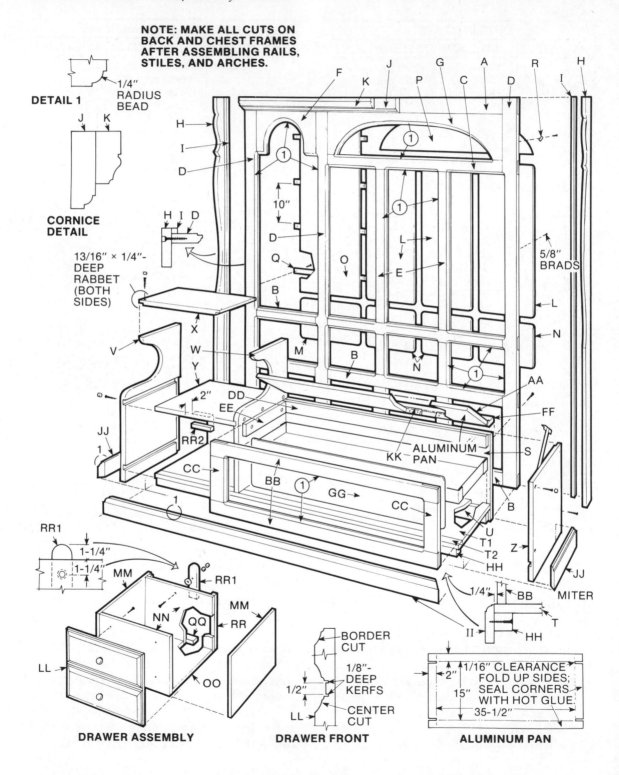

NOTE: MAKE ALL CUTS ON
BACK AND CHEST FRAMES
AFTER ASSEMBLING RAILS,
STILES, AND ARCHES.

DETAIL 1

1/4"
RADIUS
BEAD

CORNICE
DETAIL

13/16" × 1/4"-
DEEP
RABBET
(BOTH
SIDES)

10"

5/8"
BRADS

ALUMINUM
PAN

DRAWER ASSEMBLY

RR1
1-1/4"
1-1/4"

DRAWER FRONT

BORDER
CUT

1/8"-
DEEP
KERFS

1/2"

CENTER
CUT

ALUMINUM PAN

1/16" CLEARANCE
FOLD UP SIDES;
SEAL CORNERS
WITH HOT GLUE

2"
15"
35-1/2"

MITER

1/4"

① 1/4"-RADIUS BEAD

② 3/8" × 1/4"-DEEP RABBET

③ 3/8" × 11/32"-DEEP RABBET

④ 3/8" × 1/8"-DEEP RABBET

⑤ 3/4" × 3/8"-DEEP RABBET

⑥ 3/4" × 3/8"-DEEP DADO

⑦ 13/16" × 1/4"-DEEP DADO

⑧ 13/16" × 1/4"-DEEP RABBET

⑨ HALF-LAP JOINTS (TYPICAL)

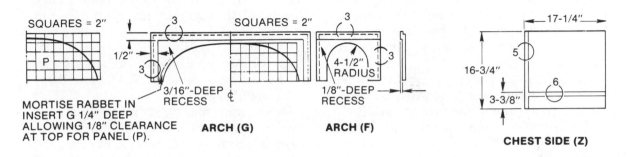

SQUARES = 2"

P

MORTISE RABBET IN INSERT G 1/4" DEEP ALLOWING 1/8" CLEARANCE AT TOP FOR PANEL (P).

1/2"

3/16"-DEEP RECESS

ARCH (G)

SQUARES = 2"

ARCH (F)

4-1/2" RADIUS

1/8"-DEEP RECESS

17-1/4"

16-3/4"

3-3/8"

5

6

CHEST SIDE (Z)

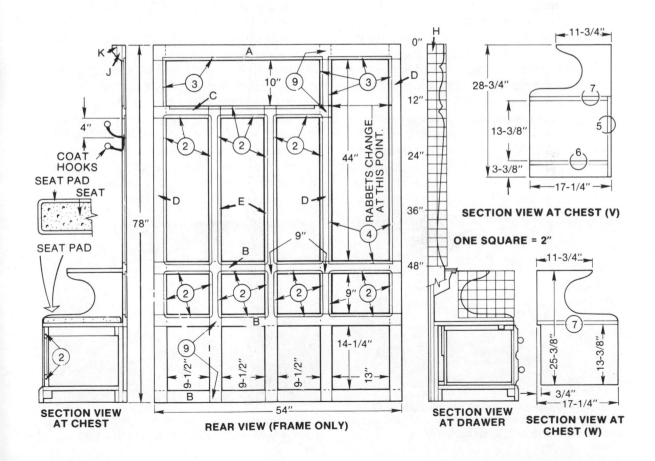

K

J

4"

COAT HOOKS

SEAT PAD

SEAT

SEAT PAD

②

SECTION VIEW AT CHEST

A

③

10"

⑨

③

D

C

② ② ②

D E D

B

9"

④

B B

② ② ② 9" ②

14-1/4"

⑨

9-1/2" 9-1/2" 9-1/2" 13"

B

78"

44"

RABBETS CHANGE AT THIS POINT.

54"

REAR VIEW (FRAME ONLY)

H

0"

D

12"

24"

36"

48"

SECTION VIEW AT DRAWER

11-3/4"

28-3/4"

13-3/8"

3-3/8"

7

5

6

17-1/4"

SECTION VIEW AT CHEST (V)

ONE SQUARE = 2"

11-3/4"

25-3/8"

13-3/8"

7

3/4"

17-1/4"

SECTION VIEW AT CHEST (W)

ing from the bottom) as shown. Next, lay in the short rail (C) that forms the bottom of the stained-glass frame. The top rail (A) follows, then the three remaining stiles (D, E).

To obtain clamp pressure in the central area where the clamps won't reach, place strips of wood over the center joints, with a double thickness over the middle rail. Bridge these strips with a long board; then clamp it down at both ends. The bowed, tensioned board will put pressure at the joints under the strips.

The assembled frame is rabbeted on the back to accommodate the plywood panel inserts (L, M, N), the solid wood arches (F, G) and mirror (O). Using a router with a 3/8" rabbeting bit will result in round inside corners. These are left round in the areas that will receive the plywood panels, with the panels cut to fit. The corners that receive the wood arches and the mirror must be squared with a chisel. Note in the drawing that the rabbet in the vertical mirror section must be cut to two depths in order to accommodate both the panel and the mirror.

The arch for the stained glass is mortised on the back in either of two patterns, depending upon whether you plan to use the real stained-glass panel or the simulated version. In either case, use a router with a mor-

tising bit to cut the recess. For the stained-glass panel, trace the curved line from the glass panel. For the simulated version, use a mirror as a backdrop and make the recess with the aid of guide strips for the straight-edge border along the sides and top.

Glue in the arched panels; then turn the frame right side up to cut the molded edge around all the openings (except the four at the bottom). Attach the plywood inserts with glue and 5/8" finishing nails. Predrill pilot holes for the nails using one of the nails with the head clipped off as a drill bit. Bore these holes about 3/8" deep.

Make the cornice by joining two pieces of stock (J, K) that have been individually pre-shaped. Secure the cornice side strips (H) with glue and screws. Note that the edges of the side strips project 1/2" to allow the unit to snug up to a wall.

If you opt to make the simulated stained glass panel, you'll need a bottle of liquid leading and a variety of clear glass stains. Normally, the stains are applied directly to a mirror or plain glass, but to obtain better visibility of the colors, apply the leading and stains to a sheet of matte Mylar (0.005 thick) purchased at an art supply store. Placed against a mirror, the matte surface disperses the light reflecting back from the mirror,

Carefully mark each frame piece for the half lap joints by laying them out as shown. Also number each member to avoid confusion later.

Clamping this bowed board into place as shown applies pressure to hard-to-reach inner joints.

resulting in a bright field that makes the colored segments brighter and more colorful.

The procedure is relatively simple. Draw the desired pattern on the dull side of the Mylar. Turn the sheet over and flow a bead of liquid leading over the outline. Allow it to dry, then apply the desired stains into each walled segment, using a separate eye dropper for each color. The work surface must be level so the stains won't flow out of bounds. When the sheet is dry, staple it into place across the top only to prevent buckling. Secure a mirror behind it.

Plywood is used for the back (S) and bottom (T1, T2) of the chest. Because a small

portion will show, add a solid oak facing (T2) to the front edge of the bottom. Cut the parts to size, but do not cut the contours until the dadoes and rabbets have been made.

Begin the chest assembly by attaching the back to the bottom with glue and finishing nails. Glue in the cleat (U), as indicated, to reinforce this joint. Dry-assemble the compartment pieces (V, W, X, Y, Z) with clamps in order to bore the pilot holes. Assemble with wood screws and glue; then attach the lid (AA) as shown.

Make the front frame (BB, CC,) as shown; clamp it into place and bore the pilot holes before routing the inside edges. The skirt

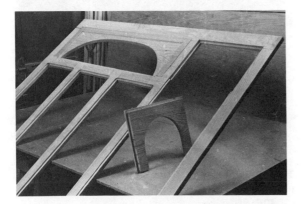

The back is rabbeted to allow for the rear panels and stained glass.

The molded edge is routed on the front of the frame after the arches have been glued into place.

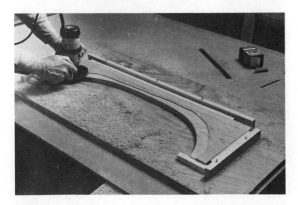

Rout the recess for the stained glass insert with a mortising bit.

Cut the plywood panels to fit the rabbeted frame and round the corners as well.

members (II, JJ) are joined with 45° miters. Cut the miters before shaping the edges or cutting the contour in the front skirt (II).

The drawer front (LL) simulates a double drawer. Use a molding head on your table or radial arm saw to make the required border and center division cuts. When the shaped cuts have been made, make two parallel, thin-blade kerf cuts across the center to form the simulated drawer divider. Construct the drawer and attach its front.

Secure the wall unit to the chest with screws only. Plug the exposed screw holes with wood filler, and sand the piece with 180-grit paper.

To make the pan for rain gear, begin by folding up the sides in a thin aluminum sheet. Draw the layout onto the metal. Cut the aluminum to size, cutting out slivers about 1/16″ wide at the corners for bending clearance. Clamp a strip of wood on the fold line, with the area to be folded overhanging

To make a stained-glass window, squeeze liquid leading out of the bottom onto the shiny side of the Mylar sheet.

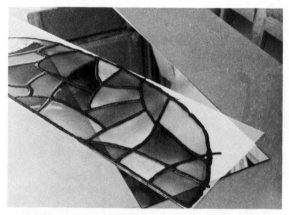

This close-up shows how the matte sheet disperses light to brighten the colors when placed on the mirror.

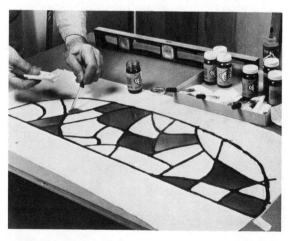

Colored stains are flowed from an eye dropper into each segment.

The finished window lends a touch of elegance to the hall butler.

the worktable. Press against the overhang with a piece of wood to form a right-angle bend.

When both ends have been folded, clamp deeper wood guide blocks along the side fold lines. Make the bends; then fold the end tabs around. Use hot-melt glue to seal the corner joints. Also lay a bead under the tabs to secure them.

To make the seat pad, fold a 35" × 38" piece of cloth in half. Stitch two sides 1/2" from the edge; then turn the cloth inside out and insert a 1" × 16-1/2" × 36-1/2" piece of foam. Close the open edge by hand stitching.

Assemble the sides of the chest as shown. Note that this section is then secured to the wall unit.

Make the tray by clamping a section of wood at the bending line. Then push up on the metal lip with another piece of wood.

Add the drawer front to the drawer. Screws and glue will hold it in place. Note the detail on the routed front.

Use hot-melt glue to seal the corner of the aluminum tray. When complete, place the tray into the unit's storage area.

Pine Chest

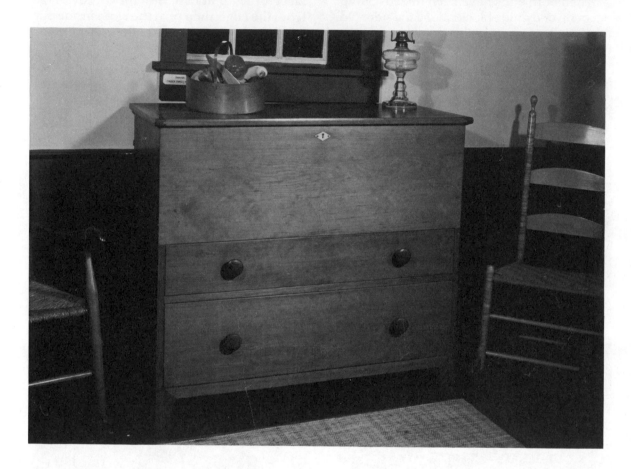

The pine chest shown here is a prime example of the Shaker ingenuity in design. With many people living in a single dwelling, it was imperative that each person have ample storage space for belongings. Hence this chest on top of two drawers. The original was made of wide pine boards; however, plywood veneer can be used just as well.

The sides (A), can be made of single pieces of plywood, with sections cut from the bottom of each to form chamfered feet. Attach the posts (C) to the inside faces of the sides.

The front posts should be flush with the front edges; the back posts should be set in 3/4" from the back edges so the back (B) can be fitted in later. The two drawers are not shown, but they should be sized to fit.

MATERIALS LIST

Hinges (2)
Lock
Drawer knobs (4)
Wood screws and/or finishing nails
Wood glue

CUTTING LIST		
KEY	**PIECES**	**SIZE AND DESCRIPTION**
A	2	3/4 × 17-3/4 × 37 sides (plywood)
B	1	3/4 × 32 × 38 back (plywood)
C	4	2 × 2 × 32 posts
D	1	3/4 × 19 × 40-1/2 top
E	6	3/4 × 1 × 33 cleats
F	1	3/4 × 15 × 39-1/2 front
G1	1	3/4 × 1 × 37-1/2 front trim
G2	1	3/4 × 1-3/4 × 37-1/2 front base trim
H	2	3/4 × 1 × 19 top trim
I	2	3/4 × 2 × 22 front legs and trim (stock)
J	3	3/4 × 17-3/4 × 38 shelves

Attach all cleats (E) to the inside faces of the sides, then install the three shelves (J). Next, fasten the front (F) of the chest, the front legs and attached trim (I), and the front trim pieces (G1, G2) with finishing nails or wood screws. Install the back, then hinge the top (D) to it. Note that the top trim pieces (H) are joined to the top with rabbet joints as shown in the illustration. Finish the piece with an antique stain or as desired.

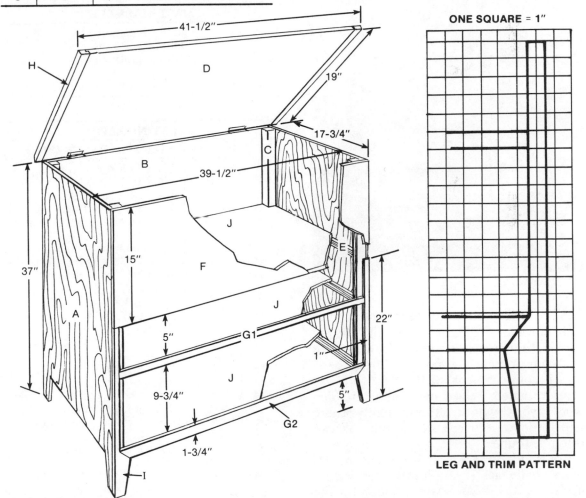

ONE SQUARE = 1"

LEG AND TRIM PATTERN

Pennsylvania Chest

sides (C), front (B), and top (A), you can substitute 3/4" plywood, concealing the edges with wood tape. Or edge-glue narrower boards together to make up the desired width.

MATERIALS LIST

6d finishing nails
4d finishing nails
Drawer pulls
Hinges
Wood glue

CUTTING LIST

KEY	PIECES	SIZE AND DESCRIPTION
A	1	3/4 × 14-3/4 × 35 top
B	1	3/4 × 16-1/4 × 33-1/2 front
C	2	3/4 × 14 × 36 sides
D	2	3/4 × 6 × 7 front legs
E	1	3/4 × 13 × 32 upper bottom
F	1	1/4 × 33-1/2 × 36 back (plywood)
G	2	3/4 × 2-1/2 × 32 front dividers
H	4	3/4 × 2-1/2 × 12 drawer runners
I	2	3/4 × 3/4 × 14-1/4 molding
J1	2	3/4 × 6-1/8 × 31-3/4 drawer front
J2	4	3/4 × 6-1/8 × 12-3/4 drawer sides
J3	2	3/4 × 6-1/8 × 30-1/4 drawer back
J4	2	1/4 × 12-1/2 × 30-1/4 drawer bottoms (plywood)
K	2	3/4 × 2 × 32 top and bottom cleats
L	4	1/2 × 3/4 × 12 side drawer cleats
M	4	1/2 × 3/4 × 28-3/4 front and back drawer cleats

The chest pictured here was a type common in Pennsylvania during the early 18th century; chests with drawers were becoming increasingly popular, but the deep upper compartment with hinged lid was often retained. Yellow pine and white pine were favorite woods, although many ornate and intricately carved samples in oak can often be found.

Construction of this chest presents no unusual challenges. If your lumber dealer does not stock 3/4" boards wide enough for the

Begin by cutting the two side panels (C), cutting a 3/4″ × 6″ notch in the bottom, and a 3/4″ × 16″ notch in the top of the front edges. Transfer the pattern from the grid to shape the scrolls. Cut the front legs (D) and attach them to the sides with glue and 6d finishing nails. Fasten cleats (K) between the sides at the rear top and bottom, then attach the 1/4″ plywood back (F) to the cleats and side panels with glue and 4d finishing nails. Glue and nail the lower and intermediate drawer runners (H) and front dividers (G) in place. Nail through the sides and back to attach the bottom (E) of the upper compartment. Glue and nail the front panel (B) in place. Round

over the sides and front edges of the top after cutting it to size. Fasten molding (I) at the ends as illustrated, then secure this to the top cleat (K) with concealed hinges. The back edge of the top is flush with the back of the chest.

Construct the drawer frames as shown and attach the cleats (L, M). Fit the plywood drawer bottoms (J4) in place, attach the drawer pulls, and you are ready to finish the piece.

Character marks—scratches and nicks accumulated during long years of faithful service—may be carefully simulated, if you wish, by gouging and scarring.

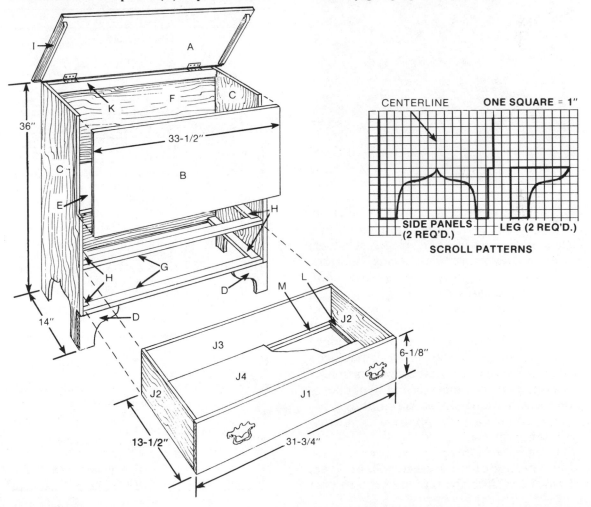

Shaker Press

S haker cabinetry was not just functional, it was big. Whole "families" (more often spiritual kin than blood relatives) shared work, prayer, and living quarters, making the furnishings they also used communally necessarily large.

The dimensions of the prototype press (Kentucky; 1850) are so huge by current standards that its presence in a modern room would be overpowering. It has been scaled down to more suitable proportions.

Because the original was made of cherry boards wider than those commonly available today, use veneer plywood or narrow cherry boards edge-glued together.

Observe the following assembly sequence after cutting the various pieces to the correct dimensions. Glue the top and bottom trim panels (A, C) to the sides (B). Attach the cleats (Q) to the inside faces of the sides with glue and nails. Attach the legs (N) to the sides, nailing and gluing all four legs with glue blocks as illustrated. Fasten the middle shelf to the cleats with glue, followed by the bottom and top shelves. The back corners of all three shelves are notched to fit around the legs. The front corners of the top and bottom

MATERIALS LIST

Glue blocks
Nails
Wood glue

CUTTING LIST

KEY	PIECES	SIZE AND DESCRIPTION
A	2	1/4 × 7-1/2 × 12 side top trim
B	2	2-3/4 × 12 × 34-1/2 sides
C	2	1/4 × 9 × 12 side bottom trim
D	1	3/4 × 6 × 34-1/2 top back
E	2	3/4 × 4 × 15-3/4 top sides
F	2	1/2 × 15-3/4 × 25 doors
G	4	1/4 × 3 × 25-1/2 door trim
H	2	1/4 × 5 × 9-3/4 bottom door trim
I	2	1/4 × 4 × 9-3/4 top door trim
J1	2	3/4 × 6-1/4 × 15-3/8 drawer front
J2	4	3/4 × 6 × 14 drawer sides
J3	2	3/4 × 6 × 13-7/8 drawer backs
J4	2	1/4 × 13-1/4 × 13-7/8 drawer bottoms
K1	2	1/2 × 15 × 33 top and bottom shelves
K2	1	1/2 × 14-1/4 × 33 middle shelf
L	1	3/4 × 16 × 36 top
M	1	3/4 × 6-1/2 × 15 drawer divider
N	4	1-1/2 × 1-1/2 × 40-1/2 legs
O	1	1-1/2 × 1-1/2 × 32 header
P	1	1/2 × 32 × 34-1/2 back
Q	6	3/4 × 3/4 × 12 cleats

shelves are notched differently than the middle shelf. Before attaching the top shelf, mark the location for the drawer divider and attach it to the shelf.

A header (O) glued across the top of the front to the insides of the legs and the top of the drawer divider completes the basic piece.

Fasten the top back (D) and sides (E) to the top (L); then glue and nail the top to the frame. Fit the drawers using butt-joint construction. Install the back (P). Construct the doors by gluing the trim pieces (G, H, I) to the doors (F). Install the hinges and hang the doors.

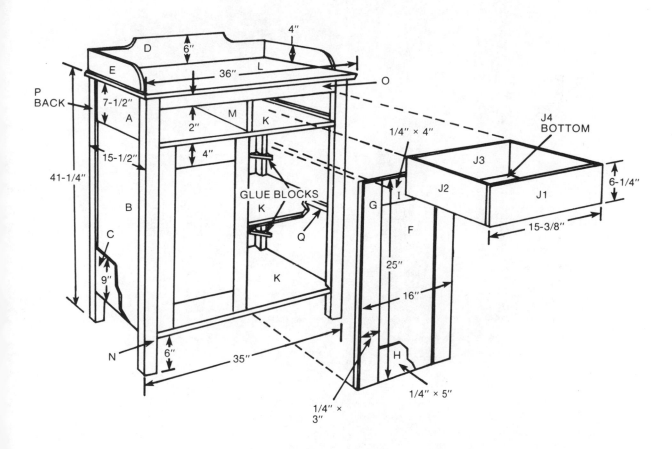

Medicine Cabinet

You can get stock bathroom medicine cabinets in a wide range of sizes, styles, and materials, but few compare with the rich oak custom-design of this handcrafted version.

Begin by cutting the ends (C) and partition trim (B2) to size. Cut at a 35° angle to make the face. For safety, make the angled face cuts on the edge of a wider board, then rip the parts to width (see photo).

Cut the remaining project parts—except the shelves (I1, J), back (D), and trim (H2, H3, H4, I2, I3, I4)—to size.

Next, cut the 35° angles on both ends of the top and bottom panels (A). Make stopped dadoes in each. Clean out the dadoes and square up their ends with a sharp chisel. Then rabbet the back edges, as indicated in the Part A Detail.

Also rabbet the edge of part C as well as B2 as illustrated.

Form the pins in the ends of part C. Use a fine-tooth saw to get a square pin. Test their fit into the top and bottoms (A). Check that the pins are not too long and that the back edge of the end is flush with the back edge of A.

Glue partition B1 to partition trim B2. Note that the trim is shorter than the partition. Center the trim to give at least a 3/8" pin at each end of the assembly. Drill 1/4" holes for the shelf pin supports into the partition.

Cut the small shelves (I1) to size and test-fit them onto partition B1. Finally, sand all the cabinet parts.

Assemble the partitions, tops and bottoms, ends, and small shelves together with carpenter's glue.

Rip the door stiles (E, G) and rails (F, H1) to size. Carefully measure the door openings in your cabinet and cut the stiles and rails to fit. Mark the dowel locations on each stile and rail. Then drill the dowel holes, apply glue, and clamp the doors together. Check that

they are square and flat. Clamp them to a flat surface while the glue dries.

Routing the moldings in long strips will make them easier to work with, and the molding will match at mitered joints. Cut a bead on the edge of the bottom molding (I2, I3, I4) and the rear crown laminate (H2, H3, H4) as shown in the detail sketches. Then cut a cove in the edge of the top part of the crown molding. Make this cut in two passes to avoid overloading your router.

MATERIALS LIST

3/8"-dia. dowels
1/4"-dia. dowels
Wood screws
Hinges (interpanel hinges for shutters)
Door pull
Magnetic latch
Pin-style shelf supports
Glass mirror
Wood glue

CUTTING LIST

KEY	PIECES	SIZE AND DESCRIPTION
A	2	3/4 × 6 × 29 top and bottom panels
B1	2	3/4 × 4-7/8 × 23-3/4 partitions
B2	2	3/4 × 1-1/4 × 23 partition trim
C	2	3/4 × 2 × 23-3/4 ends
D	1	1/4 × 23-1/2 × 28 back (oak plywood)
E	2	3/4 × 1-1/4 × 23 large door stiles
F	2	3/4 × 1-1/2 × 13 large door rails
G	4	3/4 × 1-1/4 × 23 small door stiles
H1	4	3/4 × 1-1/2 × 3-5/8 small door rails
H2	1	19˚ crown molding front (glued-up section)
H3	2	8˚ crown molding side (glued-up section)
H4	2	3˚ crown molding end (glued-up section)
I1	2	1/2 × 4-1/2 × 5-1/4 small shelves
I2	1	1/2 × 1 × 19˚ bottom molding front
I3	2	1/2 × 1 × 8˚ bottom molding side
I4	2	1/2 × 1 × 3˚ bottom molding end
J	2	1/2 × 4-5/8 × 15-1/2 shelf
K	2	1/4 × 4-3/8 × 20-3/4 door back
L	1	1/4 × 13-3/4 × 20-3/4 door back

˚Cut to rough size and then miter for exact fit.

Glue the two parts of the crown molding together with C-clamps. There should be about 1/8″ space between the edge of the bead and the bottom of the cove. When the glue is dry, cut the molding to the exact width of 1-1/4″.

Miter the molding so you have a 17-1/2° angle for the front joints and 27° for the rear ones (see illustration). Test the fit with scrap before cutting your molding. Then glue and nail it in place. Glue scrap blocks behind the top crown for additional strength.

Make two rabbets all around the inside door edges. One accommodates the door backs (K, L) and the other holds the mirror. Finally, route a 1/4″ bead around the inside front edge of the doors.

Install the mirrors and door backs and hang the doors.

Transfer the dowel hole locations from the small shelf (I1) to the partition. Then dowel and glue the shelves in place.

Make angled face cuts in Parts B2 and C on the edge of a wider board, for safety.

Cut stopped dadoes in Part A and then square them with a wood chisel. Use a stop block as shown, clamped to the table saw's edge.

Test fit the partition and end (C) into their dadoes. Note the dowel in the end of I1 rests in hole drilled in the end.

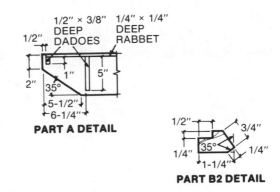

PART A DETAIL

PART B2 DETAIL

PART C DETAIL

Glue scrap blocks behind the crown molding for additional support after gluing and nailing the molding in place.

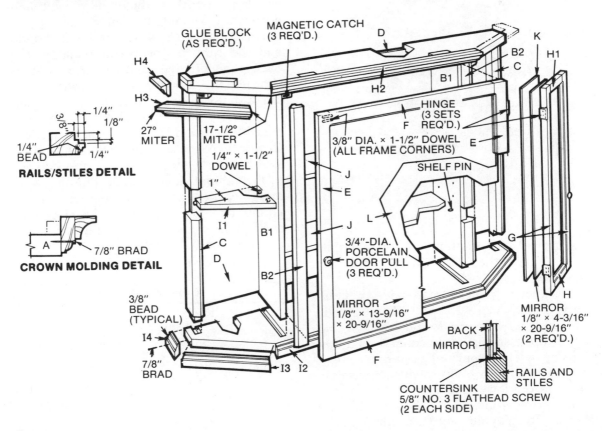

RAILS/STILES DETAIL

CROWN MOLDING DETAIL

Country-Style Sewing Cabinet

Thread, scissors, thimbles, and materials all have their place in this charming oak cabinet.

Designed to fit into a small space, the cabinet is 16-3/4" deep × 25-1/2" wide × 45" high. The project features a drop-down desk that opens up to storage drawers and a lid that flips up to let you pull out a removable tray. You can also store bulky sewing materials in the spacious lower cabinet.

If sewing is not your hobby, modify the cabinet to suit your specific needs. Without the scissors organizer on the lid and the tray, it makes an interesting desk. Or, omit the scissors organizer, tray, and drawers and you'll have a nice-looking bar.

The project calls for fir and oak veneer plywood and solid oak lumber. But other materials, such as pine, can be easily substituted for the oak.

Begin by cutting the rails (A), stiles (B), and panels (C) for the cabinet sides. Glue and dowel the stiles and rails together, along with the inserted panels. Next, cut the shelf dado and the rabbets for accommodating the back panels (N, P3) and the brace (D), as shown in the cross section illustration.

Cut the shelves for the lower cabinet and the parts for the support shelf (E1). Then cut the edge trim and glue it onto the shelf edges (I2) for the lower cabinet shelves; E2 for the shelf support). Attach the shelf supports (H) to the cabinet sides with 3d finishing nails and glue. Then assemble the basic cabinet by gluing the support shelf and lower cabinet shelf to the sides. Also, glue the back brace (D) and square the entire unit.

MATERIALS LIST
Knobs
2" pin hinge
Decorative door hinge
Drop lid support
Magnetic door latch
3/4" brads
3/8"-dia. dowels
3d finishing nails
Wood glue

KEY	PIECES	SIZE AND DESCRIPTION
		CUTTING LIST
A	4	3/4 × 5-1/4 × 11-1/2 rails
B	4	3/4 × 1-3/4 × 39 stiles
C	2	1/4 × 12 × 29 panels (oak plywood)
D	1	3/4 × 5-1/4 × 23 back brace
E1	1	3/4 × 12 × 23 support shelf (fir plywood)
E2	1	3/4 × 3 × 23 shelf trim
E3	1	3/4 × 3/4 × 22-1/2 cleat
F	2	3/4 × 2 × 20-1/2 stiles
G	1	3/4 × 2 × 24 rail
H	4	3/4 × 2 × 14-3/4 shelf supports
I1	2	3/4 × 14 × 22-1/2 shelves (oak plywood)
I2	2	3/4 × 3/4 × 22-1/2 shelf trim
J	1	3/4 × 5-1/4 × 25-1/2 base front
K	2	3/4 × 5-1/4 × 16-1/8 base sides
L1	2	3/4 × 2 × 22-1/2 base braces
L2	2	3/4 × 2 × 15-3/4 base braces
L3	2	3/4 × 1 × 14-1/4 base braces
M	1	3/4 × 15-3/4 × 24 base (oak plywood)
N	1	1/4 × 23 × 23 back (oak plywood)
O1	1	3/4 × 12 × 22-1/2 drawer top (oak plywood)
O2	1	3/4 × 3/4 × 22-1/2 drawer trim
P1	2	3/4 × 9 × 11-3/4 drawer sides (oak plywood)
P2	2	3/4 × 3/4 × 9 drawer trim
P3	1	1/4 × 9 × 22-1/2 drawer unit back (fir plywood)
Q1	3	1/2 × 11-3/4 × 21-3/4 drawer dividers (fir plywood)
Q2	3	1/2 × 3/4 × 21-3/4 divider trim

KEY	PIECES	SIZE AND DESCRIPTION
		CUTTING LIST (continued)
R1	3	1/2 × 2-1/2 × 12 drawer divider (fir plywood)
R2	3	1/2 × 3/4 × 2-1/2 divider trim
S1	4	3/4 × 2-3/8 × 4-3/4 drawer fronts
S2	4	3/4 × 2-3/8 × 4-3/4 drawer backs (oak plywood)
S3	8	1/2 × 2-3/8 × 12 drawer sides (fir plywood)
S4	4	1/4 × 4-1/4 × 11-1/2 drawer bottoms (fir plywood)
T1	2	3/4 × 2-3/8 × 20-7/8 drawer fronts
T2	2	3/4 × 2-3/8 × 20-7/8 drawer backs (oak plywood)
T3	4	1/2 × 2-3/8 × 12 drawer sides (fir plywood)
T4	2	1/4 × 11-1/2 × 19-7/8 drawer bottoms (fir plywood)
U1	2	3/4 × 3-1/2 × 21-1/2 tray sides
U2	2	3/4 × 3-1/2 × 11-1/4 tray sides
U3	1	3/4 × 4 × 12 tray handle
U4	1	1/4 × 11 × 20-1/2 tray bottom (oak plywood)
V1	4	3/4 × 2 × 6 door rails
V2	4	3/4 × 2 × 20-1/2 door stiles
V3	2	1/4 × 6-1/2 × 17 door panels (oak plywood)
W1	2	3/4 × 2 × 22 drop desk rails
W2	2	3/4 × 2 × 15-3/4 drop desk stiles
W3	1	1/4 × 12-1/4 × 20-1/2 drop desk panel (oak plywood)
X1	2	3/4 × 2 × 21-1/2 lid rails
X2	2	3/4 × 2 × 16-1/2 lid stiles
X3	1	1/4 × 13 × 22 lid panel (oak plywood)
X4	1	1/4 × 3/4 × 6 lid handle
X5	1	3/4 × 5-1/2 × 21-1/2 holder

Next, attach the cleat (E3) and the stiles (F) and rail (G) to the cabinet. The cleat hides any visible gap between E1 and G and also strengthens this area of the cabinet.

Cut the braces (L1, L2, L3) and the front (J) and sides (K) for the base unit. Miter both ends of the base as shown. Lay out and cut the scroll designs. Then assemble the braces and base pieces with nails and glue. Cut out the top of the base (M) from oak plywood and rabbet the edge for the back (N) as illustrated. Then glue it to the base unit.

Glue the cabinet to the base unit. Sand the bottom of the lower cabinet so it sits properly on the base. When the glue dries, insert and glue the back.

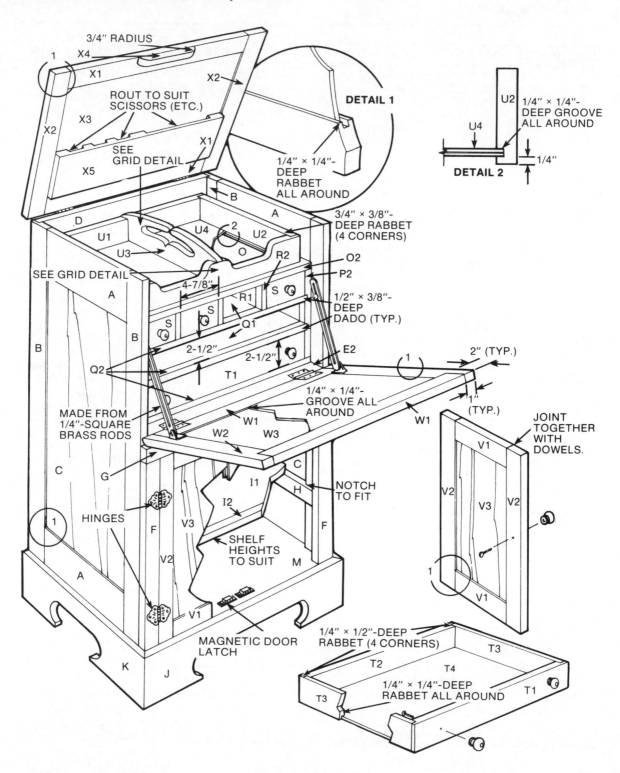

3/4" RADIUS

X4
X1
X2
X2
X3
X5
X2
X1

ROUT TO SUIT
SCISSORS (ETC.)

SEE
GRID DETAIL

DETAIL 1

1/4" × 1/4"-
DEEP
RABBET
ALL AROUND

U2
U4

1/4" × 1/4"-
DEEP GROOVE
ALL AROUND

1/4"

DETAIL 2

B
A
D
U1
U4
U3
2
O
U2

3/4" × 3/8"-
DEEP RABBET
(4 CORNERS)

SEE GRID DETAIL
4-7/8"
R2
R1
S
S
Q1
S
S

O2
P2
S

1/2" × 3/8"-
DEEP
DADO (TYP.)

A
B
B
2-1/2"
2-1/2"
T1
Q2
E2

1
2" (TYP.)

1/4" × 1/4"-
GROOVE ALL
AROUND

1" (TYP.)

MADE FROM
1/4"-SQUARE
BRASS RODS

W1
W2
W3
W1

JOINT
TOGETHER
WITH
DOWELS.

V1
V2
V3
V2

C
G
I1
I2
C
H
F

NOTCH
TO FIT

HINGES
F
V3
V2
M

SHELF
HEIGHTS
TO SUIT

A
V1
1
V1

K
J

MAGNETIC DOOR
LATCH

1/4" × 1/2"-DEEP
RABBET (4 CORNERS)

T3
T2
T4
T3
1/4" × 1/4"-DEEP
RABBET ALL AROUND
T1

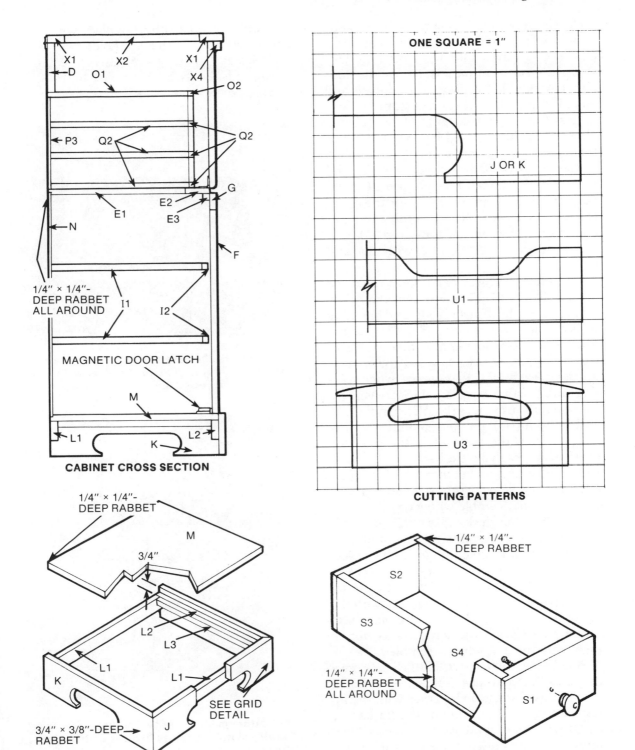

X1
X2
X1
D
O1
X4
O2
P3
Q2
Q2
E2
G
E1
E3
N
F
1/4" × 1/4"-
DEEP RABBET
ALL AROUND
I1
I2
MAGNETIC DOOR LATCH
M
L1
L2
K

CABINET CROSS SECTION

ONE SQUARE = 1"

J OR K

U1

U3

CUTTING PATTERNS

1/4" × 1/4"-
DEEP RABBET
M
3/4"
L2
L3
L1
K
L1
J
SEE GRID
DETAIL
3/4" × 3/8"-DEEP
RABBET

1/4" × 1/4"-
DEEP RABBET
S2
S3
S4
1/4" × 1/4"-
DEEP RABBET
ALL AROUND
S1

Cut the door rails (V1), stiles (V2), and door panels (V3) to suit the lower cabinet opening. Cut 1/4" grooves into the rails and 1/4" stopped grooves into the stiles for the door panel. Assemble the doors with dowels and glue. Plane each door for a custom fit.

The drawer unit consists of oak edging glued onto the oak and fir plywood cut to form the sides, top and bottoms, and dividers of the unit. Cut all of the pieces to size and glue the oak trim onto the plywood. Cut dadoes and rabbets into the side for the dividers (Q1) as shown. Next, assemble the unit consisting of the sides (P1, P2), top (O1, O2), and dividers (Q1, Q2, R1, R2) with glue and nails.

Cut out the drawer parts and rabbet the drawer fronts (S1, T1) and backs (S2, T2). Then groove the drawer fronts and backs, as well as the drawer sides (S3, T3), for the drawer bottoms (S4, T4). Assemble the drawers with glue. Avoid using too many nails during the assembly to minimize wood splitting, and be sure to square the drawers.

Cut out the tray sides (U1, U2), handle (U3), and bottom (U4). Lay out and cut the tray designs from the patterns in the grid diagram. Then notch out the handle as shown in the diagram and rabbet the ends of the sides (U1). To complete tray construction, groove the sides and assemble with glue.

Join the drop desk stiles (W2) and rails (W1) by cutting the joints, then trimming the cutouts with a wood chisel to create a nice-looking joint. Groove the stiles and rails as shown and assemble the unit with the inserted panel (W3). Glue it together with the aid of bar clamps and make sure that it sets on a flat surface. Otherwise, it may not be flush with the unit when assembled.

Finally, cut out the parts for the lid. Groove the stiles (X2) and rails (X1) as seen in Detail 1, and dowel and glue together with the inserted panel (X3). Then cut the lid handle (X4) to size and round over its edges. Glue it onto the lid as shown in the diagram. Use a

C-clamp to keep it snugly in place while the glue dries. Cut out the lid's holder (X5) and rout designs to suit your scissors or other sewing aids. A core box bit is ideal for routing these grooves.

Glue and nail the base unit together. Notice the interlocked braces. The plywood base (M) fits inside of the recessed lip.

The bottom cabinet has two stationary shelves. The hinged doors are kept in place with magnetic latches.

Dado the sewing cabinet sides to accommodate the support shelf (E1, E2). Then glue the cabinet to the base.

The drawer unit is assembled separately and is then inserted into the upper section of the cabinet assembly.

Early American Sewing Machine Cabinet

This sewing machine cabinet is an adaptation of a dry sink. It has the praiseworthy quality of providing a place for a modern sewing machine in a country-style piece.

The materials consist largely of 3/4" pine boards, doweled and edge-glued to make up the necessary widths. Pine plywood may be used for the wider pieces, providing the edges are finished with wood trim. The top rails (B, C) are made from solid pine because it must be cut to the patterns indicated on the graph. It would be difficult to conceal plies on curves such as these.

Construction uses dadoes and rabbet joints as shown in the illustration. The joints are nailed and glued. If you lack power tools, joints can be butted and reinforced with glue blocks.

The cabinet is a simple box with solid sides (E) and back (F) and a double top (A, D). Part of the face is a dummy drawer (G) that conceals the sewing head when it is stored. Below that, a large cabinet door (J) hung on piano hinges gives access to the machine controls, spool holders (K) and shelf (L, M). The door is made of doweled and edge-glued boards. Select them carefully for grain pattern.

The box has a double top. The fixed portion is cut from 3/4" plywood. The opening is tailored to fit the particular machine. Special hardware and hinges are sold by many sewing machine distributors. The sequence by which the machine is lowered is shown in Detail 1.

The top shelf (A) is attached on the left side of the sewing table (D) with three hinges mortised into the wood. Cut the rails as shown in the patterns and attach them to the shelf with glue and nails before attaching the shelf to the box. The pieces are joined with mitered joints.

MATERIALS LIST
22" piano hinge
Brass hinges
Doorknobs
1/4"-dia. dowels
Screws
Finishing nails
Wood glue

CUTTING LIST		
KEY	**PIECES**	**SIZE AND DESCRIPTION**
A	1	3/4 × 16-1/2 × 26 top shelf
B	1	3/4 × 3 × 26 back rail
C	2	3/4 × 3 × 16-1/2 side rails
D	1	3/4 × 16-1/2 × 26 sewing table (plywood)
E	2	3/4 × 16-1/2 × 30 sides
F	3	3/4 × 24-1/2 × 30 back
G	1	3/4 × 7-1/4 × 26 false top drawer
H	3	3/4 × 2-1/2 × 25-1/2 long cleats
I	2	3/4 × 2-1/2 × 13 short cleats
J	1	3/4 × 22-3/4 × 26 cabinet door
K	2	1-1/2 × 1-1/2 × 20 spool holders
L	2	1/2 × 2-1/2 × 3 shelf sides
M	1	1/2 × 2-1/2 × 18 shelf front

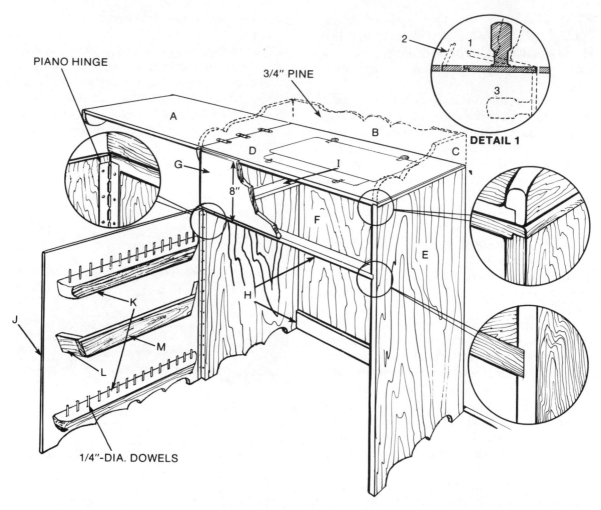

PIANO HINGE

3/4" PINE

2

1

3

DETAIL 1

A

B

C

D

G

I

8"

F

E

H

J

K

M

L

1/4"-DIA. DOWELS

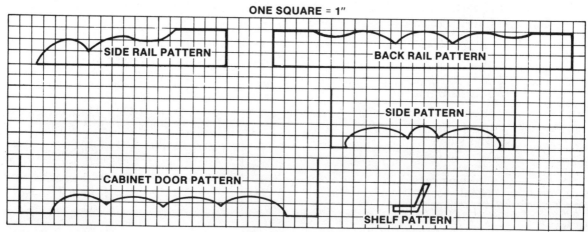

ONE SQUARE = 1"

SIDE RAIL PATTERN

BACK RAIL PATTERN

SIDE PATTERN

CABINET DOOR PATTERN

SHELF PATTERN

Wardrobe

This adaptation of Abraham Lincoln's wardrobe has plenty of adjustable shelves to store clothing, linen, and other items.

The original wardrobe was constructed of light-colored walnut. This adaptation uses glued-up pine and plywood for economy and strength.

To begin, glue up 1" × 8" pine boards sufficiently to fabricate the sides (C), doors (L), six shelves (S, T), and the interior partition (D) of the wardrobe. Because this adaptation departs from the time-honored joinery of rail-and-stile paneled construction, it is important that seasoned, dry wood be used to eliminate warping and twisting after construction.

Mark the facing edges to be jointed and carefully plane each edge straight for a smooth, tight fit. Then apply glue to both edges. Clamp with equal pressure and use a straightedge or carpenter's square to assure that the assembled boards are flat.

While the glue is drying, lay out the top (A) and bottom (E) on 3/4" plywood. Then lay out the back (B) on 1/2" plywood. Plan these components so the good face is exposed. Do your drawing and cutting on the back side.

Unclamp the glued-up pieces and sand, being especially careful to smooth the glued joints so they will accept stain evenly. Then, lay out each component and cut all of the pieces to size.

Assemble the box of the wardrobe face-down on a flat surface. Mark the location on the sides of the bottom. Then glue and nail the sides to the bottom. Locate and fit the partition and glue and nail this to the bottom. Finally, position the top, and glue and nail it, making sure you correctly position the partition.

Next, draw a line on the rear face of the back panel showing the center of the partition. The assembly will square up when you glue and nail the back in place. Place nails every 8" to 10" to secure all glued components. Use the same separation when nailing through the back into the partition and through the sides into the back.

When the glue dries, sand the assembly with rough- and medium-grit sandpaper.

MATERIALS LIST

Clothes bar brackets
Shelf clips
6d finishing nails
4d finishing nails
Roller catches
Wood knobs
Brass butt hinges
Wood glue

With the cabinet on its back, cut and apply the base (F) and top fascia (X, Z). Turn the cabinet so that one side is up and apply the base sides (G) and top trim (V). Cut, glue, and nail the cleats (H). Apply the side trim (M, N) with glue and 3/4" brads (see illustration), or by clamping. Repeat on the opposite side.

Next, drill shallow 1/4"-diameter holes for the shelf clips where shown in the diagram. Test-fit the shelves (S, T) along with their respective shelf clips. Then glue and nail the shelves in position.

Use a miter box to saw the cove molding (Q, Y) for the top edge of the cabinet. Sand

CUTTING LIST

KEY	PIECES	SIZE AND DESCRIPTION
A	1	3/4 × 48 × 20-1/4 top (plywood)
B	1	1/2 × 48 × 81-3/4 back (plywood)
C	2	3/4 × 20 × 82-1/2 sides
D	1	3/4 × 20-1/2 × 74-1/2 partition
E	1	3/4 × 19-3/4 × 48 bottom (plywood)
F	1	3/4 × 7-1/4 × 51 base
G	2	3/4 × 7-1/4 × 20-1/4 base sides
H	2	3/4 × 2 × 19-3/4 cleats
J	4	1/4 × 3-1/2 × 69-1/4 door trim
K	4	1/4 × 3-1/2 × 18-3/8 door trim
L	2	3/4 × 24-3/8 × 69-1/4 doors
M	4	1/4 × 3-1/2 × 69-1/2 side trim
N	4	1/4 × 3-1/2 × 13 side trim
P	1	3/4 × 5-1/2 × 55-7/8 top trim
Q	1	3-1/4 × 55-3/8 cove molding
R	1	3/4 × 57-3/8 quarter-round molding
S	2	3/4 × 19 × 23-5/8 shelves
T	4	3/4 × 19 × 23-3/8 shelves
U	1	1-5/8 dia. × 23-3/8 clothes bar
V	2	1/4 × 5-1/2 × 17-15/16 top trim
W	2	3/4 × 24-3/16 quarter-round molding
X	2	3/4 × 5-3/4 × 20-1/4 side fascia
Y	2	3-1/4 × 23-3/16 cove molding
Z	1	3/4 × 5-3/4 × 51 fascia

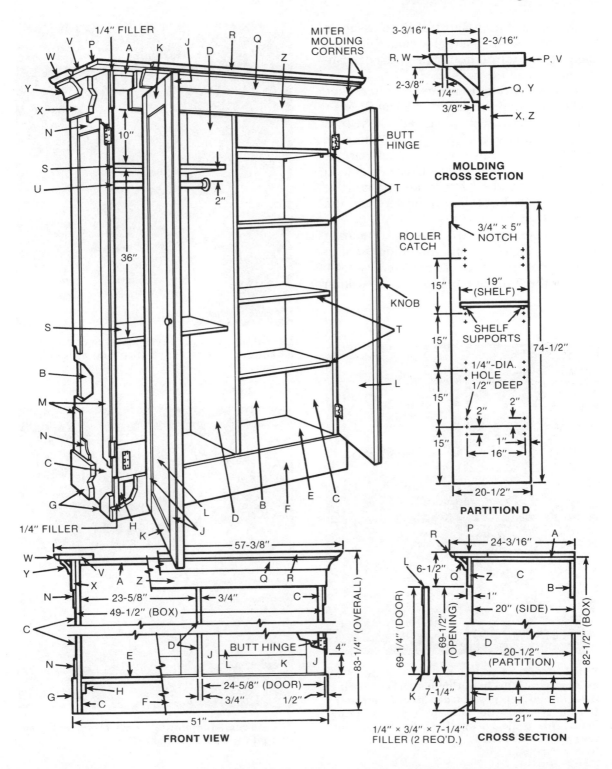

1/4" FILLER

MITER MOLDING CORNERS

BUTT HINGE

ROLLER CATCH

KNOB

1/4" FILLER

MOLDING CROSS SECTION

3-3/16"
2-3/16"
R, W
P, V
2-3/8"
1/4"
Q, Y
3/8"
X, Z

PARTITION D

3/4" × 5" NOTCH
19" (SHELF)
SHELF SUPPORTS
1/4"-DIA. HOLE 1/2" DEEP
74-1/2"
15"
15"
15"
15"
2"
2"
2"
1"
16"
20-1/2"

FRONT VIEW

57-3/8"
83-1/4" (OVERALL)
23-5/8"
3/4"
C
49-1/2" (BOX)
BUTT HINGE
4"
24-5/8" (DOOR)
3/4"
1/2"
51"

CROSS SECTION

24-3/16"
6-1/2"
69-1/4" (DOOR)
69-1/2" (OPENING)
20" (SIDE)
1"
20-1/2" (PARTITION)
82-1/2" (BOX)
21"
7-1/4"
1/4" × 3/4" × 7-1/4" FILLER (2 REQ'D.)

each end carefully and test-fit to assure a tight miter joint. Then glue and nail these pieces to the top of the cabinet with 6d finishing nails. Sink the nails.

Now, attach the top trim (P). Miter, glue, and nail on quarter-round molding (R, W).

To complete the doors (L), attach the trim (J, K) as shown in the illustrations. Make sure that the doors are straight, without warp or twist. Lay them on a flat surface when you glue on the lattice. Then locate and mortise out the hinge locations on the door and the cabinet frame.

Complete the wardrobe by attaching hinges to the doors and mounting them to the cabinet. Also, cut a clothes bar dowel (U), mount the hanger hardware, and position the bar.

Lay the plywood good-face-up when cutting with a handsaw, and facedown if cutting with a circular saw.

This 19th century walnut armoire was used daily by Abraham Lincoln during his years in Springfield, Illinois. It is preserved in his bedroom at the Lincoln Home National Historic Site in Springfield. This project simplifies construction and uses pine for economy.

Prepare edges for jointing by machining each one straight for a smooth, tight fit.

Draw a line showing the center of the partition (D) on the rear face of the back panel (B). Place nails every 8" to 10" through the back into the partition.

Cut the lattice trim (M, N) to size. Glue and nail them to the sides. Then fill the nail holes with putty.

Sand the assembly after the glue has dried and put it on its back. Nail on the base (F) and top fascia (X, Z).

Miter 3-1/4" cove molding (Q, Y) to length and sand and fit edges. Glue and nail to the cabinet's top.

Stacked Bookcase

The stacked bookcase is like fine wine— it gets better with age. It's that rare piece of furniture that looks equally attractive in a home or an office setting. The bookcase consists of modular units stacked one upon the other. The glass doors of this easy-to-build project swing up and back into the oak unit.

Determine the number of units that you are going to build; then cut the bookcase sides (B) from the same piece of lumber so that the grain pattern will appear unbroken. If you plan on building more units later, purchase enough material to cut these extra sides all at the same time.

Cut the top (A), bottom (C), and back (D), as well as the base members (G, H, I,), as described in the cutting list. Round over the showing edges of the top, sides, base top (G), and base sides (I).

Assemble the base unit (G, H, I) first with dowel pins and glue. In a similar manner, assemble each unit's top, bottom, and sides. Use bar clamps when gluing.

Next, rabbet the recess for the back panel (D) as shown in the cross-section view. Round over the edges of the back panel to fit into this recess.

Finally, assemble the door frames. Use half-lap joints for the rails (E) and stiles (F). Assemble each door frame with glue and clamp each of the joints. Again, round over the showing edges of the door panel and make a rabbet in the back of the door (see diagram) for fitting the glass.

Sand the entire unit and install the special door panel hardware according to the manufacturer's instructions. Drill holes for the porcelain knobs in the door. Apply the finish before finally mounting the hardware. Then reattach the hardware.

Finally, cut the glass or plexiglass windows to fit the rabbeted door frame. Attach with glass retaining pins to finish the project.

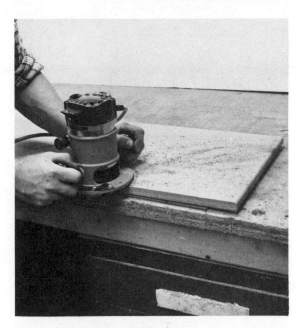

Prior to assembling the project, round over the showing edges of the project with a rounding-over bit and router.

MATERIALS LIST (One Unit)

1/8″ × 10-1/8″ × 43-3/8″ plexiglass
1/4″ × 14″ × 48″ oak plywood
Doorknobs
Door slide hardware
Glass retaining pins
3/8″-dia. dowels
Wood glue

CUTTING LIST (One Unit)

KEY	PIECES	SIZE AND DESCRIPTION
A	1	3/4 × 14-1/2 × 50 top
B	2	3/4 × 13-3/4 × 13-3/4 sides
C	1	3/4 × 13 × 47 bottom
D	1	1/4 × 13-1/2 × 47-1/2 back panel (oak plywood)
E	2	3/4 × 2 × 46-7/8 door rails
F	2	3/4 × 2 × 13-5/8 door stiles
G	1	3/4 × 14-1/2 × 50 base top
H	2	3/4 × 2-1/2 × 47 base front and rear
I	2	3/4 × 2-1/2 × 13-3/4 base sides

Make a dowel drill jig by drilling perpendicular holes into scrap wood with a drill press. The stop lets you align the holes for drilling.

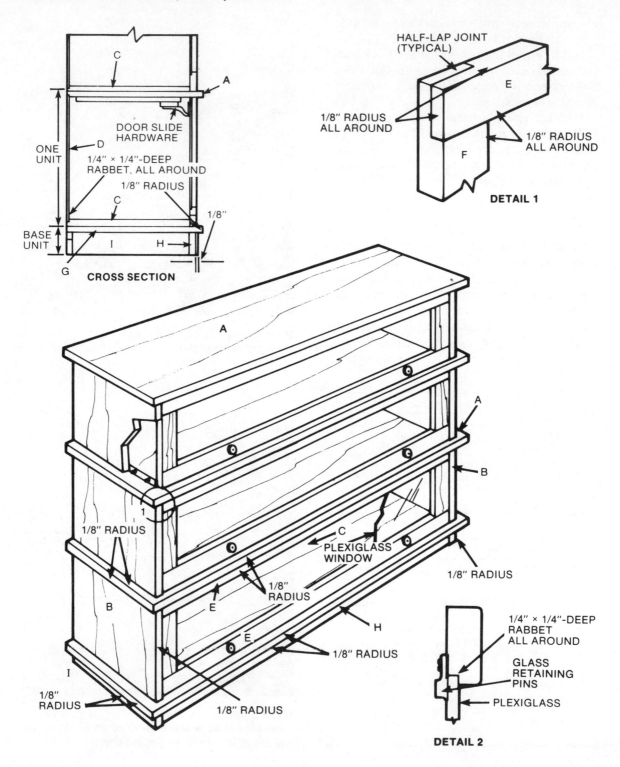

C

A

DOOR SLIDE
HARDWARE

ONE
UNIT

D

1/4" × 1/4"-DEEP
RABBET, ALL AROUND

1/8" RADIUS

C

BASE
UNIT

1/8"

I

H

G

CROSS SECTION

HALF-LAP JOINT
(TYPICAL)

E

1/8" RADIUS
ALL AROUND

1/8" RADIUS
ALL AROUND

F

DETAIL 1

A

A

B

1

1/8" RADIUS

C

PLEXIGLASS
WINDOW

B

1/8"
RADIUS

E

E

1/8" RADIUS

H

I

1/8"
RADIUS

1/8" RADIUS

1/8" RADIUS

1/4" × 1/4"-DEEP
RABBET
ALL AROUND

GLASS
RETAINING
PINS

PLEXIGLASS

DETAIL 2

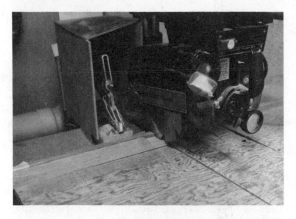

A radial arm saw's dado blade can be used to make the door's half-lap joints by making repeated cuts. Clean the cuts with a wood chisel.

Part of the door hardware mounts in the routed holes. Two of these are needed for each door panel.

You'll need to rout a circle, using a straight bit with guide bushing and a round template to mount the door hardware.

Mount the hardware; then connect them with scrap wood as shown. This smooths the gliding and retraction operations.

Oak Book Cabinet

Begin by ripping 3/4" oak stock to the dimensions shown in the cutting list.

Build the cabinet's sides first. Clamp the stiles (C) and rails (D) together temporarily, then use a 1/4" rounding-over bit to form the inside profiles. Next, mill the 1/4" × 1/2" slots in the stiles as shown in the detail drawings.

Cut 1/2"-long tenons on the side rails (D). Adjust the depth of cut carefully. Also cut the mortises for the hinges in the front stiles.

Assemble the sides by inserting the panels (I) and rail tenons into the slots. Glue only the frame joints. Check for squareness and clamp securely. Once the glue dries, drill holes in the stiles for the shelf hangers, then sand the assemblies.

Next, lay out the door components and mark them to indicate the faces and outside edges. Round over the outer edges of the door stiles (E) with a 3/8"-radius rounding-over bit.

Build this cabinet and show off your skills as well as your books. Frame and panel sides, combined with simple glass panel doors, give this project a light, airy feeling, while a hand-rubbed finish shows off the oak grain.

MATERIALS LIST

Single-strength glass
5/16"-dia. dowels
3/8"-dia. plugs
3/8"-dia. bullet catches
2-1/2" × 1-17/32" brass hinges
3" brass wire door pulls
No. 8 × 1-1/4" wood screws
No. 6 × 3/4" brass wood screws
Brass shelf clips
No. 18 × 3/4" brass pins
Wood glue

Drill mating holes for the dowel pins in the rails (F) and stiles, then assemble the door frames. Check squareness carefully.

While the frames are drying, make the retaining moldings. Round over one edge of a length of 3/8"-thick stock with the 1/4"-radius bit, as shown in the door frame through section detail, then rip the molding off on your saw.

Once the frames have dried, rabbet the inside of the doors with a 3/8" rabbeting bit. Finish the corners by hand with a sharp chisel. Round over the inner edges of the door faces with the 1/4"-radius rounding-over bit as illustrated in the through section.

Sand the door and moldings, then lay the glass panels in the rabbets. Install the moldings with brass pins after drilling 1/16" pilot holes through the moldings.

Assemble the shelf pieces (B1, B2) and top (A) with dowels and wood glue as shown. Use

a doweling jig to help you drill accurate holes for the dowel pins. Glue and clamp securely.

Sand the components well, then form the bullnosed edges with two passes of the 3/8"-radius rounding-over bit as shown in the detail drawing.

Cut the profile of the cabinet's kick rail (G), then round over the contour and the ends with the 3/8" bit. Do the same for the top rail (H).

Begin final assembly by building the base assembly as shown in the diagram. Drill pilot holes in the cleats (M, N, O) and attach them to the bottom shelf (B1) and the kick rail (G) with screws and glue.

On level sawhorses, clamp the sides to the base assembly. Align the components and mark the correct positions as well as the location of the screw holes. Disassemble and apply glue to the edges of the base and the cleats. Add the sides, clamp securely, then install the screws.

Glue the top rail (H) in position and clamp. Measure the diagonals of the cabinet to check its squareness. Counterbore pilot holes, then screw the cabinet top in place. Fill all screw holes with wood plugs.

Now, turn the case over and rabbet the side stiles and top for the back panel as indicated in the main sketch. Finish the corners by hand and install the back panel.

Turn the case over once more and carefully hang the doors. Clamp the center supports in place while marking the hinge positions on the door frames.

Once the doors are hung, drill holes for the pulls and install the bullet catches. The striker plates fit in shallow mortises chiseled into the rails.

Remove the doors and give all components a final sanding before finishing. Once the finish has dried, install the shelves, rehang the doors, and install the door pulls.

CUTTING LIST		
KEY	**PIECES**	**SIZE AND DESCRIPTION**
A	2	3/4 × 6-1/2 × 38 top
B1	2	3/4 × 5-1/2 × 34-1/2 bottom shelf pieces
B2	10	3/4 × 5-1/2 × 34-1/4 shelf pieces
C	4	3/4 × 2 × 71-1/4 side stiles
D	4	3/4 × 2 × 8-1/4 side rails
E	4	3/4 × 2 × 65 door stiles
F	4	3/4 × 2 × 13-15/16 door rails
G	1	3/4 × 4 × 36 kick rail
H	1	3/4 × 2 × 36 top rail
I	2	1/4 × 8 × 68 panels (oak plywood)
J	1	1/4 × 35-1/8 × 68-3/8 back (oak plywood)
K	4	3/8 × 3/8 × 61-3/4 molding
L	4	3/8 × 3/8 × 13-15/16 molding
M	1	3/4 × 3/4 × 33 cleat
N	2	3/4 × 3/4 × 10-1/4 cleats
O	2	3/4 × 3/4 × 3-1/4 cleats

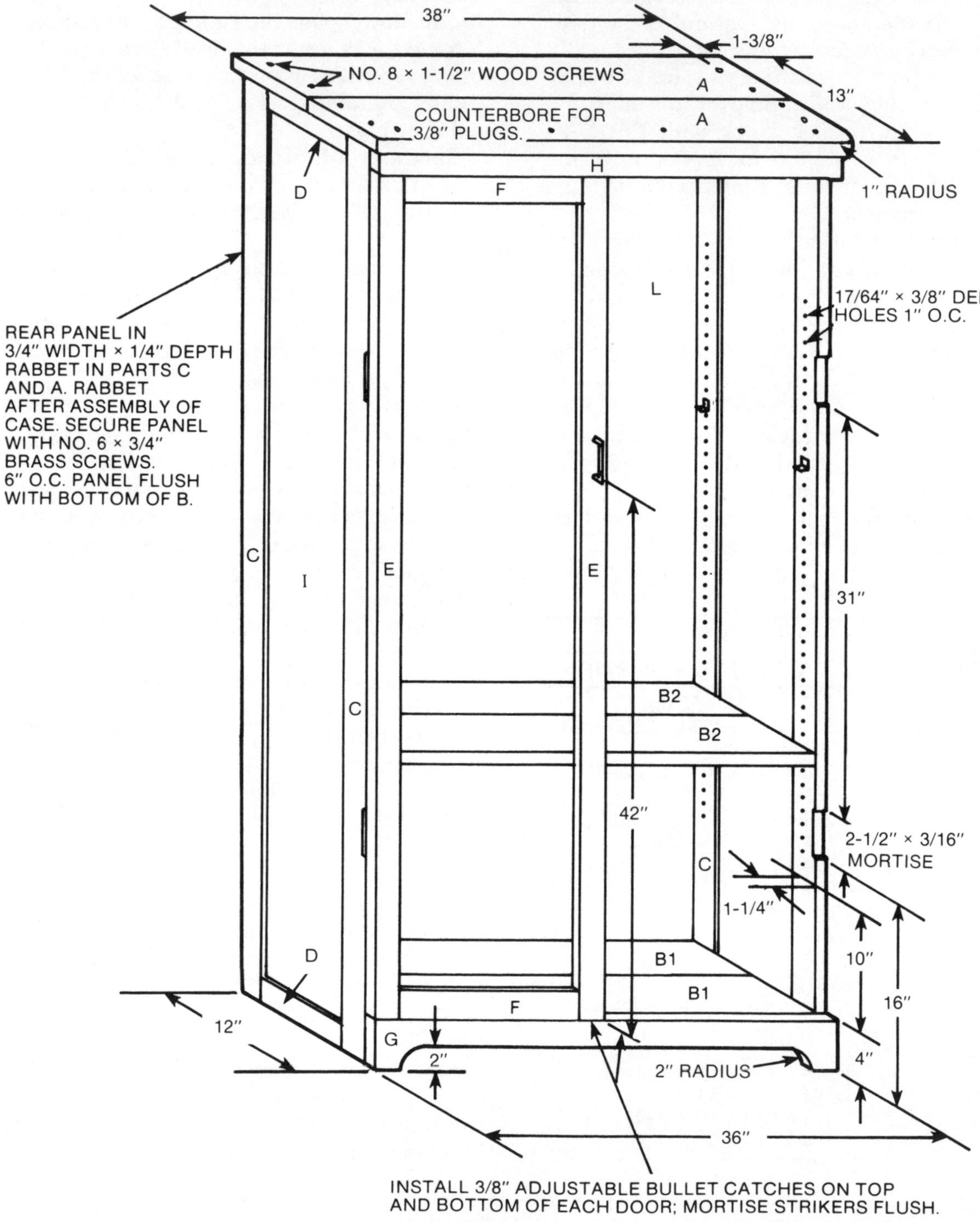

38"

1-3/8"

NO. 8 × 1-1/2" WOOD SCREWS

A

A

13"

COUNTERBORE FOR
3/8" PLUGS.

H

D

F

1" RADIUS

L

17/64" × 3/8" DEEP
HOLES 1" O.C.

REAR PANEL IN
3/4" WIDTH × 1/4" DEPTH
RABBET IN PARTS C
AND A. RABBET
AFTER ASSEMBLY OF
CASE. SECURE PANEL
WITH NO. 6 × 3/4"
BRASS SCREWS.
6" O.C. PANEL FLUSH
WITH BOTTOM OF B.

C

I

E

E

31"

C

B2

B2

42"

2-1/2" × 3/16"
MORTISE

C

1-1/4"

10"

D

B1

16"

12"

F

B1

G

4"

2"

2" RADIUS

36"

INSTALL 3/8" ADJUSTABLE BULLET CATCHES ON TOP
AND BOTTOM OF EACH DOOR; MORTISE STRIKERS FLUSH.

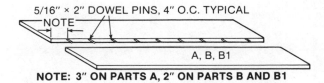

5/16″ × 2″ DOWEL PINS, 4″ O.C. TYPICAL
NOTE

A, B, B1

NOTE: 3″ ON PARTS A, 2″ ON PARTS B AND B1

ATTACH CLEATS WITH NO. 8 × 1-1/4″ SCREWS AND GLUE.

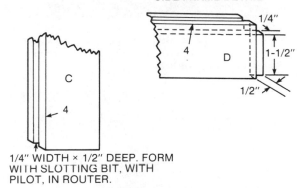

G
O
M
3/4″
N

BASE ASSEMBLY VIEW FROM BELOW

SIDE FRAME DETAIL

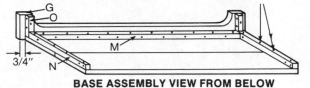

1/4″
4
D
1-1/2″
1/2″

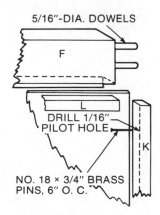

C
4

1/4″ WIDTH × 1/2″ DEEP. FORM WITH SLOTTING BIT, WITH PILOT, IN ROUTER.

5/16″-DIA. DOWELS

F
L
DRILL 1/16″ PILOT HOLE
K

NO. 18 × 3/4″ BRASS PINS, 6″ O. C.

DOOR FRAME DETAIL

**DETAIL 1 SECTION
TOP AND SHELVES**
FORM WITH TWO PASSES OF 3/8″ RADIUS ROUTER BIT, WITH PILOT.

1

**DETAIL 2 SECTION
G, H, AND TWO OF E**
FORM WITH 3/8″ RADIUS ROUTER BIT WITH PILOT.

2

THROUGH SECTION DOOR FRAME

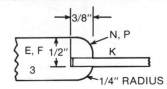
3/8″
N, P
E, F 1/2″ K
3
1/4″ RADIUS

THROUGH SECTION SIDE FRAME

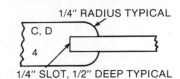
1/4″ RADIUS TYPICAL
C, D
4
1/4″ SLOT, 1/2″ DEEP TYPICAL

NOTE: MILL RADIUSES BEFORE SLOT

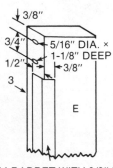
3/8″
3/4″ 5/16″ DIA. × 1-1/8″ DEEP
1/2″ 3/8″
3
E

FORM RABBET WITH 3/8″ RABBETING BIT, WITH PILOT AFTER ASSEMBLY OF FRAME. FINISH CORNERS WITH CHISEL.

A dado blade in a radial arm or table saw works best for cutting hinge mortises in the side stiles.

A 1/4″ × 1/2″ slotting bit can be used in a table-mounted router to form the panel grooves *after* the edges are milled.

Clamp side stiles and rails together temporarily to round off the inside edges with a router.

The tenons on the side rails must be formed accurately. Clamp a stop to the saw fence and adjust cutting depth carefully.

When rounding the ends of the top and kick rails, clamp scrap to the sides to prevent tearing out.

After assembly of the cabinet, form a 3/8″ × 1/4″ rabbet on the back for the back panel.

After rabbeting the door frames, use a chisel to square up the rounded corners left by the router bit.

Moldings hold the glass in place. Fasten them with brass escutcheon pins. Drill pilot holes to prevent splitting.

Colonial Bookcase

This colonial-style bookcase will provide ample space for an evergrowing collection of books. Most of the components are constructed of edge-glued maple.

Joint the edges of the stock to prepare them for gluing. Cut the boards to length and lay out the pairs that form the sides (A) and shelves (B). Alternate the direction of the end grain to prevent warping.

Mark the faces and mating edges of each set of boards, and use a doweling jig to drill 5/16"-diameter holes for the dowels. Drill the holes 1-1/8" deep to allow space for excess glue.

Assemble each component with wood glue and clamp the assemblies until they are completely dry. While the panels are drying, rip the bottom trim (D) and top trim (E), then cut them to length. Sand the cut edges, then round off the edges with a 1/4" rounding-over bit in a router.

Once the sides have dried, cut the shelf dadoes as shown in the diagram. Now, lay

out the rounded cutouts on these side panels. Cut out the curved areas with a saber saw; note the 1/4" gap between the curves and the dadoes. Round over the edges with a router as shown in the photo. *Note:* Some edges are rounded over after assembly.

Next, drill 5/16"-diameter dowel holes in the ends of the trim pieces, on the top edge of

MATERIALS LIST

5/16"-dia. dowels
Finishing nails (optional)
180-grit sandpaper
Wood glue

CUTTING LIST

KEY	PIECES	SIZE AND DESCRIPTION
A	4	3/4 × 5-1/2 × 36 sides
B	6	3/4 × 5-1/2 × 34-1/4 shelves
C	2	3/4 × 6 × 37 top pieces
D	1	3/4 × 4 × 33-1/2 bottom trim
E	1	3/4 × 3 × 33-1/2 top trim

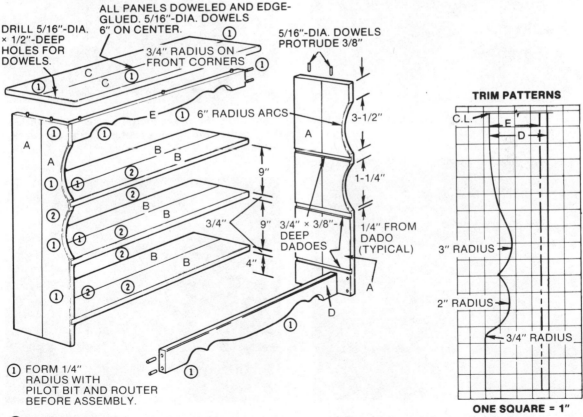

DRILL 5/16"-DIA. × 1/2"-DEEP HOLES FOR DOWELS.

ALL PANELS DOWELED AND EDGE-GLUED. 5/16"-DIA. DOWELS 6" ON CENTER.

3/4" RADIUS ON FRONT CORNERS

5/16"-DIA. DOWELS PROTRUDE 3/8"

E — 6" RADIUS ARCS

3-1/2"

9"

9"

3/4"

4"

1-1/4"

3/4" × 3/8"-DEEP DADOES

1/4" FROM DADO (TYPICAL)

① FORM 1/4" RADIUS WITH PILOT BIT AND ROUTER BEFORE ASSEMBLY.

② FORM 1/4" RADIUS AFTER ASSEMBLY.

TRIM PATTERNS

C.L.

E

D

3" RADIUS

2" RADIUS

3/4" RADIUS

ONE SQUARE = 1"

the sides, and on the top edge of the top trim. Make the holes 1-3/4″ deep. Glue and install the dowels so they protrude approximately 3/8″.

Drill mating holes 1/2″ deep in the sides and the top. Use care when laying out the holes. Assemble all the components, except the top pieces (C), using wood glue. Square and securely clamp the assembly while it stands on a level surface. When the glue dries, add the top.

Remove any hardened excess glue with a sharp chisel, then round over the remaining edges, as shown in the diagram. Sand the whole assembly with 180-grit paper to prepare it for finishing.

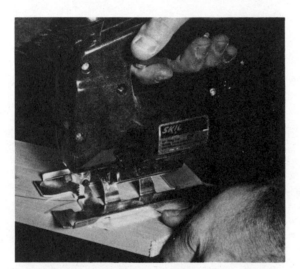

Lay out the enlarged pattern for the top and bottom trim, then cut out.

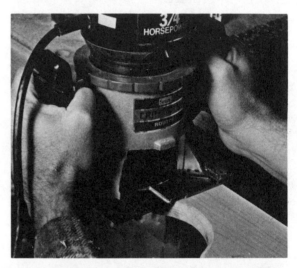

Round off the edges of the curved sides with a 1/4″ radius bit in your router. Clamp the workpiece securely.

Cut the shelf dadoes in one pass with a dado blade, or substitute with a router, straight bit, and straightedge guide.

Assemble the bookcase upright on a level surface and clamp it securely, using at least six clamps. Add the top later.

Vegetable Bin _____

This vegetable bin fits just as comfortably into a kitchen of 1850 as it does into a modern kitchen. This pine prototype measures 11-1/4″ × 36″ × 36″.

With its well-ventilated, roomy cabinet, you will no longer have to store your fruits and vegetables under the sink or on the cellar stairs. Four separate compartments let you keep produce orderly, and the see-through, hardware cloth-covered doors let you see what you have.

The doors also provide good ventilation; nevertheless, don't place the bin near a heat source, such as a south-facing window or an oven. Choose a cool corner and stock the bin with only one week's provisions at a time.

Begin by cutting the pieces to the sizes specified. Dado and rabbet the sides (B) to accommodate the back (O) and shelves (C, D).

Lay out the design for the decorative scroll on the bottom of the sides and cut them. Do the same for the base rail (L) and bottom braces (Q), following the patterns provided.

Before assembling the shelves, cut notches in the center and the ends of the top shelf as shown in the detail drawings. Attach the two shelves with wood screws or finishing nails, then plug with wood filler. Whatever method of fastening you choose, use wood glue for extra strength.

Fasten the lower divider (F) with wood screws. The upper divider (E) is glued into the dado on the top shelf and screwed to the top rail (J). Attach the stiles (K, M) and rails (J, L) to the face of the cabinet and to one another. (For greater authenticity, use dowel or mortise-and-tenon joints to join the rails and stiles.) Braces (P, Q) are used to strengthen the corners where the stiles and rails meet.

Use lap joints for each of the doors and glue them together. After the glue has dried, cut a rabbet along the inside back edge to set in the hardware cloth (N5). Rout all of the visible outside edges of the cabinet, doors, and top with a 3/8" rounding-over bit.

Attach the top (A) and trim (G, H). Nail and glue the door braces (R) to the lower cabinet bins. The top braces (P) also serve as door-stops because they overlap the door frame by 1/4".

MATERIALS LIST

Pin hinges (8)
Doorknobs (4)
Wood screws and/or finishing nails
Wood filler
Brads
Wood glue

Do all staining before fastening the hardware and back (O).

The door strips are mitered and nailed to the door frame.

KEY	PIECES	SIZE AND DESCRIPTION
		CUTTING LIST
A	1	3/4 × 11-1/4 × 36 top
B	2	3/4 × 9 × 35-1/4 sides
C	1	3/4 × 9-1/2 × 31-3/4 shelf
D	1	3/4 × 8-3/4 × 31-3/4 shelf
E	1	3/4 × 8-3/4 × 17-1/2 divider
F	1	3/4 × 8-3/4 × 14-3/4 divider
G	1	3/4 × 3/4 × 34-1/2 trim (cove molding)
H	2	3/4 × 3/4 × 10-1/2 trim (cove molding)
I	4	1/4 × 3/4 × 1-3/4 latches
J	1	3/4 × 2-1/2 × 28 top rail
K	2	3/4 × 2-1/2 × 35-1/4 stiles
L	1	3/4 × 2-1/2 × 28 base rail
M	1	3/4 × 2 × 30-1/4 center stile
N1	8	3/4 × 2 × 13 door frames
N2	8	3/4 × 2 × 14-3/4 door frames
N3	8	3/16 × 3/4 × 10-1/2 door strips
N4	8	3/16 × 3/4 × 12-1/4 door strips
N5	4	1/16 × 10 × 11-3/4 hardware cloth
O	1	1/4 × 32-1/4 × 33-1/2 back (plywood)
P	2	3/4 × 2-3/4 × 15-3/8 top braces
Q	2	3/4 × 1-3/4 × 5 bottom braces
R	2	1/4 × 3/4 × 15-3/8 door braces

Paint the hardware cloth, if you desire, and install. Use brads to fasten the holding strips (N3, N4) onto the back of the door.

When your vegetable bin is complete, install the hinges and other hardware.

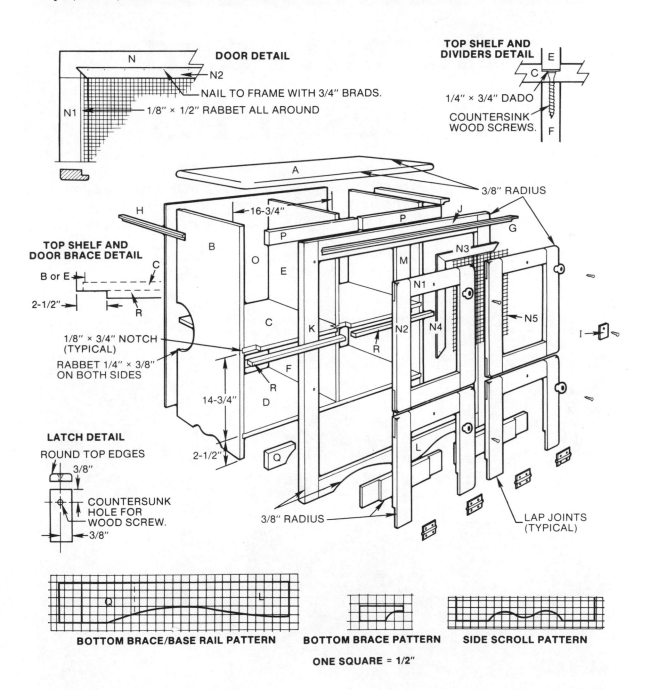

DOOR DETAIL

N2

NAIL TO FRAME WITH 3/4" BRADS.

N1

1/8" × 1/2" RABBET ALL AROUND

TOP SHELF AND DIVIDERS DETAIL

1/4" × 3/4" DADO

COUNTERSINK WOOD SCREWS.

TOP SHELF AND DOOR BRACE DETAIL

B or E

2-1/2"

R

1/8" × 3/4" NOTCH (TYPICAL)

RABBET 1/4" × 3/8" ON BOTH SIDES

14-3/4"

2-1/2"

LATCH DETAIL

ROUND TOP EDGES

3/8"

COUNTERSUNK HOLE FOR WOOD SCREW.

3/8"

3/8" RADIUS

16-3/4"

3/8" RADIUS

LAP JOINTS (TYPICAL)

BOTTOM BRACE/BASE RAIL PATTERN

BOTTOM BRACE PATTERN

SIDE SCROLL PATTERN

ONE SQUARE = 1/2"

Section IV
Accents and Accessories

Whether or not the home decor is country, individual country-style accents and accessories are always welcome for practical purposes and as conversation pieces. The following pages give you an abundance of choices, whatever the reason for your need.

As always, wood selection and dimensions are up to you. However, each project has accurate finished dimensions that can be followed, and many suggest appropriate types of wood.

Free-standing Mirror

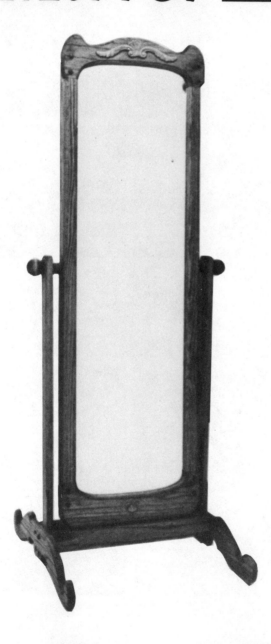

An attractive and useful free-standing mirror like this can be built in a few hours at only a fraction of the cost of a similar mirror purchased in a furniture store. It can be built in two stages: the frame and the stand.

Starting with the mirror frame, make the sides (E), with the edges routed to suit your taste. The top and bottom (D) of the mirror

MATERIALS LIST

Carriage bolts
Teenuts
Brads
1"-dia. dowels
3/8"-dia. dowels
3/8"-dia. dowel caps
Mirror
Wood screws
2"-dia. wood knobs (2)
Wood glue

CUTTING LIST

KEY	PIECES	SIZE AND DESCRIPTION
A	2	3/4 × 5-1/2 × 27 feet
B	2	3/4 × 2-1/2 × 35 upright supports
C	2	3/4 × 2-1/2 × 20-1/2 cross supports
D	2	3/4 × 5-1/2 × 18 mirror frame
E	2	3/4 × 1-1/2 × 47-1/2 mirror frame
F	2	3/4 × 1-1/2 × 54 frame
G	2	3/4 × 1-1/2 × 17-3/4 frame
H	1	1/4 × 18 × 54 backing (plywood or oak paneling)
I	1	3/4 × 2-1/2 × 19 support stretcher

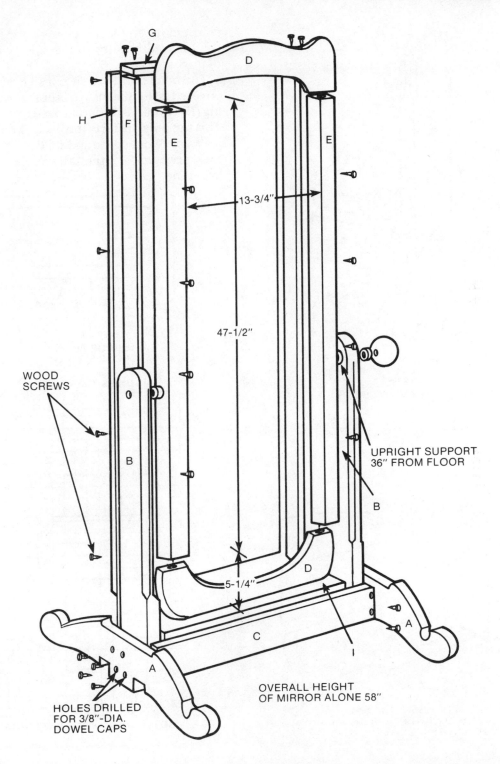

WOOD
SCREWS

13-3/4"

47-1/2"

UPRIGHT SUPPORT
36" FROM FLOOR

5-1/4"

HOLES DRILLED
FOR 3/8"-DIA.
DOWEL CAPS

OVERALL HEIGHT
OF MIRROR ALONE 58"

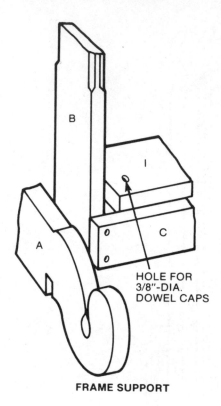

HOLE FOR
3/8"-DIA.
DOWEL CAPS

FRAME SUPPORT

frame have the same edge routing. Attach the top and bottom to the sides with 3/8"-diameter dowels.

The back of the frame consists of a "box," covered (after the mirror is put in) with backing (H) to match the wood used on the frame. This not only protects the back of the mirror, it also provides space and solid anchoring for the carriage bolts that attach the frame to the stand.

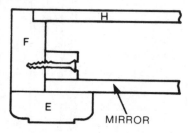

MIRROR

**MIRROR FRAME
CROSS SECTION**

ONE SQUARE = 1"

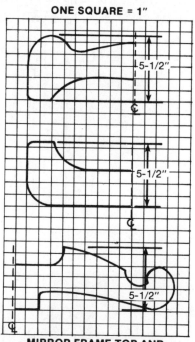

5-1/2"

5-1/2"

5-1/2"

**MIRROR FRAME TOP AND
BOTTOM AND FOOT PATTERNS**

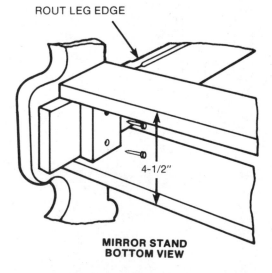

ROUT LEG EDGE

4-1/2"

**MIRROR STAND
BOTTOM VIEW**

Drill a 5/16″-diameter hole on each side of the box for the carriage bolts, centered on the side and halfway up. To make the pivot, start with a pair of 2″-diameter wood knobs. Drill a 3/8″-diameter hole about 3/4″ deep in each knob to provide clearance for the bolt. Then fit the knob with a 5/16″ teenut (a nut that has teeth to grip into wood and that mounts flush). To make sure the nut will stay in place, you might want to drill two or three small holes in it and nail it into the knob.

Make the spacers to go between the stand and frame by drilling a 3/8″-diameter hole through the centers of two short pieces of 1″-diameter doweling, measured to fit exactly between the frame and stand. Construct the stand as shown, being sure to use both wood glue and screws to make it sturdy. Use the pattern for the legs shown here or design your own. Note that all screw heads are covered with dowel caps.

After the frame and stand are assembled, sand everything smooth and finish as desired. This mirror was first treated with a natural oak stain, then finished with two coats of tung oil. When the finish has dried completely, lock the mirror in place with several small wood blocks screwed into the sides of the back frame box.

Insert the carriage bolts from the inside of the frame, put in the spacers, and mount the unit to the stand. Tighten the pivot knobs enough to keep the mirror from swinging. The last step is to put on the backing, using small brads. The result is a fine-looking mirror made to your own taste.

Scroll Mirror/ Picture Frame

Decorative scrollwork makes this mirror and picture frame two charming additions to your home. Use black walnut to highlight the intricate scroll patterns. Construction is the same for both pieces, the only difference being the dimensions.

Begin by making the frame; it can be done on a circular saw without the use of special molding cutters. Cut a single piece of crown molding stock long enough to make two vertical and two horizontal pieces. Rabbet the back of the molding to hold the mirror/picture. Miter the corners; then nail and glue the frame together.

Make the scrollwork pieces from 1/2" black walnut; the edges should be finely finished. Plane and sand a board of well-seasoned stock large enough to make the scrolled top (C), bottom (D), and sides (E and F for mirror, E for picture frame). Make full-sized templates from the patterns provided. Glue the scroll pieces to the frame, aligning the rear surface of these pieces with the rear surface of the frame.

Next, make the tempered hardboard plates that are screwed to the back of the frame to hold the mirror/picture and backing in place. Drill pilot holes in the frame for the wood screws, then screw on the plates. Even though they will have to be removed to put in the mirror/picture after the finish is applied, they will serve to secure the joints while the finishing is being done.

Finally, finish the piece(s) as desired. A natural finish is suggested, with a good filler rubbed into the pores of the wood beforehand.

MATERIALS LIST
8-5/8" × 12-5/8" mirror or
8-5/8" × 10-5/8" picture
Wood screws
80-grit sandpaper
Wood filler
Wood glue

CUTTING LIST (Mirror)

KEY	PIECES	SIZE AND DESCRIPTION
A	2	3/4 × 7/8 × 14 frame
B	2	3/4 × 7/8 × 10 frame
C	1	1/2 × 3 × 11 top scroll piece
D	1	1/2 × 2-1/2 × 10 bottom scroll piece
E	2	1/2 × 1-1/4 × 4 side scroll pieces
F	2	1/2 × 1-1/2 × 3-1/2 side scroll pieces
G	1	1/4 × 8-5/8 × 12-5/8 backing (hardboard)
H	2	1/8 × 2-1/2 × 2-3/4 mirror and backing supports (hardboard)
I	2	1/8 × 2 × 3-1/2 mirror and backing supports (hardboard)
J	2	1/8 × 1-1/2 × 2 mirror and backing supports (hardboard)

CUTTING LIST (Picture Frame)

KEY	PIECES	SIZE AND DESCRIPTION
A	2	3/4 × 7/8 × 12 frame
B	2	3/4 × 7/8 × 10 frame
C	1	1/2 × 5 × 10-1/2 top scroll piece
D	1	1/2 × 2-5/8 × 10 bottom scroll piece
E	4	1/2 × 1-1/4 × 4 side scroll pieces
F	1	1/4 × 8-5/8 × 10-5/8 backing (hardboard)
G	2	1/8 × 2-1/2 × 2-3/4 picture and backing supports (hardboard)
H	2	1/8 × 2 × 3-1/2 picture and backing supports (hardboard)
I	2	1/8 × 1-1/2 × 2 picture and backing supports (hardboard)

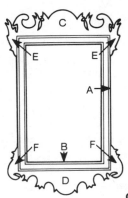

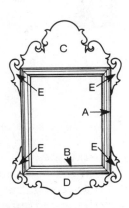

ONE SQUARE = 1″

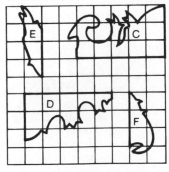

MIRROR SCROLLWORK PATTERNS

ONE SQUARE = 1″

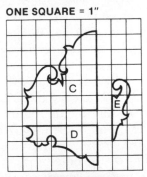

**PICTURE FRAME
SCROLLWORK PATTERNS**

Shaker Pegboard Rails

No discussion of country-living storage would be complete without mentioning Shaker peg rails—the original hang-alls. Chairs, cabinets, garments, utensils, just about anything that wasn't in constant use, could be stored out of the way but be always at hand, ready for service. The shelves and racks shown here can be used in conjunction with a typical Shaker peg rail. The storage units may be held directly on pegs or hung from the pegs by leather thongs.

The pegboard hanging rail itself may be either 3"- or 4"-wide clear pine. The edges may be sanded slightly to remove sharp corners, or they may be beaded. Holes for pegs (1/2" diameter) may be bored 6" or 12" apart depending on the holding method. The pegs may be purchased ready-made from a woodworking supply shop or may be turned from maple following the pattern given here. Install the pegs on the rail with glue and

finish with a clear varnish or stain as desired. Then secure the pegboard rail to the wall studs with screws or nails.

The four units illustrated here are constructed basically the same. That is, begin by cutting out the sides of the units with a band-saw or saber saw.

When cutting the shelf units, bevel the showing edges slightly to conform with the sides. Assemble the shelves to the sides with glue and finishing nails.

When assembling one of the rack units, cut the dowels to length and bore in the sides

MATERIALS LIST

4d finishing nails
3/4"-dia. dowels
Shaker pegs
1" × 3" clear pine pegboard
Leather thongs (2)
Wood glue

with a spade bit. Also assemble the hanging dowels with glue and finishing nails.

The major difference in the construction of shelves and racks is how they are held on the pegboard. The companion shelf and rack units are held directly by the pegs. Bore 1"-diameter holes into the hangers for the pegs.

The hanging shelves shown here are hung from the peg rail by leather thongs. Bore the two holes in the sides for the thongs. The towel rack is mounted over the pegs and held in place by gravity.

Finish all of the pieces with a clear varnish or stain as desired.

Hanging shelves are held in place by leather thongs on the peg.

CUTTING LIST (Hanging Shelves)

KEY	PIECES	SIZE AND DESCRIPTION
A	2	3/4 × 7 × 25 sides
B	1	3/4 × 5 × 26-1/4 shelf
C	1	3/4 × 6 × 26-1/4 shelf
D	1	3/4 × 7 × 26-1/4 shelf

CUTTING LIST (Hanging Towel Rack)

KEY	PIECES	SIZE AND DESCRIPTION
A	1	3/4 × 1 × 24 top hanger
B	2	3/4 × 3/4 × 24 towel hangers
C	2	3/4 × 4 × 16 sides

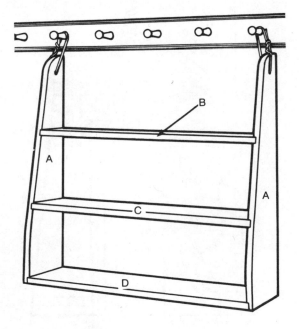

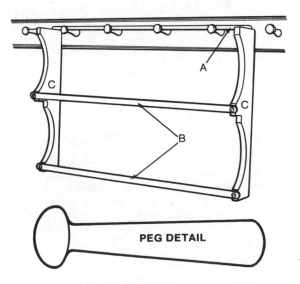

PEG DETAIL

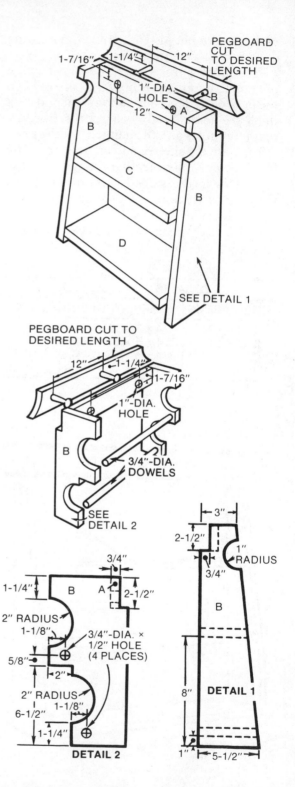

The towel rack is held on the pegs by a hanger which is screwed to the top of the unit. The screws used to hold the towel hangers may be fastened as shown or concealed by wood plugs.

CUTTING LIST (Peg-held Shelves)

KEY	PIECES	SIZE AND DESCRIPTION
A	1	3/4 × 2-1/2 (or 3-1/2) × 18 hanger
B	2	3/4 × 5-1/2 × 17-1/2 sides
C	1	3/4 × 4-9/16 × 18 shelf
D	1	3/4 × 5-3/8 × 18 shelf

CUTTING LIST (Peg-held Rack)

KEY	PIECES	SIZE AND DESCRIPTION
A	1	3/4 × 2-1/2 × 20 hanger
B	2	3/4 × 5-1/2 × 17-1/2 sides

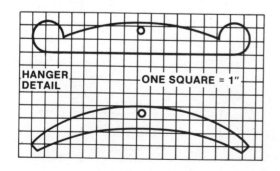

The companion peg-held units are the shelf (left) and rack (right).

An abrasive grinder does a great job of sanding the shelves' curves and edges.

The companion units are hung on two Shaker pegs. Mounting the units locks them into place.

Drill holes into both sides of the peg-held rack and glue the dowels into place.

In many Shaker homes, closets were at a minimum. As a result, pegboards were used in bedrooms. The maple clothes hangers were held on the pegs by leather thongs. The shaping of the hangers is shown on the grid.

Shaker Candle Sconce

place and clamp until dry. Finish the candle sconce as desired, and it's ready for use.

MATERIALS LIST
Wood glue

	CUTTING LIST	
KEY	**PIECES**	**SIZE AND DESCRIPTION**
A	1	3/4 × 5-1/2 × 6 base
B	1	1/2 × 3-1/2 × 18 back

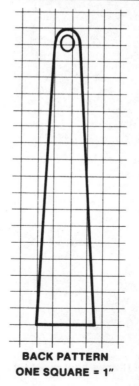

BACK PATTERN
ONE SQUARE = 1"

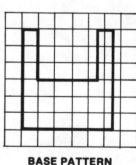

BASE PATTERN
ONE SQUARE = 1"

Beautiful in its simplicity, this pine candle sconce was placed at a convenient height in hallways and bedrooms of Shaker homes. While the sconce was originally designed to hang on a Shaker pegboard, it can be easily mounted on any peg or rail. Construction is quite simple; it's just a matter of gluing the two pieces together.

Cut the back (B) using the pattern provided. A keyhole saw can be used to make the oval in the top of the back for hanging the sconce. The base (A) is open on one end to fit the 3-1/2"-wide back into it. Glue the back in

Coatrack Hall Mirror

To build it, first enlarge the scale drawing and make a pattern on heavy cardboard. The frame is doweled together from four pieces of glued 6"-wide stock. The design utilizes two pieces to eliminate wasted material where the center of the frame would be. Joint to make sure all edges are smooth. Position them on a flat, smooth surface; then lay the cardboard pattern in place.

Make sure the frame is square with the lengthwise run of the glue joints or the entire frame will appear to be crooked when cut. Trace the frame, marking the dowel locations. Cut the inside of the oval; then slice away the outside of the frame, leaving a few square blocks on each end for clamping purposes.

Using a doweling jig and 3/8"-diameter dowels, join and glue the frame pieces (A, B, C). Clamp securely until dry. Clamp the center to hold the frame flat while the glue sets; this prevents pulling the frame out of square with the long bar clamps.

After overnight drying, remove the clamps and clamping blocks from the ends of the

MATERIALS LIST
1/4"-dia. dowels
3/8"-dia. dowels
Mirror
Hardboard backing
Wood screws
Porcelain knobs (4)
Hanging wire or hooks
180-grit sandpaper
Wood glue

An old-fashioned hall mirror can add a touch of antique charm to any room in the home, and it's an inexpensive workshop project. Although the frame can be fashioned from a variety of woods, white pine or quarter-sawn oak were the pick of most old-time craftsmen.

frame. Sand the inside with a drum sander in a drill press or radial arm saw, then sand all joints thoroughly. Shape the inside and outside edges; then cut a 1/2"- or 1/4"-deep recess in the back of the frame to hold the mirror and backing. The depth of the cut depends on the thickness of the mirror and hardboard backing.

The shelf (D), railing (F), and shelf support (E) are cut from 3/4" white pine with the edges sanded smooth. The railing supports (G) are turned with a 1/4" hole bored through each of the turnings to accommodate the dowels. Cut the railing and run both sides of the railing top through a quarter-round shaper. Round the front ends to get a nice finish.

Assemble the shelf with glue and 1/4"-diameter dowels fitted in stopped holes in the shelf and railings. Clamp and glue the shelf securely, then glue and screw it to the mirror frame.

Sand the frame with 180-grit paper; then finish as desired. Attach porcelain knobs on both sides of the frame.

Finally, insert the mirror into the back of the frame; then screw the hardboard backing securely to the back. Hanging wire or hooks will put your finished product on the wall and in the spotlight.

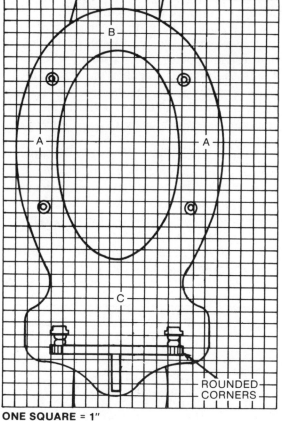

ONE SQUARE = 1"

CUTTING LIST		
KEY	**PIECES**	**SIZE AND DESCRIPTION**
A	2	1-1/4 × 6 × 32 frame sides
B	1	1-1/4 × 4 × 6 frame top
C	1	1-1/4 × 6 × 11-1/2 frame bottom
D	1	3/4 × 5 × 11-1/2 shelf
E	1	3/4 × 3 × 4-1/2 shelf support
F	2	3/4 × 1-1/2 × 5 railing
G	2	1-1/4 × 1-1/4 railing supports

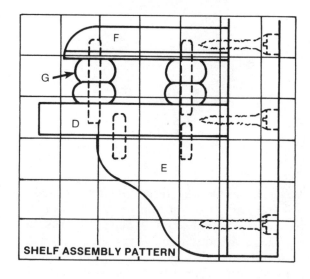

SHELF ASSEMBLY PATTERN

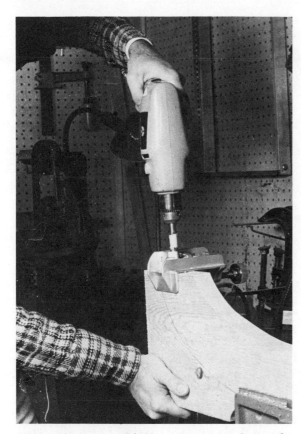

Use a saber saw or bandsaw to cut out the inside oval, then dowel and glue the pieces together.

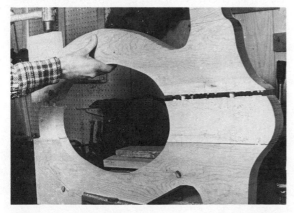

Square ends are left on each part of the frame to make clamping easier. These are cut away later.

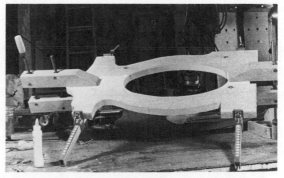

The two center clamps will prevent the frame from buckling or warping.

After the glue has set, saw off the clamping blocks. Use a drum sander in a drill press or radial arm saw to smooth all edges.

After inserting the mirror into back of the frame, fasten with hardboard backing. Measure and attach the hanging wire.

Step Stools

Step stools are a must in every home.
Those featured here combine a variety
of uses and designs, and all are attractive as
well as practical.

Kitchen Step Stool

The recipe calls for a pinch of basil and
the jar is on the top shelf, in the back,
where you can't reach it. Though it's too late
for this recipe, be prepared next time by constructing this cherry kitchen step stool.

Because the sides (A) measure 17" wide,
you'll probably want to edge-glue several
narrower boards together. After the glue

dries, rip the sides to the finish width, but cut
to length later.

Cut the top (B) and bottom (C) to size. Now
you are ready to cut the finger, or box, joints.
Set up your table saw to make a 1/2" dado
cut with the aid of the homemade jig.

The jig is a 3/4" piece of plywood measuring about 3" high by 13" long. Set the dado
blade to cut 13/16" deep. Then, holding the
jig firmly against the saw's miter gauge, run
the jig past the blade. Make another dado
spaced 1/2" away from the first one. Attach
the jig to the miter gauge so the inner dado
cut falls directly over the dado blade. Then
make a wooden spacer block the exact width
of the dado cut and place it in the jig's out-
ermost dado cut.

Check the quality of the jig by cutting box
joints in scrap wood. All the fingers should fit
tightly. When they do fit you're ready to start
on the real thing. Align one of the sides to cut
a full 1/2" groove. After the first cut, use the
spacer to space the second cut as shown in
the photo. Continue making these cuts until
you've cut all the fingers in the side, then
repeat on the second side.

Now place the top against the spacer—it
starts with a finger, not a groove. Then space
each cut as you did for the sides.

Next, cut the stopped dado in each of the sides for the bottom with the dado blade reset to 3/4" wide and 1/2" deep. Because this is a stopped dado, square the cut with a wood chisel.

Enlarge the side pattern and transfer it to the workpieces. Cut the sides to shape, and sand all of the pieces before assembly. Then glue and clamp the stool together.

After the glue dries, drill three 3/8"-diameter holes, 1/4" deep, into the sides in line with the bottom. Then drill the pilot hole for the No. 6 × 1-1/2" wood screws. Fill in the holes with wood plugs.

Because the top and bottom were cut square, they need to be planed at the correct angle. Do this with a hand plane. Round over all the corners slightly, then sand the stool before finishing.

MATERIALS LIST

No. 6 × 1/2" wood screws
Wood plugs
Wood glue

CUTTING LIST

KEY	PIECES	SIZE AND DESCRIPTION
A	2	3/4 × 18 × 20 sides
B	1	3/4 × 8 × 16 top
C	1	3/4 × 8 × 15 bottom

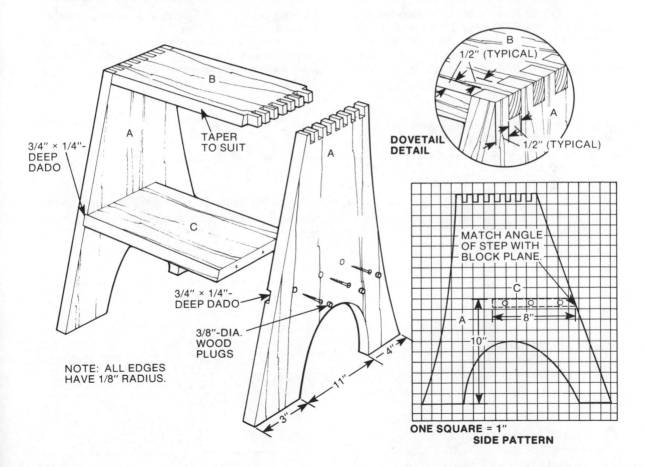

3/4" × 1/4"- DEEP DADO

TAPER TO SUIT

3/4" × 1/4"- DEEP DADO

3/8"-DIA. WOOD PLUGS

NOTE: ALL EDGES HAVE 1/8" RADIUS.

DOVETAIL DETAIL

1/2" (TYPICAL)

1/2" (TYPICAL)

MATCH ANGLE OF STEP WITH BLOCK PLANE.

ONE SQUARE = 1"
SIDE PATTERN

Construct the jig from a 3″ × 13″ piece of plywood. Make one 1/2″ wide dado cut and then another 1/2″ away from the first. Cut a spacer block so it fits snugly in the dado. Glue sandpaper on the jig to keep the wood from sliding.

Clamp the side to the jig after determining your first cut, then dado. Place this cut dado over the jig's spacer block as shown. Repeat for each cut. Dado the top by making the first cut with the piece placed against the spacer block

Shaker Step Stool

A clever Shaker innovation, this step-stool was designed with a long back so

it could be carried easily and hung neatly on the wall when not in use. Note the dovetailing in the front; this gave the stool the strength required to perform many duties in the Shaker household.

Cut the components to size; use the patterns provided to shape the ends (A) and

CUTTING LIST		
KEY	**PIECES**	**SIZE AND DESCRIPTION**
A	2	3/4 × 7-1/2 × 9 ends
B	1	1 × 7-1/2 × 13 seat
C	1	3/4 × 5 × 24 back
D	1	3/4 × 13 support rail (dowel)

back (C). Cut dovetail joints in one of the ends and the seat (B) as shown. Then drill a

---

MATERIALS LIST

180-grit sandpaper
Wood glue

3/4"-diameter hole completely through each end to accommodate the support rail (D). Likewise, drill a 3/4"-diameter hole through the back as shown for hanging the stool.

The entire stepstool can be assembled using wood glue. Sand down with 180-grit sandpaper, then finish as desired.

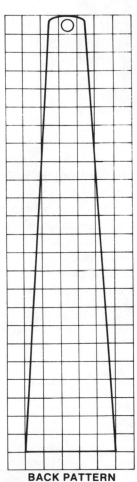

BACK PATTERN
ONE SQUARE = 1"

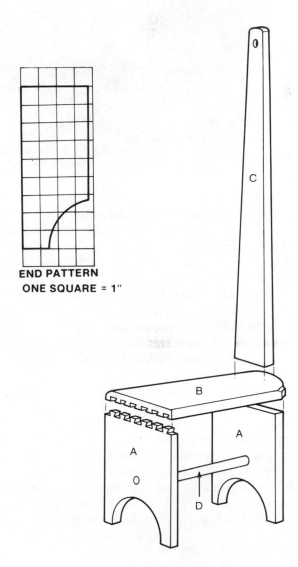

END PATTERN
ONE SQUARE = 1"

Storage Step Stool

This step stool combines its basic purpose with that of storage. The entire project is constructed from 3/4" pine.

Cut out the lengths and widths of each component. Next, cut a 6° taper on each leg (A). Measure in 1-1/2" from the top corners on both legs and draw a straight line from this point to the bottom corner to make the appropriate taper for each leg. Also, locate and cut out the handles and the 3-1/2" radius on the bottom of each leg.

The sides (B) have a 6° slope on the top and on each end. The bottom (C) has a 6° taper on all four sides. The top (D) is made with straight cuts; it is not tapered.

Begin assembly by gluing and nailing the bottom to the sides. Check to be sure the slant of the top of the sides is parallel with the floor. To square the unit, nail one side completely and place only one nail in the middle on the other side. Then turn the piece top down on a flat surface and finish nailing in that position.

Secure the legs with glue and No. 8 × 1-1/2" wood screws. After assembly, fill the screw holes with wood filler. Rout the top to give it a finished appearance.

Finish the stool as desired, then secure the top with two strap hinges. Add a hinge hasp for looks and security.

MATERIALS LIST

Finishing nails
No. 8 × 1-1/2" wood screws
Strap hinges (2)
Hinge hasp
Wood filler
Wood glue

CUTTING LIST		
KEY	**PIECES**	**SIZE AND DESCRIPTION**
A	2	3/4 × 11-1/4 × 15-5/16 legs
B	2	3/4 × 8-5/16 × 20-7/8 sides
C	1	3/4 × 7-1/4 × 20-7/8 bottom
D	1	3/4 × 11-1/4 × 24 top

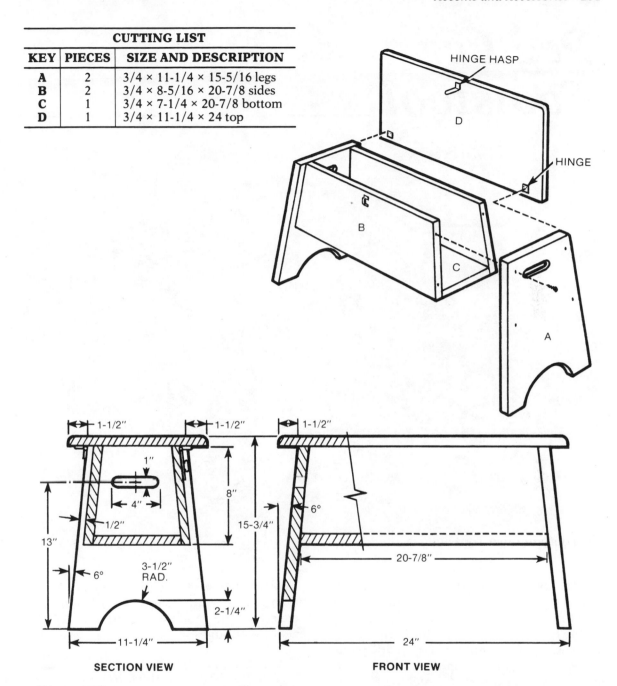

HINGE HASP

D

HINGE

B

C

A

1-1/2"   1-1/2"   1-1/2"

1"

8"

4"

1/2"

15-3/4"

13"

6"

6"

3-1/2"
RAD.

2-1/4"

20-7/8"

11-1/4"

24"

SECTION VIEW   **FRONT VIEW**

Peg Leg Footstool

For solid comfort, there's nothing to beat a footstool and a favorite chair. Here's one that can be made in no time at all.

The legs (B) are tapered as desired; exact dimensions don't matter. Drill 1"-diameter holes 1" deep in the top of each leg to accommodate dowels. Drill matching 1"-diameter holes in the top (A) and glue the legs in place with lengths of dowel about 3" long.

Cut off whatever excess dowel protrudes above the top and sand flush. Round the edges of the stool with a wood rasp to achieve a rough-hewn look.

MATERIALS LIST

1"-dia. dowels
Wood glue

CUTTING LIST		
KEY	**PIECES**	**SIZE AND DESCRIPTION**
A	1	1-1/2 × 8-1/4 × 13 top
B	4	1-1/2 × 1-1/2 × 7-1/2 legs

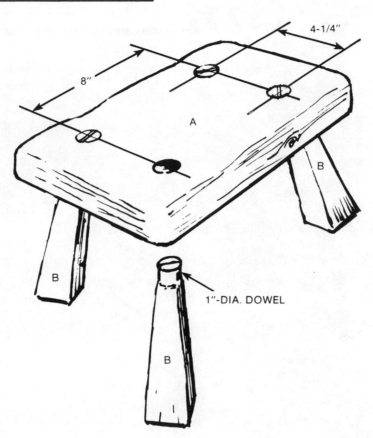

1"-DIA. DOWEL

Country Feed Bin

This feed bin lends itself to all sorts of storage uses around the home. Of course, the length may be altered to suit your needs.

Cut all components to size; note that 1″ stock is used throughout. When making the five dividers (C), cut the first one according to the dimensions shown in the exploded drawing. Then use this as a template for cutting the other four.

To assemble the bin, first lap the back (B) over the bottom (D) and secure it with screws and wood glue. Attach the dividers

---
MATERIALS LIST

Wood screws and/or finishing nails
Butt hinges (8)
Wood glue
---

next; you can space them at irregular intervals if you want compartments of different sizes. The front (A) and the ledge (E) can be secured next.

Construct the four lids (G) by nailing or screwing the edging (F) in place; then attach the lids with butt hinges as shown. The slight overhang of the lids makes handles unnecessary.

CUTTING LIST		
KEY	**PIECES**	**SIZE AND DESCRIPTION**
A	1	1 × 7-7/8 × 56 front
B	1	1 × 11-5/8 × 56 back
C	5	1 × 6-5/8 × 11-5/8 dividers
D	1	1 × 7-5/8 × 56 bottom
E	1	1 × 1-5/8 × 56 ledge
F	8	1 × 2 × 9-5/8 edging
G	4	1 × 9-5/8 × 12 lids

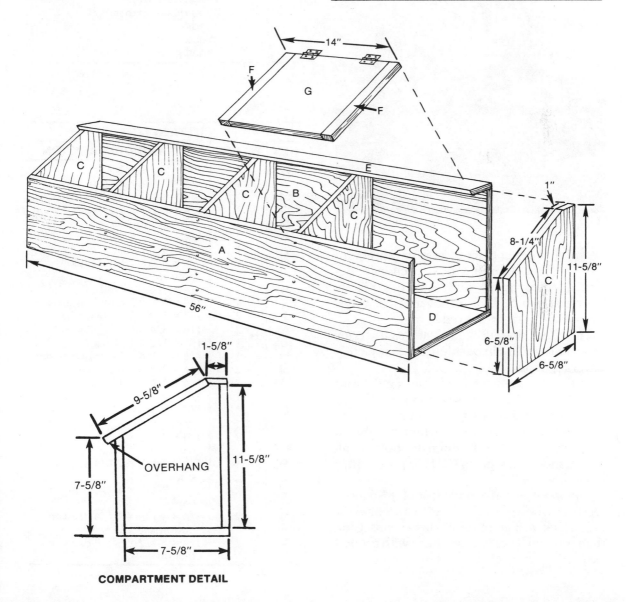

COMPARTMENT DETAIL

Sewing Boxes

MATERIALS LIST

1/8"-dia. dowels
Pin cushion
Drawer knobs (3)
120-grit sandpaper
Brads
Wood filler
Wood glue

CUTTING LIST

KEY	PIECES	SIZE AND DESCRIPTION
A	2	1/4 × 5 × 9-1/2 sides
B	1	1/4 × 7-1/4 × 12 top
C1	1	1/4 × 9-1/2 × 11-1/2 shelf
C2	1	1/4 × 2-1/2 × 7-1/4 divider
D	1	1/2 × 11 × 13 base
E	2	1/4 × 1-1/2 × 13 feet
F	1	1/4 × 5 × 12 back
G	1	1/4 × 3/4 × 10-1/2 rack bottom
H	1	1/4 × 3/4 × 11 rail
I	4	1/4 × 3/4 × 3 rack supports
J	2	1/4 × 3/4 × 5-1/2 rack base
K	2	1/4 × 3/4 × 6-1/8 rails
L	1	1/4 × 1/2 × 11 trim
M	1	1/4 × 2-3/4 × 11 drawer front
N	2	1/4 × 2-3/4 × 9 drawer sides
O	1	1/4 × 2-3/4 × 11 drawer back
P	1	1/4 × 9 × 11 drawer bottom
Q	1	1/4 × 2-3/4 × 11-1/2 drawer facing
R	2	1/4 × 2-1/2 × 4-7/8 drawer fronts
S	4	1/4 × 2-1/2 × 7-1/4 drawer sides
T	2	1/4 × 2-1/2 × 4-7/8 drawer backs
U	2	1/4 × 4-7/8 × 7-1/4 drawer bottoms
V	2	1/4 × 2-1/2 × 5-1/8 drawer facing

What better place to keep sewing equipment than in a box specifically designed for that purpose? Because this utilitarian piece can be built in a variety of ways, two designs are presented here.

The first sewing box features exterior spool pins and a pin cushion that completely covers the top.

Cut out all pieces first and sand them smooth. Join the sides (A) with the shelf (C1), using glue and brads for all joints. Add the divider (C2), and then attach the assembly to the base (D). Drill 1/8"-diameter holes in all of the spool rack parts (G, H, I, J, K) before assembly.

The spool pins are made from 1/8"-diameter hardwood dowels fitted with cubes of 1/2" stock, drilled to fit the dowel ends. Glue them on and let dry, then shape with a wood rasp.

The drawers are constructed in the butt style. Since all stock is 1/4″, facing (Q, V) is added to provide a base for the knobs.

Round the exposed edges of the box roughly with a rasp, then sand smooth. Fill the nail holes with wood filler, then stain as desired.

The pin cushion is a small bag full of sawdust, kapok, ground cork, or pine needles mounted on cardboard and made to fit the recess on the cabinet. It is then covered with chintz, denim, or other material. In this way, the cushion is removable for washing.

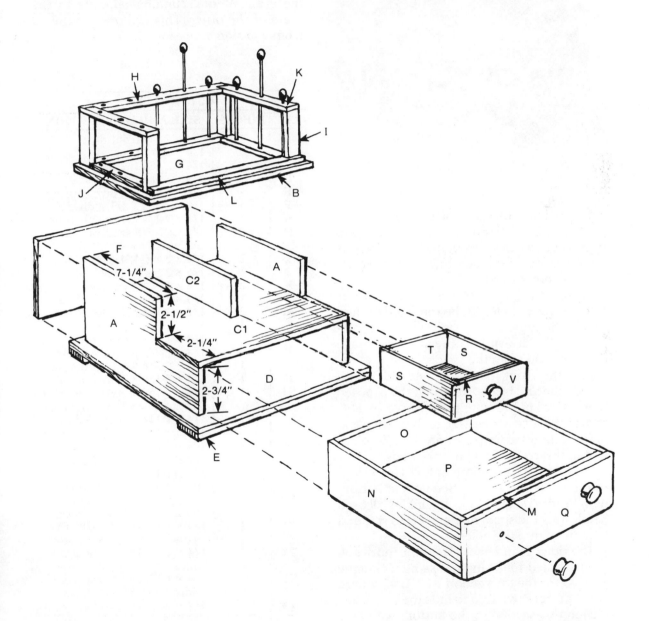

The same procedure is used for the sides (M) and back (N) of the bottom drawer frame. Here, corner pieces (O) are again used. Finally, attach the bottom (P) of the unit with glue and brads.

The lid is made of two pieces (Q, R) with the grain of one running opposite to the grain of the other. This will prevent the lid from warping.

A variation of the first sewing box follows: The basic unit—spool storage and frame for the top and bottom drawers—is made by starting assembly at the top and working downward.

After cutting all the pieces to size, drill four 1/8″-diameter holes in the top front (A) and two of the same size in each side (C) as indicated in the drawing. These are for passage of the thread from the spools.

Join the front, back (B), and sides with wood glue and brads. Note that the exposed front edges of the sides are covered by 1/4″ square corner strips (D) to hide the end grain. The dividers (E, F) are held in place within this frame by glue and brads.

Drill eight 3/16″-diameter holes in the bottom (G) for the spools. Secure the bottom with brads and glue, countersinking all brad heads. Cut the spool holders (H) to size and glue them into the holes.

The sides (I) and back (J) for the top drawer are joined following the same technique as used for the top section with 1/4″-square corner pieces (K) used to hide the end grain. Fasten this section to the bottom with glue and brads and add the bottom (L) of this section to the underside.

CUTTING LIST		
KEY	**PIECES**	**SIZE AND DESCRIPTION**
A	1	1/4 × 2 × 8 front
B	1	1/4 × 2 × 8 back
C	2	1/4 × 2 × 5-1/2 sides
D	2	1/4 × 1/4 × 2 corners
E	1	1/4 × 1-1/2 × 8 divider
F	1	1/4 × 1-1/2 × 1-3/4 divider
G	1	1/4 × 7-1/4 × 10-1/2 bottom
H	8	3/16 × 1-5/8 spool holders (dowels)
I	2	1/4 × 2 × 6-1/4 sides
J	1	1/4 × 2 × 9-1/4 back
K	2	1/4 × 1/4 × 2 corners
L	1	1/4 × 7-3/4 × 11-1/2 bottom
M	2	1/4 × 2 × 6-3/4 sides
N	1	1/4 × 2 × 10-1/2 back
O	2	1/4 × 1/4 × 2 corners
P	1	1/4 × 7-3/4 × 11-1/2 bottom
Q	1	1/4 × 6-3/8 × 9-1/8 outer lid
R	1	1/4 × 5-1/8 × 7-3/4 inner lid
S1	1	1/4 × 1-15/16 × 9-1/8 drawer front
S2	1	1/4 × 1-11/16 × 8-5/8 drawer back
S3	2	1/4 × 1-15/16 × 6 drawer sides
S4	2	1/4 × 1-15/16 × 5-3/4 drawer dividers
S5	1	1/4 × 6 × 8-5/8 drawer bottom
T1	1	1/4 × 1-15/16 × 10-3/8 drawer front
T2	1	1/4 × 1-11/16 × 9-7/8 drawer back
T3	2	1/4 × 1-15/16 × 6 drawer sides
T4	1	1/4 × 1-15/16 × 9-7/8 drawer divider
T5	1	1/4 × 6-1/2 × 9-7/8 drawer bottom

MATERIALS LIST

220-grit sandpaper
Brads
Clothespins (4)
Pin cushion
Wood glue

The pin cushion is fastened to the lid by inserting one long brad or a small screw directly through the cushion into the center of the lid. The cover is not hinged, but instead fits loosely into the top section in which the spools are stored.

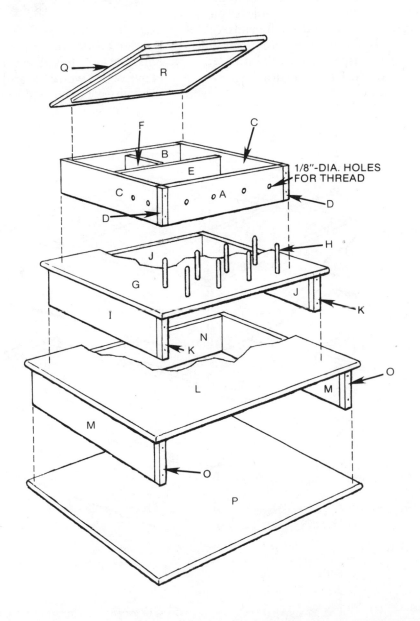

The fronts (T1, S1) of both drawers have rabbets cut along the outside edge to receive the sides (T3, S3), as shown. The backs (T2, S2) of both drawers are cut 1/4″ shallower than the fronts and the sides. The backs rest on the bottoms.

The divider (T4) in the bottom drawer fits into dadoes cut into the sides. The dividers (S4) in the top drawer are also held in place by dadoes cut in the front and back. All parts are secured with glue and small brads.

Cut the knobs from clothespin heads. File the ends with a rasp until they fit into 3/16″-diameter holes drilled in the drawer fronts. Secure with glue.

After all the parts have been assembled and the glue has dried, round all exposed edges with a wood file and then with 220-grit sandpaper. Finish as desired.

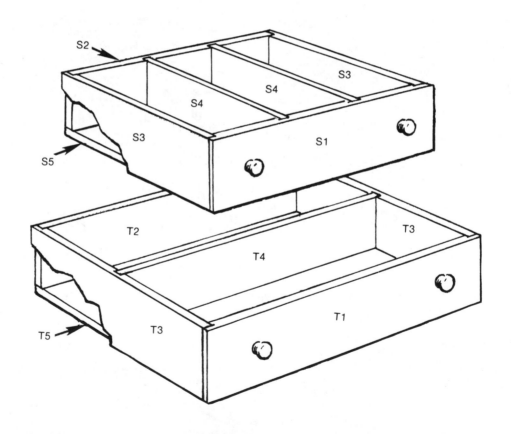

Letter Rack ―――――――――

Here is a replica of an antique letter rack that will add grace and charm to any home; hang it in the entrance hall or foyer. The three drawers can hold stamps, keys, or other small articles. Maple, pine, or birch are all good stock from which to build the rack.

Cut all of the pieces to the sizes specified in the cutting list. Use the patterns to cut the top and bottom curves of the back (A) and the sides (B). Cut three 1/8"-deep dadoes 5/16" wide in each side to accommodate the shelves (C).

Cut a 1/8"-deep dado 5/16" wide in the underside of the top shelf and the top of the center shelf as shown to accommodate the divider (E). Bevel the edges of the letter holder (D); then cut slots for the letters with a backsaw.

Cut 1/8"-deep rabbets 1/4" wide along the outside edge of the drawer fronts (F, J) so that the drawer sides (G, K) fit flush. Secure the sides to the fronts with glue and brads. Use three brads driven at an angle; counter-set the heads.

Set the backs (H, L) between the sides so that their top edge is flush with the sides. Use glue and brads to hold. Insert the drawer bottoms (I, M) between the sides and nail and glue in place. Use a wood screw to attach a drawer pull to each of the fronts.

Glue and nail the sides of the rack to the back with brads spaced about 2" apart. Apply glue along the edges of the shelves and slide them into the dadoes cut in the sides. Use two or three brads per shelf as added support.

Slide the divider into position after applying glue to the top and bottom edges. Secure the letter holder with wood screws driven through the rear of the back into the holder. Countersink the screw heads.

After the glued parts are thoroughly dry, sand and file all edges. Finish the letter rack to suit your taste. If desired, insert a brass hanger in the back as shown.

MATERIALS LIST
Wood screws
Brads
Brass hanger (1)
220-grit sandpaper
Wood glue

CUTTING LIST

KEY	PIECES	SIZE AND DESCRIPTION
A	1	5/16 × 10-1/2 × 17-1/2 back
B	2	5/16 × 6-1/16 × 17-1/2 sides
C	3	5/16 × 5-3/4 × 10-3/4 shelves
D	1	3/4 × 2 × 9-3/4 letter holder
E	1	5/16 × 2 × 5-3/4 divider
F	1	5/16 × 1-11/16 × 10-3/8 drawer front
G	2	1/4 × 1-11/16 × 5-1/2 drawer sides
H	1	1/4 × 1-7/16 × 9-7/8 drawer back
I	1	1/4 × 5-3/8 × 9-3/4 drawer bottom
J	2	5/16 × 1-11/16 × 5 drawer fronts
K	4	1/4 × 1-11/16 × 5-1/2 drawer sides
L	2	1/4 × 1-7/16 × 4-1/2 drawer backs
M	2	1/4 × 4-1/2 × 5-3/8 drawer bottoms

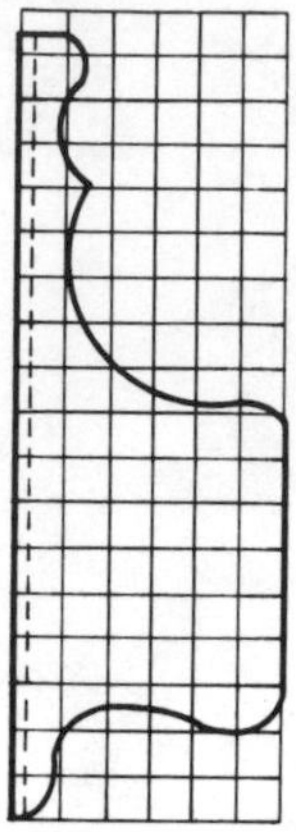

SIDE PATTERN

ONE SQUARE = 1"

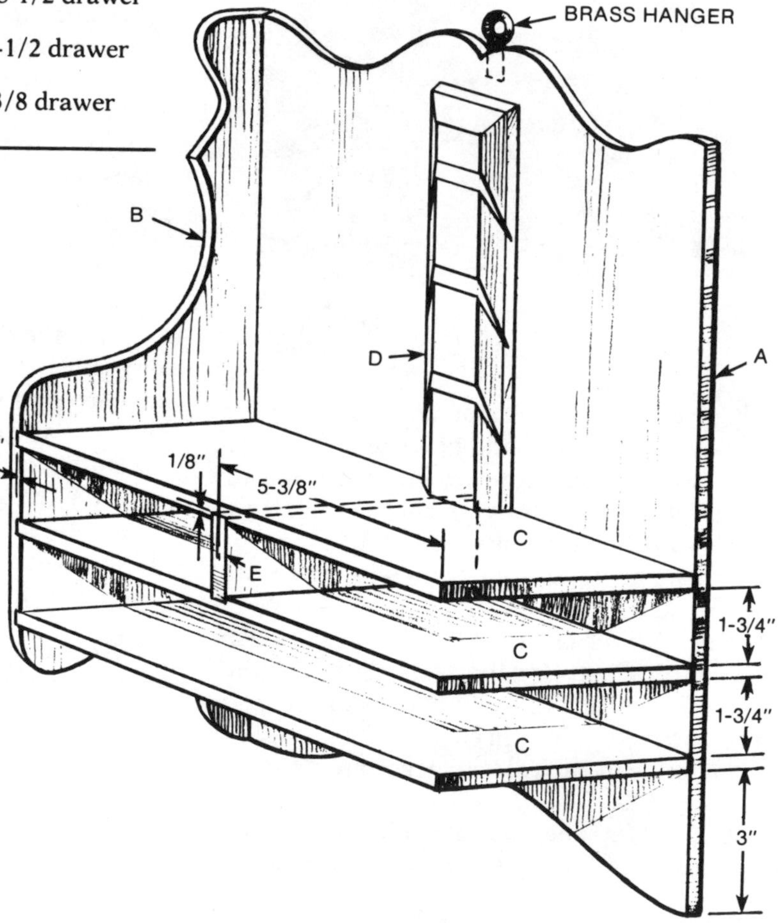

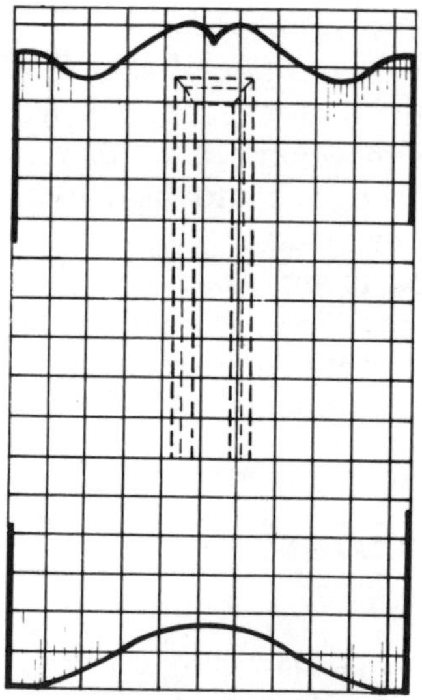

BRASS HANGER

B

D

A

1/8"

1/8"

5-3/8"

C

E

C

1-3/4"

C

1-3/4"

3"

BACK PATTERN

ONE SQUARE = 1"

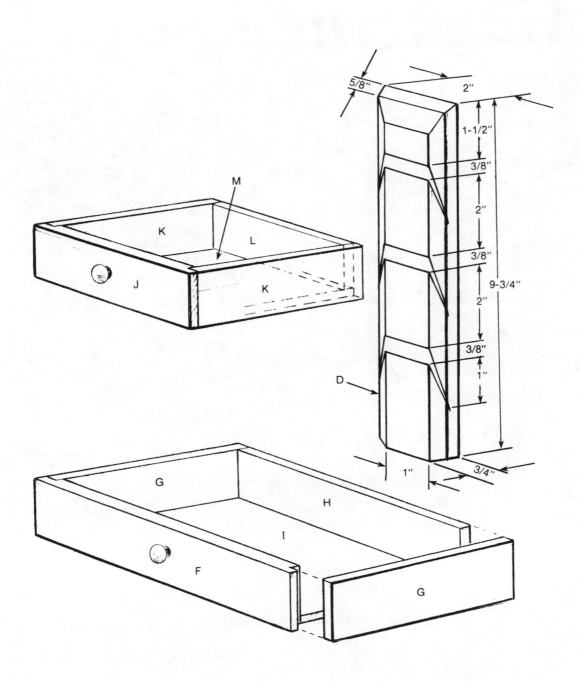

Magazine Rack

This 3/4″ oak magazine rack is 10″ wide × 19″ long × 14-5/8″ high and is designed for long, heavy use. In fact, it should last a lifetime if you use hardwood material. The darker magazine rack in the photo was given a coat of Spanish oak stain. Both racks were finished with two coats of satin polyurethane, sanded between coats. Make sure to use extra fine sandpaper when sanding.

You'll need a total of fourteen 1-1/2″ screws to hold the rack together. Five screws are used for each end (C) and four under the

MATERIALS LIST

5/8″-dia. wood plugs (10)
No. 8 × 1-1/2″ wood screws
220-grit sandpaper

base (D) to secure the ends to the base. To avoid splitting the wood, predrill the holes for each screw. Putting a little wax or soap on the screws will make the job easier.

Use a 5/16" rounding-over bit to rout the base, ends, and handle (A), and a 3/8" cove trim to groove the sides.

If you are ambitious, you can cut out a design such as a diamond or heart shape on the ends. Sanding, cutting out, drilling, and assembling will take approximately seven hours with the use of power tools.

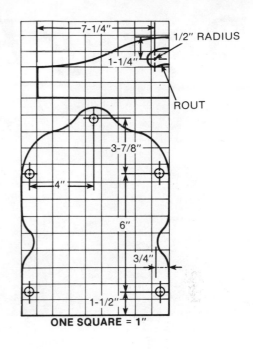

ONE SQUARE = 1"

CUTTING LIST

KEY	PIECES	SIZE AND DESCRIPTION
A	1	3/4 × 3-1/2 × 16-1/2 handle
B	4	3/4 × 3 × 16-1/2 handle
C	2	3/4 × 9 × 12-1/2 ends
D	1	3/4 × 10 × 19 base

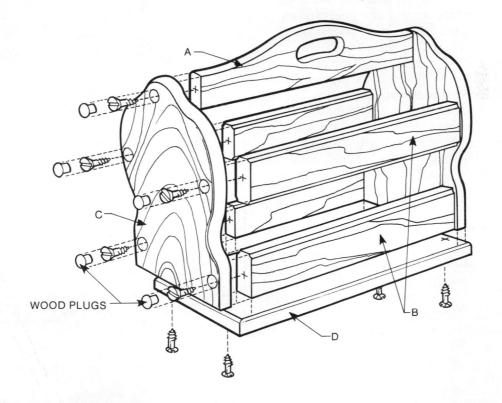

WOOD PLUGS

Drying Racks

Round exposed edges of all parts irregularly with a wood rasp, then sand smooth before finishing.

CUTTING LIST		
KEY	PIECES	SIZE AND DESCRIPTION
A	2	1 × 10 × 28 ends
B	2	1 × 2 × 24 crosspieces

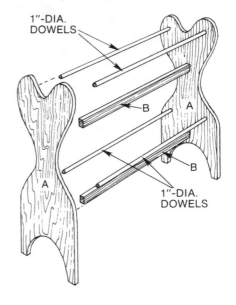

Few pieces can be so easily reproduced as this one or, when finished, can blend so gracefully into almost any background. Both useful and ornamental, drying racks will brighten a bleak corner with a display of fine linen.

Cut all pieces to size from clear pine. The pattern for the traditional Shaker heart design of the end pieces (A) must be enlarged to full scale and transferred to 1 × 10 stock. Cut out with a scroll or coping saw or with a jig, band, or saber saw.

Attach all crosspieces (B) and dowels with counterset wood screws put through the ends, two screws into each end of the 1 × 2 pieces.

MATERIALS LIST (Both Racks)

1-1/2" wood screws
1"-dia. dowels (4)
Wood glue

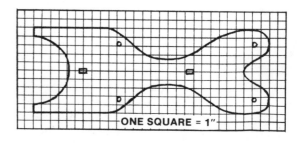

ONE SQUARE = 1"

mortise-and-tenon joints are open with the exception of those joining the two uprights (C) to the base and top. The top pieces are joined with simple butt joints. All the joints are nailed and glued.

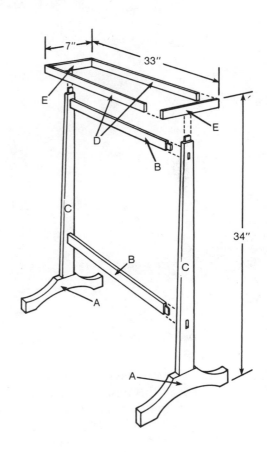

This Shaker drying rack offers a beautiful contrast to the humdrum racks you see today. The method of building this rack, once the wood is cut, is obvious from the drawing. A pattern for shaping the base of this rack is given in the base pattern.

All the joints with the exception of the top pieces (D, E) are mortise and tenon. All of the

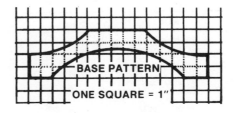

CUTTING LIST		
KEY	**PIECES**	**SIZE AND DESCRIPTION**
A	2	1 × 15 bases
B	2	1 × 2 × 33 leg supports
C	2	1 × 3 × 29-1/2 uprights
D	2	1 × 1-1/4 × 31 top pieces
E	2	1 × 1-1/4 × 7 top pieces

Catwalk Plate Rack

From the earliest days of the country, plate racks of this type have been used to display the family's prized chinaware—ironstone, willoware, and other such pieces—which rarely found their way into everyday use. The passage of time has not lessened the pride felt in showing off prized possessions, and this piece still serves its purpose as ably as ever.

Construction is simple. First, cut the various pieces to size. The patterns on the sides (A) and the bottom brace (E) can be cut by hand, although any power saw suited to curve cutting will do. Round all exposed edges with a wood rasp, then sand smooth. Cut the V-shaped beads in the shelves (B, C); these are needed to hold the plates upright.

Join the shelves and the top brace (D) to the sides with 10d finishing nails and wood glue; counterset the nails. Drill 1/2"-diameter holes in the bottom brace to accommodate the cup pegs (F), and square them with a rasp or sharp chisel. Attach the bottom brace in the same way the shelves were attached and secure the pegs with glue. Fill all nail holes with wood filler.

After finishing the rack, attach the brackets to the upper ends of the sides. Use 60-pound picture hangers to mount the piece.

MATERIALS LIST

10d finishing nails
Brackets (2)
60-lb picture hangers (2)
Wood filler
150-grit sandpaper
Wood glue

CUTTING LIST

KEY	PIECES	SIZE AND DESCRIPTION
A	2	1 × 4-3/4 × 23-1/2 sides
B	1	1 × 3-1/2 × 34-1/2 top shelf
C	1	1 × 4-1/2 × 34-1/2 bottom shelf
D	1	1 × 1-1/4 × 36 top brace
E	1	1 × 3 × 34-1/2 bottom brace
F	4	1/2 × 2-3/4 cup pegs

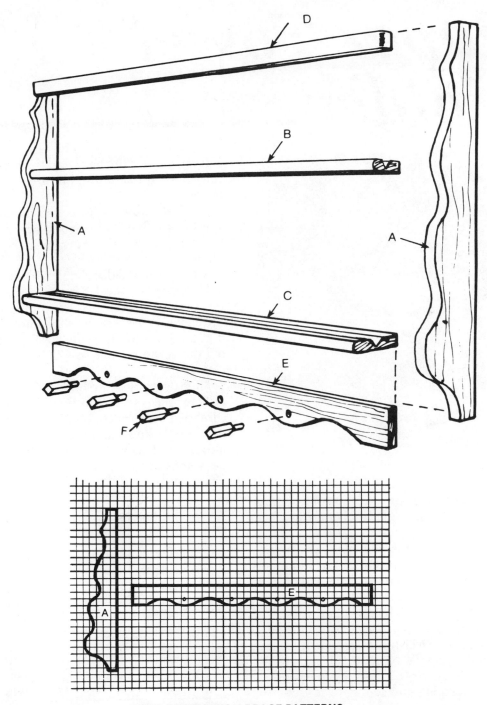

SIDES AND BOTTOM BRACE PATTERNS

Paper Towel Holder

Next, cut out the back and the sides. Use a fine-toothed blade to minimize wood splintering.

Sand all showing faces and assemble the sides to the back with wood screws. Cover the counterbored screw holes with oak plugs.

Attach wooden doorknobs to both ends of a 1"-diameter dowel. They are available in most hardware stores and home centers. Thread a knob screw into the knob and glue it into place. After the glue has hardened, cut off the screw's head so 1/2" of the thread remains.

Then drill holes into both ends of the dowel 1/16" narrower than the diameter of the threaded screws. Glue only one end of the dowel to a knob after threading the knob into place. This will allow the other knob to be removed when adding a new roll of towels.

A holder for paper towels is an essential accessory in any kitchen. But that doesn't mean you need to hang something ugly on your wall. Instead, make this country-style oak towel bar that can be mounted horizontally, as shown, or vertically on the wall.

Begin by cutting out the blanks for the sides (A) and back (B). Then lay out the pattern for them. Drill the holes into the side pieces with a spade bit. Use a drill press or drill guide to ensure a hole that is perpendicular to the wood's surface.

MATERIALS LIST
1"-dia. dowel
Doorknobs (2)
No. 10 × 1-1/2" wood screws
1/2"-dia. plugs
Wood glue

CUTTING LIST		
KEY	**PIECES**	**SIZE AND DESCRIPTION**
A	2	3/4 × 5-1/4 × 5-3/4 sides
B	1	3/4 × 5 × 13-1/2 back

Drill a starter hole and cut out the long slot with a saber saw. A bench vise does a nice job of holding the work while sawing.

File the dowel hole to smooth the scratches left by drilling. Filing will enlarge the hole enough to allow the dowel to slide easily.

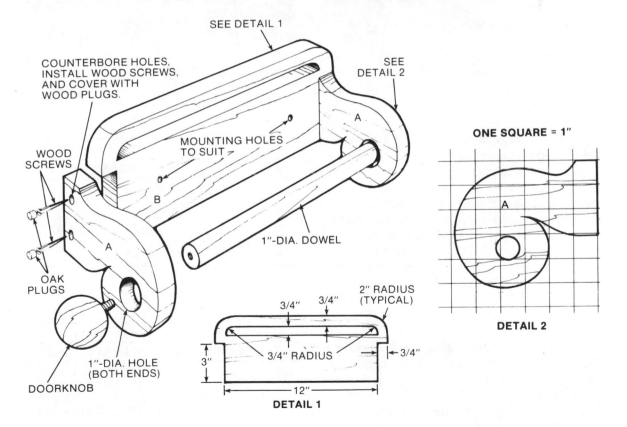

SEE DETAIL 1

COUNTERBORE HOLES,
INSTALL WOOD SCREWS,
AND COVER WITH
WOOD PLUGS.

SEE
DETAIL 2

WOOD
SCREWS

MOUNTING HOLES
TO SUIT

A

B

1"-DIA. DOWEL

OAK
PLUGS

A

1"-DIA. HOLE
(BOTH ENDS)

DOORKNOB

ONE SQUARE = 1"

A

DETAIL 2

3/4"   3/4"

2" RADIUS
(TYPICAL)

3/4" RADIUS

3/4"

3"

12"

DETAIL 1

Cranberry Scoop —

Build it large or build it small; both sizes of the cranberry scoop are attractive and useful examples of the craftsman's skill. Scoops such as these have been in use for centuries and continue to be used to harvest cranberry crops simply by running the comb edge through the plants. They make great country conversation pieces, or can serve practical purposes. The miniature can be used as a wall planter; the larger is suited for use as a magazine rack next to your favorite chair. The smaller is made from 1/4" stock, except for the handle, which is 1/2". The larger one is made of 1/2" stock throughout. Backs (A) are of one piece; the slots are cut into them by making parallel saw cuts. Shape the pointed teeth with a rasp, then assemble with brads and glue. Fasten handles (E) with glue and screws, attaching them before fastening the fronts.

CUTTING LIST (Small Scoop)		
KEY	**PIECES**	**SIZE AND DESCRIPTION**
A	1	1/4 × 8 × 8-1/2 back
B	2	1/4 × 2-1/2 × 8-1/2 sides
C	1	1/4 × 2-3/4 × 8-1/2 front
D	1	1/4 × 2-1/2 × 8 bottom (not shown)
E	1	1/2 × 2 × 5-1/2 handle

CUTTING LIST (Large Scoop)		
KEY	**PIECES**	**SIZE AND DESCRIPTION**
A	1	1/2 × 15 × 15-1/2 back
B	2	1/2 × 4 × 15 sides
C	1	1/2 × 7-1/2 × 16-1/2 front
D	1	1/2 × 4 × 15-1/2 bottom (not shown)
E	1	1/2 × 2-1/2 × 8 handle

MATERIALS LIST

Wood Screws
Brads
Wood glue

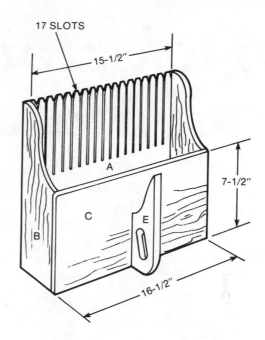

17 SLOTS

15-1/2"

7-1/2"

16-1/2"

A

B

C

E

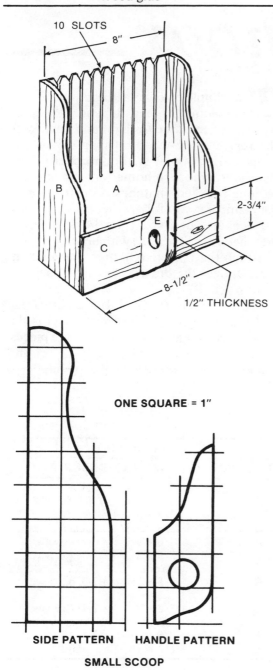

10 SLOTS

8"

B

A

C

E

2-3/4"

8-1/2"

1/2" THICKNESS

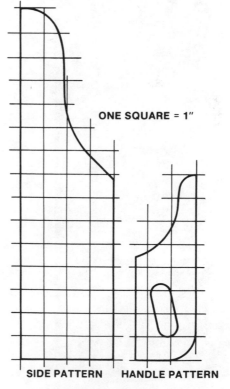

ONE SQUARE = 1"

SIDE PATTERN   HANDLE PATTERN

SMALL SCOOP

ONE SQUARE = 1"

SIDE PATTERN   HANDLE PATTERN

LARGE SCOOP

Wick Holder and Matchbox

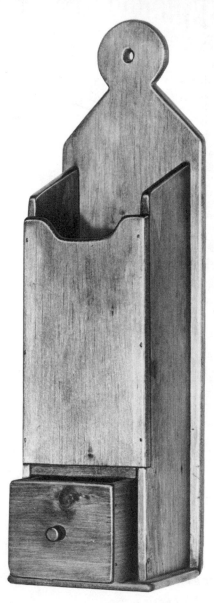

T his simple box was a ubiquitous fixture in colonial homes, dependent as they were on open flame for light and heat. With the regrowth of wood-burning stoves and fireplaces in popularity, they are useful additions in the modern home for storing wicks or long-handled matches. Construction is very simple if you follow these instructions.

Pieces are cut to size, then the sides (B) are attached to the back (A) with brads and glue.

Attach the bottom (C), then the small insert (D) over the drawer. Finally, attach the front piece (E).

Drawer pieces (F, G, H, I) are cut to size and glued together. The front panel is dadoed on the edges to receive the side pieces.

Cut the drawer knob from a dowel and shape with a wood rasp or sharp knife.

CUTTING LIST		
KEY	**PIECES**	**SIZE AND DESCRIPTION**
A	1	3/8 × 4 × 15 back
B	2	3/8 × 3 × 10-7/8 sides
C	1	3/8 × 3-1/4 × 4 bottom
D	1	3/8 × 2-3/4 × 3 insert
E	1	3/8 × 3-1/2 × 6-1/2 front
F	1	3/8 × 2-5/8 × 2-3/4 drawer front
G	1	3/8 × 1-7/8 × 2-3/4 drawer back
H	2	3/8 × 2-3/4 × 2-3/4 drawer sides
I	1	3/8 × 1-7/8 × 2-1/4 drawer bottom

MATERIALS LIST

3/8"-dia. dowel
Brads
Wood glue

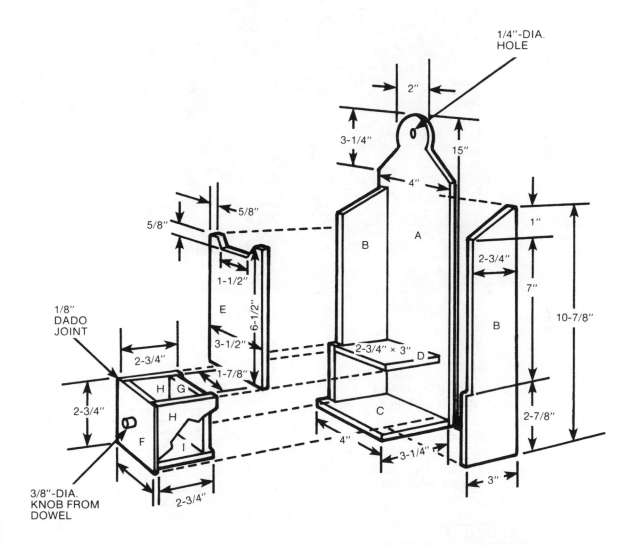

Wall Caddy

This wall caddy is a delight to make. Just be sure to bevel the hinge side of the lid (A) and the top edge of the front panel (E). A rabbet joint is shown for the drawer face (G) for variety's sake, but you can make a butt joint if it's more convenient. The remainder of the joints used in construction are glued and nailed butt joints.

MATERIALS LIST

Hinges
Brass drawer pull
Finishing nails
Wood glue

CUTTING LIST

KEY	PIECES	SIZE AND DESCRIPTION
A	1	1/2 × 5-1/2 × 14 lid
B	1	1/2 × 1-1/2 × 14 top
C	2	1/2 × 6 × 14 sides
D	1	1/4 × 13 × 14 back (plywood)
E	1	1/2 × 6 × 13 front panel
F1	1	1/2 × 5-3/4 × 13 shelf
F2	1	1/2 × 5-1/4 × 13 shelf
G	1	1/2 × 4 × 13 drawer face
H	1	1/2 × 4 × 12 drawer back
I	2	1/2 × 4 × 5-1/2 drawer sides
J	1	1/8 × 4-3/4 × 12 drawer bottom (plywood)

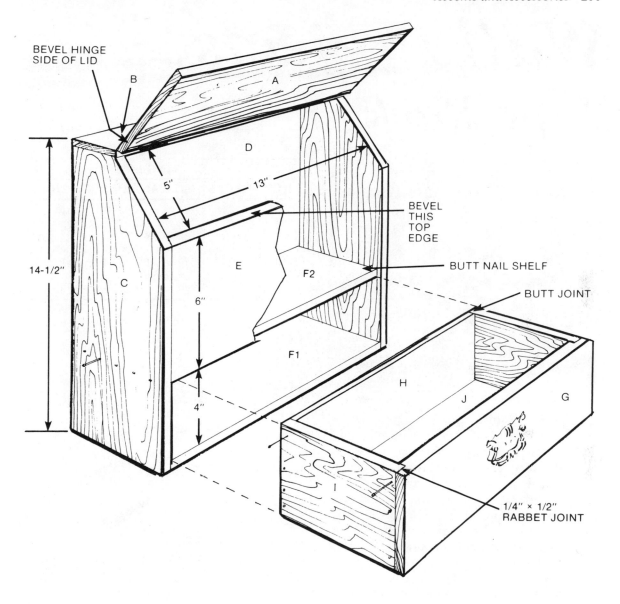

BEVEL HINGE
SIDE OF LID

B

A

D

5"

13"

BEVEL
THIS
TOP
EDGE

14-1/2"

C

E

F2

BUTT NAIL SHELF

6"

BUTT JOINT

F1

H

J

G

4"

I

1/4" × 1/2"
RABBET JOINT

Wall Projects
Pipe Rack

CUTTING LIST		
KEY	**PIECES**	**SIZE AND DESCRIPTION**
A	2	1/2 × 4-1/2 × 10-1/4 sides
B	1	1/2 × 1-1/2 × 10-1/2 top crossbar
C	2	1/2 × 4-1/2 × 10-1/2 shelves
D	2	1/2 × 3-1/2 × 4-1/2 shelf dividers
E	3	1/2 × 3 × 3-1/2 drawer fronts

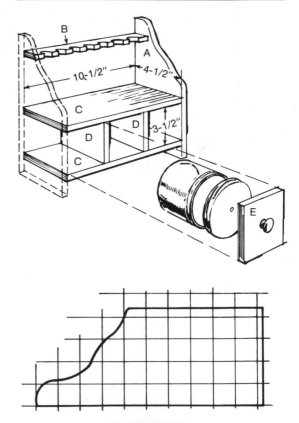

SIDE PATTERN
ONE SQUARE = 1"

Made to order for a pipe-smoking friend, this is a place where he'll be able to store his favorite pipes and tobaccos. The false drawers are deceiving; the fronts (E) conceal small food jars about 3" in diameter with screw caps. Drill a small hole through the cap and fasten it to the front with the same screw that holds the drawer pull in place. To make the pipe rack, use 1/2" stock and butt joints throughout. Assemble with brads and glue. The crossbar (B) has 1/2" × 1/2" notches spaced at 1-1/2" intervals, beginning 3/4" from the end of the crossbar.

MATERIALS LIST
Drawer pulls
Brads
Jars with screw caps
Screws
Wood glue

Spice Shelf with Rack

CUTTING LIST		
KEY	**PIECES**	**SIZE AND DESCRIPTION**
A	1	1/2 × 5-1/2 × 11-1/2 top
B	2	1/2 × 4-1/2 × 15 sides
C	2	1/2 × 4-1/2 × 11-1/2 shelves

This is a piece at home in any kitchen. The shelves (C) display the spices, and the dowel is removable so that a roll of paper towels can be placed on it. To make the spice rack, cut all pieces to size from 1/2″ stock and fasten together with butt joints and brads and glue. Drill the dowel at both ends, making a 1/4″ hole all the way through. In one hole, glue a 1/4″ peg. In the other, fit another peg that's been sanded to a taper. It should fit tightly, but must be easily removable. To remove the dowel from the rack, withdraw the tapered peg and slide the dowel out.

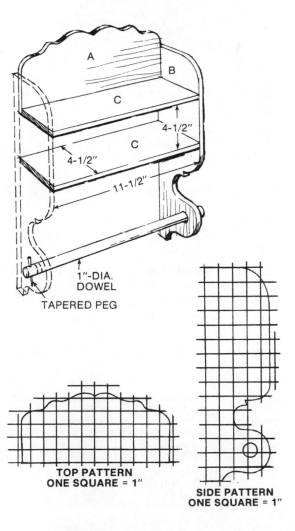

1″-DIA. DOWEL

TAPERED PEG

TOP PATTERN
ONE SQUARE = 1″

SIDE PATTERN
ONE SQUARE = 1″

MATERIALS LIST

1/4″-dia. dowel pegs
1″-dia. dowel
Brads
Wood glue

Fisherman's Friend with Rack

CUTTING LIST		
KEY	**PIECES**	**SIZE AND DESCRIPTION**
A	1	1/4 × 8-1/2 × 15-1/4 back
B	2	1/4 × 4-1/2 × 12 sides
C	4	1/4 × 4-1/2 × 8 shelves
D	3	1/4 × 1-5/8 × 8-1/4 drawer fronts
E	3	1/4 × 1-3/8 × 7-1/2 drawer backs
F	6	1/4 × 1-3/8 × 4-1/2 drawer sides
G	3	1/4 × 4-1/4 × 7-1/2 drawer bottoms

The fisherman's friend is well worth the small effort required for its simple construction. The drawers are for hooks, feathers, dressing, and all the other apparatus of the fisherman. Call it a fly tier's cabinet and you'll get the idea. It will hold all the supplies the avid sportsman needs. The drawers (D, E, F, G) can be made as shown or subdivided into small compartments. The pegged dowel across the bottom holds the spools of thread used for tying lures. Quarter-inch stock is used throughout. The 1"-diameter dowel is held in place with 3/4" wood screws driven through the sides (B). Glue and small brads are used with butt joints everywhere else. The 1/4"-diameter pegs on the dowel are 2" long, glued into 1/2"-deep holes in the dowel.

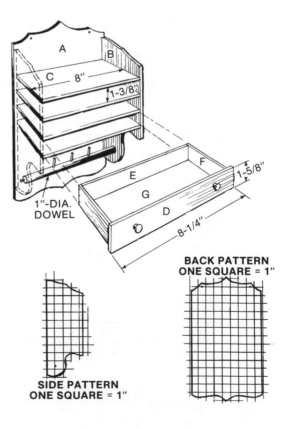

MATERIALS LIST

1/4"-dia. dowel pegs
1"-dia. dowel
3/4" wood screws
Brads
Porcelain drawer knobs
Wood glue

Spice Chest

CUTTING LIST		
KEY	**PIECES**	**SIZE AND DESCRIPTION**
A	1	1/2 × 18 × 28 top
B	2	1 × 7 × 25-1/2 sides
C1	3	1 × 7 × 19 shelves
C2	1	1 × 8-3/8 × 19 top shelf
D	4	1/2 × 2-1/2 × 22 door frame sides
E	4	1/2 × 2-1/2 × 6 top and bottom frames
F	2	1/4 × 6-1/2 × 16-1/2 door panels (plywood)
G	2	1 × 1-1/2 × 19 base front and back
H	2	1 × 1-1/2 × 7 base sides

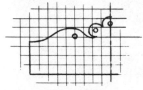

TOP PATTERN
ONE SQUARE = 1"

The doors on this spice chest are beveled panels in a tongue-and-groove assembly. The chest is built with the shelves (C1) ripped to a width of 7". The top shelf (C2) is 8-3/8" wide, with a bead routed along the front edge as shown. Door frames (D, E) are 1 × 3s grooved to receive 1/4" plywood panels (F). Grooves are cut with a dado blade or kerfed on a table saw. The doors are rabbeted to overlap and are recessed into a rabbet on the top shelf as shown. Secure the base (G, H) with glue and finishing nails. Attach molding of your choice to the base as shown.

MATERIALS LIST

Nails
Molding
Hinges
Doorknobs
Wood glue

*Hanging Cabinet_*

the bottom two shelves as shown. Attach the shelf trim (B) with finishing nails.

The drawers are constructed in the butt style. Hardwood drawer pulls can either be purchased or formed from scrap stock. Finish the cabinet as desired, after first sanding it with 220-grit paper.

CUTTING LIST		
KEY	**PIECES**	**SIZE AND DESCRIPTION**
A	1	1/4 × 18 × 22 back (plywood)
B	2	1/2 × 2 × 18 shelf trim
C	4	1/2 × 4 × 18 shelves
D	2	1/2 × 4 × 22 sides
E	1	1/2 × 3 × 4 divider
F	2	1/2 × 3 × 8-1/4 drawer fronts
G	2	1/2 × 3 × 7-1/4 drawer backs
H	4	1/2 × 3 × 3 drawer sides
I	2	1/2 × 3 × 7-1/4 drawer bottoms

Hanging cabinets gained popularity when the American pioneers, having become settled in their new environment, were able to give some attention to decorating their homes. Here is an easily copied example that will look good most anywhere in the home.

Cut all the components as shown. The shelves (C) are glued into 1/4″ dadoes in the sides (D). The divider (E) is set into dadoes in

MATERIALS LIST
Drawer pulls (2)
Finishing nails
220-grit sandpaper
Wood glue

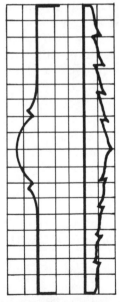

BACK AND SHELF TRIM PATTERNS
ONE SQUARE = 1″

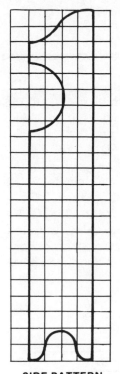

SIDE PATTERN

ONE SQUARE = 1"

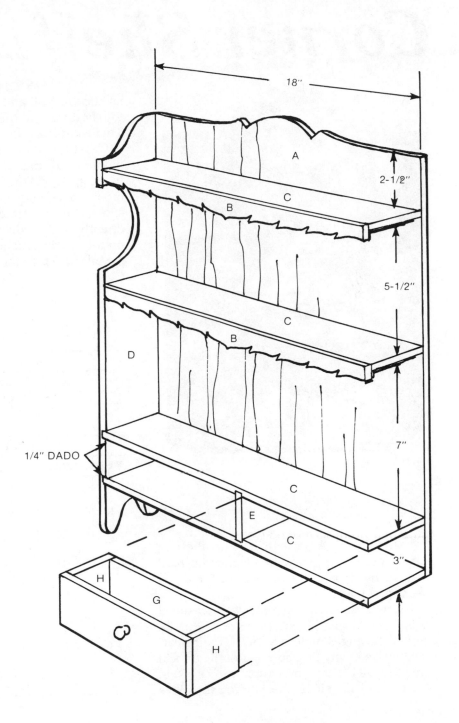

18"

A

2-1/2"

C

B

5-1/2"

C

B

D

7"

1/4" DADO

C

E

C

3"

H

G

H

Corner Shelf

as shown. Nail and glue the back (L) to the top, bottom, and the back edges of the sides. This completes the basic box.

Cut the two shelves (D), trimmed to pointed ends to fit exactly the confines of the interior, supporting them with cleats (E, F) on the back and on the short bar of the L sides. Cut and attach the front trim (G, H) directly to the edges of the sides, top, and bottom, adding, at last, the five strips of horizontal trim (I, J) and the crown or head piece (K).

MATERIALS LIST

Finishing nails
Wood glue

CUTTING LIST

KEY	PIECES	SIZE AND DESCRIPTION
A	2	1/2 × 6 × 35 angled sides, narrow pieces
B	2	1/2 × 20 × 35 angled sides, wide pieces
C	2	1/2 × 19 × 41 six-sided top and bottom
D	2	1/2 × 18 × 40 shelves
E	2	1/2 × 2 × 16 back cleats
F	4	1/2 × 2 × 20 side cleats
G	1	1/2 × 2-1/2 × 18 front trim, top
H	2	1/2 × 3 × 35 trim
I	1	1/2 × 1 × 35 trim
J	4	1/2 × 1 × 6 trim
K	1	1/2 × 5 × 35 crown
L	1	1/2 × 16 × 35 back (plywood)

This Early American corner shelf is especially practical for displaying small articles because of the absence of the usual V-shaped back.

Use 1/2″ stock throughout—well-seasoned beech, pine, maple, cherry, or ash. Put together the angled sides (A, B) first, fabricating two L's. (Only the short bars of the L's will show.) Nail the top and bottom pieces (C) to the ends of the sides, overlapping the sides

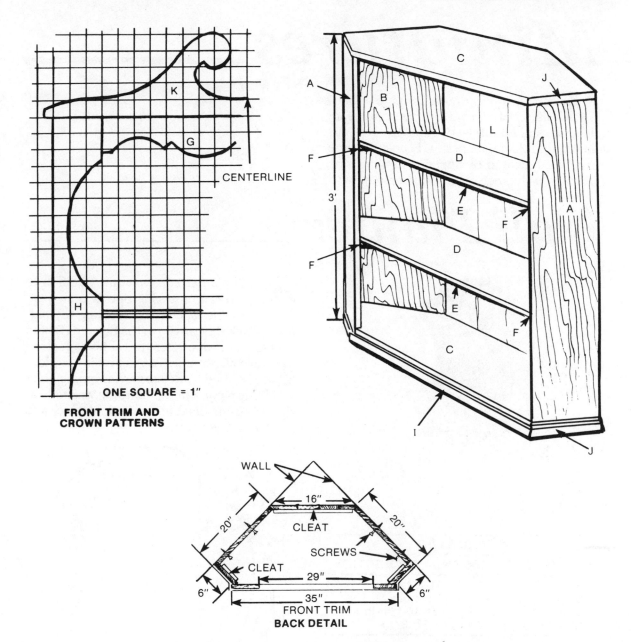

CENTERLINE

ONE SQUARE = 1"

**FRONT TRIM AND
CROWN PATTERNS**

3'

WALL

16"

CLEAT

20"

20"

SCREWS

CLEAT

29"

6"

35"

6"

FRONT TRIM

BACK DETAIL

Miniatures

With a minimum amount of tools, materials, and effort, you can create these lasting country-style tokens. The soft patina that distinguishes early colonial pine can be duplicated by applying antique pine stain on each piece after it's complete.

Wall Planter

A wall planter is a welcome addition to any room, and this one is a snap to make. Cut the pieces to size using the patterns. Tack the rail (D) to the bottom (B) and drill the 1/4"-diameter dowel holes togther to insure alignment. The hearts in the sides (C) are formed by drilling overlapping holes and filing a point in the bottom. Assemble as shown using finishing nails and glue, and sand all edges round.

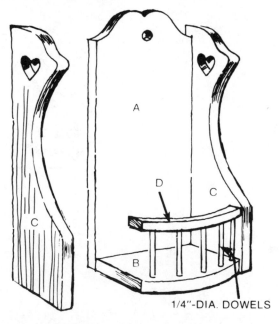

1/4"-DIA. DOWELS

CUTTING LIST

KEY	PIECES	SIZE AND DESCRIPTION
A	1	1/2 × 5 × 11-1/4 back
B	1	1/2 × 4 × 5 bottom
C	2	1/2 × 3-1/2 × 10-1/4 sides
D	1	1/2 × 1/2 × 5 rail

MATERIALS LIST

1/4"-dia. dowels
Finishing nails
180-grit sandpaper
Wood glue

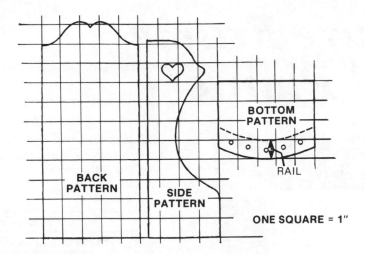

BACK
PATTERN

SIDE
PATTERN

BOTTOM
PATTERN

RAIL

ONE SQUARE = 1"

Tote Box Serving Tray

You select the curves that lend grace to this tote box serving tray. Cut all the pieces to size. The uprights (C) are tapered at a slight 6° angle as shown. Drill 3/4"-diameter holes for the handle with the uprights tacked together to assure alignment. Assemble the tray with butt joints as shown, using wood glue and finishing nails for sturdy construction. Horseshoe nails in the handle add a rustic touch.

CUTTING LIST

KEY	PIECES	SIZE AND DESCRIPTION
A	2	3/4 × 3-1/4 × 8-7/8 sides
B	2	3/4 × 3-1/4 × 21-5/8 sides
C	2	3/4 × 8-7/8 × 14-1/2 uprights
D	5	1/4 × 1-1/4 × 21-5/8 slats

MATERIALS LIST

3/4"-dia. dowel
Finishing nails
Horseshoe nails
Wood glue

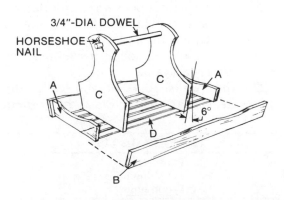

3/4"-DIA. DOWEL

HORSESHOE
NAIL

Picture Frame Wall Planter

and glue and nail the trim to the box. The half-round molding, cut to fit, is attached with finishing nails.

CUTTING LIST

KEY	PIECES	SIZE AND DESCRIPTION
A	2	1/2 × 2-5/8 × 8 box top and bottom
B	2	1/2 × 2-5/8 × 13 box sides
C	1	1/2 × 4 × 8 back
D	2	1/2 × 3-1/2 × 14-1/2 trim
E	2	1/2 × 3-1/2 × 17 trim
F	2	1/2 × 7-3/4 frame (half-round molding)
G	2	1/2 × 10-1/2 frame (half-round molding)
H	4	1/2 × 5 frame (half-round molding)

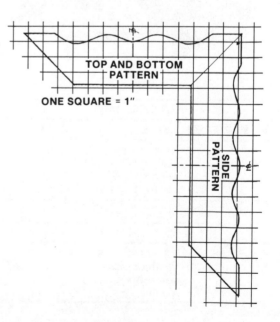

TOP AND BOTTOM PATTERN

ONE SQUARE = 1"

SIDE PATTERN

This wall planter boasts a unique design. The basic box (A, B) is built first, with the back (C) nailed in place as shown. The plant box should be noncorrosive metal or plastic and removable.

Cut the trim pieces (D, E) and scallop the edges in pairs to match. Bevel the corners

MATERIALS LIST

Plant box
Finishing nails
Wood glue

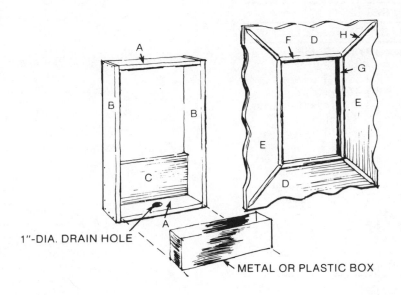

1"-DIA. DRAIN HOLE

METAL OR PLASTIC BOX

Hanging Cabinet _____

This miniature cabinet is quite a conversation piece. The sides (A) are laid out first. Cut 3/8" dadoes on 3-9/16" centers

in both sides to accommodate the shelves (G) and the horizontal dividers (H), as shown in the drawing. Add the back (B, C), nailing and gluing the pieces to the sides, shelves, and dividers.

Cut the parts for one drawer after the cabinet is together. Use these as models for the other drawers. The metal grill is nailed across the back. The trim is nailed and glued at the top (D), bottom (E), and front (F). Tiny drawer pulls are attached as shown to enable the cabinet to be hung.

MATERIALS LIST
Doorknobs (8)
Metal grill
Drawer pulls
Finishing nails
Wood glue

CUTTING LIST

KEY	PIECES	SIZE AND DESCRIPTION
A	2	3/8 × 3-1/8 × 17 sides
B	2	3/8 × 4 × 13-1/2 back
C	2	3/8 × 2-1/2 × 8 back
D	1	3/8 × 3 × 16 top trim
E	1	3/8 × 1-1/2 × 16 bottom trim
F	1	3/8 × 2 × 8 front trim
G	2	3/8 × 3-1/8 × 16 shelves
H	6	3/8 × 3-1/8 × 3-1/2 dividers
I	2	3/8 × 3-1/8 × 13-1/2 dividers
J	8	3/8 × 2-7/8 × 3-1/4 drawer fronts
K	8	3/8 × 2-1/2 × 2-7/8 drawer backs
L	16	3/8 × 2-3/4 × 2-7/8 drawer sides
M	8	3/8 × 2-3/4 × 3-1/4 drawer bottoms

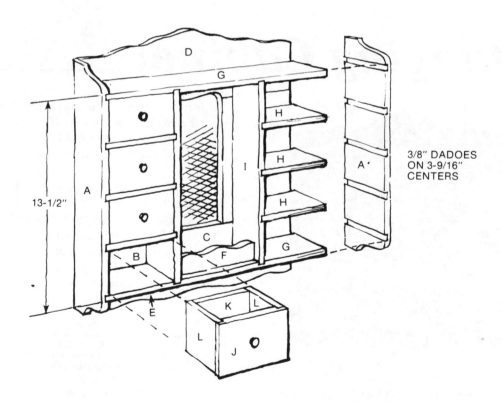

3/8" DADOES
ON 3-9/16"
CENTERS

Switch Plate

Assembly of this switch plate is easy. To begin, first cut the back **(A)** from masonite or a similar hardboard. Mark and cut out openings for the wall switch and screws. To make the square opening for the switch, drill a starter hole, then cut with a coping saw. Use the pattern to cut the sides **(C)**.

The handle is turned from a 1″-diameter dowel. Before assembling the switch plate, drill a 3/8″-diameter hole in the center of the bottom **(B)** and the handle for a dowel. At-

tach the handle by gluing and inserting the dowel. Attach the bottom, sides, and front **(D)** to the back as shown, using wood glue and finishing nails.

Use a wood rasp and 180-grit sandpaper to get that handmade antique look. Brass pins furnish a final touch.

MATERIALS LIST

3/8″-dia. dowel
1″-dia. dowel
Finishing nails
180-grit sandpaper
Brass pins (2)
Wood glue

CUTTING LIST

KEY	PIECES	SIZE AND DESCRIPTION
A	1	1/8 × 4 × 7-1/2 back hardboard)
B	1	1/2 × 1-1/2 × 3-1/2 bottom
C	2	1/2 × 2-1/8 × 6-1/4 sides
D	1	1/2 × 2-1/2 × 4 front

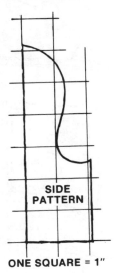

SIDE PATTERN

ONE SQUARE = 1″

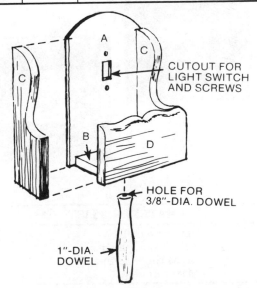

CUTOUT FOR LIGHT SWITCH AND SCREWS

HOLE FOR 3/8″-DIA. DOWEL

1″-DIA. DOWEL

Plaques

Deliberate crudeness in the construction of these plaques adds to their appeal. Cutting lists are provided for two different sizes; you may wish to make modifications to suit your own taste.

Blunt the corners of the outer frame molding (A) with 80-grit sandpaper. Fasten the outer frame by driving small finishing nails into the face of the plywood backing (B).

On the large plaque, narrow molding (C), mitered at the corners, adds to the quiet beauty of the flying ducks on the ceramic

CUTTING LIST (Small Plaque)		
KEY	**PIECES**	**SIZE AND DESCRIPTION**
A	4	3/8 × 7/8 × 9 outer frame (molding)
B	1	1/4 × 9 × 9 backing (plywood)
C	4	3/4 × 3/4 × 3 inner frame

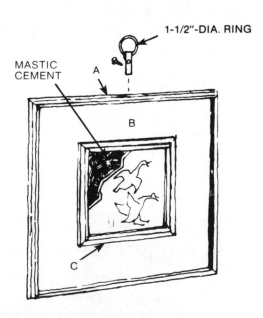

MATERIALS LIST

Finishing nails
80-grit sandpaper
Brass ring and metal strip
Mastic cement

tile. The small plaque utilizes 3/4" flat stock (C) to make the inner frame. Bend a narrow strip of thin metal around a brass ring to mount the plaques.

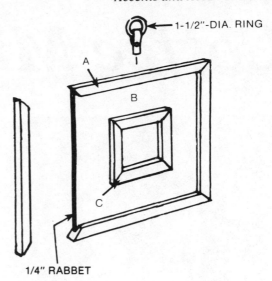

CUTTING LIST (Large Plaque)		
KEY	**PIECES**	**SIZE AND DESCRIPTION**
A	4	3/8 × 3/8 × 12 outer frame (molding)
B	1	1/4 × 12 × 12 backing (plywood)
C	4	1/2 × 1/2 × 6 inner frame (molding)

Coffee Mill

This cherry wood project reproduces the design of a 19th century coffee mill and, best of all, it really works.

The box and drawer are assembled with finger or box joints. The increased glue area makes this a very strong joint, although it's used here primarily for visual appeal.

The joint is not difficult to make, although it calls for accurately spaced notches and fingers of uniform width. The procedure can be used equally well on a variety of other projects, such as drawers, chests, and boxes.

Using a simple jig on a table saw, begin by cutting all the stock to size; then replace the saw blade with a dado head set up for a 1/4"-wide and 1/2"-deep cut. Attach a fresh piece of wood to the miter gauge with screws and nuts, then make a pass to cut a notch into it.

Next, apply a piece of masking tape to the table, positioned so that it bridges the notch in the fence. Accurately mark the tape to indicate the cutting path. Unscrew the fence from the miter gauge and draw a pencil mark exactly 1/4" away from the edge of the notch (toward the end opposite the miter gauge). Position this mark on the tape mark so you can make a second notch cut, spaced 1/4" from the first. Make the cut, then erase the pencil mark.

Turn the fence upside down and glue a 1/4" × 1/2" block into the second notch. This block should be long enough so it projects a little more than twice the thickness of the work. Use a square to accurately draw two pencil lines, one through the center of the first notch and a second centered between each notch. Attach the fence to the miter gauge so that it is in its original position. This completes the setup of the jig.

Make test cuts in two scraps of wood by placing the previously cut notch over the guide block. If the test pieces mate properly, you can proceed with the work. If not, it will be an indication that the guide block is not correctly located.

Break off a finger from the test piece to use as a spacer. Hold a back (B) and side (A) member together, offset side to side by the thickness of the spacer. Use a few strips of masking tape to keep the mated pieces from shifting. Place them against the fence.

Align the edge of the projecting back member with the centerline between the notches in the fence; then clamp the work to

---

MATERIALS LIST

Coffee mill mechanism
Drawer knob
No. 6 × 1" wood screws
Wood glue

CUTTING LIST

KEY	PIECES	SIZE AND DESCRIPTION
A	2	1/2 × 4-1/2 × 5-1/4 side
B	1	1/2 × 4-1/2 × 5-1/4 back
C	1	1/2 × 2-3/8 × 5-1/4 front
D	1	1/2 × 6-1/2 × 6-1/2 base
E	1	1/2 × 2-1/8 × 4-3/16 drawer front
F	2	1/2 × 1-7/8 × 4-3/4 drawer side
G	1	1/2 × 1-7/8 × 4-3/16 drawer back
H	1	1/8 × 3-15/16 × 4-1/2 drawer bottom (plywood)

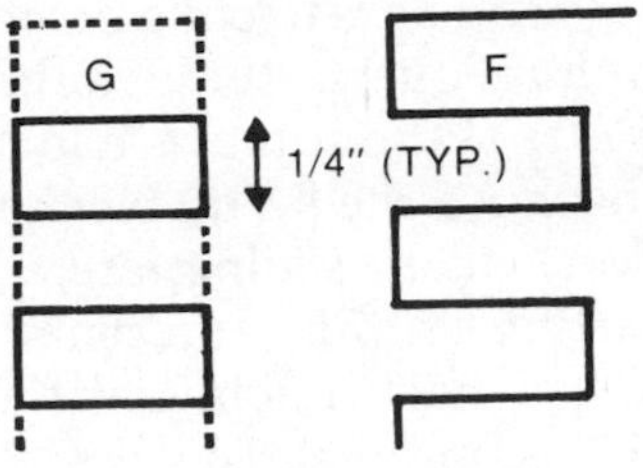

G F 1/4" (TYP.)

DETAIL 1

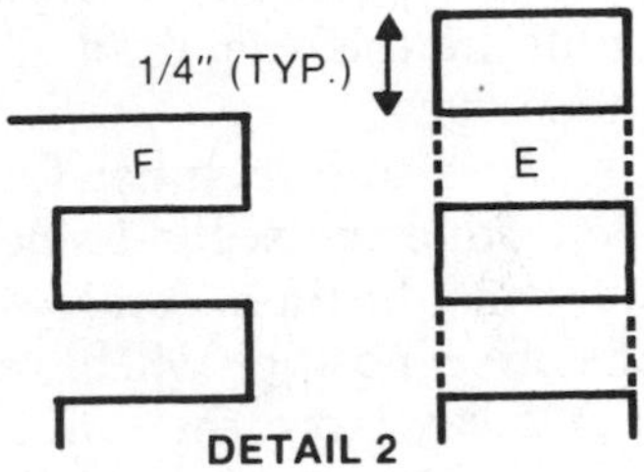

1/4" (TYP.) F E

DETAIL 2

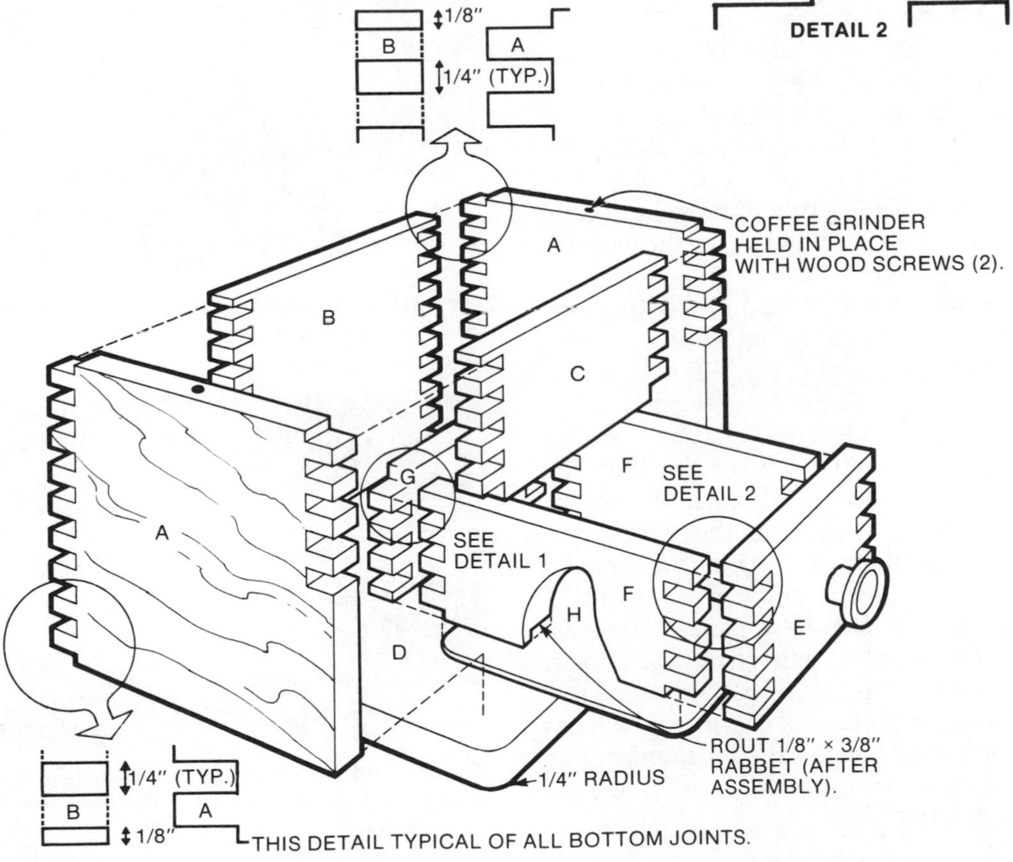

B A 1/8" 1/4" (TYP.)

COFFEE GRINDER HELD IN PLACE WITH WOOD SCREWS (2).

A B C G F SEE DETAIL 2 SEE DETAIL 1 H F E D

ROUT 1/8" × 3/8" RABBET (AFTER ASSEMBLY).

1/4" RADIUS

B A 1/4" (TYP.) 1/8"

THIS DETAIL TYPICAL OF ALL BOTTOM JOINTS.

the fence. Make a pass to cut a notch in both pieces simultaneously. Remove the clamp. The remainder of the cuts are made without clamping because the guide block will prevent the work from sliding laterally. Note that by starting on the centerline between the notches, a half notch and finger are formed. This is optional. To start with a full notch, simply disregard the line and snug the work up to the guide block to make the first cut.

Place the previously cut notch over the guide block to position the work for the next cut. Continue this step until all the notches have been cut.

Detach the side member from the back member. Tape the second side member to the back to make the second set of cuts. This time the offset position will be reversed—the member away from the fence will extend; therefore, align the edge of the setback member with the other centerline, the one directly over the notch in the fence.

Repeat the procedure with the front piece (C), alternately taped to one side member, then to the other. Here you must be sure to cut only enough notches to span the width of the front member.

Since glue must be applied to so many surfaces, a slow-setting hide glue is recommended for assembling the joints.

The bottom of the drawer is rabbeted to receive a plywood panel (H). Use a router with a 3/8" rabbeting bit for this cut. The resulting rounded inside corners can be squared with a chisel, but this is optional. You can leave the corners round, and round the corners of the insert panel to match.

Sand the box and base panel before assembly, then apply the finish of your choice.

Attach the grinding mechanism to the box with two screws. Made of cast iron which has a rich gray-black color, the mechanism can be used as is or you may opt to give it an antique white finish.

To obtain the antiqued finish, apply several light coats of antique white spray enamel to the cast iron, allowing each coat to dry thoroughly. Follow with a brushed-on coat of gold paint. Do not allow the gold paint to dry. Dampen a cloth lightly with paint thinner, roll it into a small, tight pad, and wipe the gold paint off the high spots of the relief design and the wood handle. Treat the drawer knob in the same manner. The result will be a warm, white highlighting nicely complemented by the gold in the depressed areas.

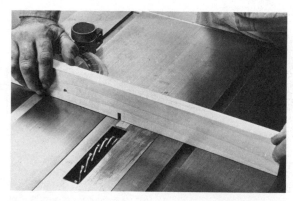

Attach a wood fence to the miter gauge; make a dadoed notch and mark the notch location on masking tape.

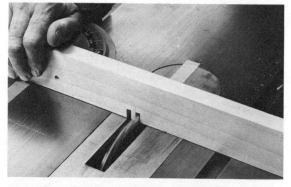

Detach and shift the fence 1/4" to the right by using the tape to mark the slot location. Cut a second notch.

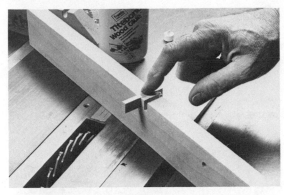

Glue a guide block into the second notch. It must be sized exactly the same as the notch in thickness and width.

Use protective wood pads and two clamps for each assembly. Check for squareness—an off-center clamp axis can cause problems.

Use a scrap finger from a test piece as a guide to offset a back and side member 1/4". Tape to maintain alignment.

To cut the rabbet for the drawer bottom panel, use a rabbeting bit. Round the corners of the bottom to fit.

Align the edge with the centerline nearest the guide block. Use a clamp to make the first notch.

A wing nut holds the grinding mechanism together. The top is held in place with two wood screws.

Collectors' Cabinet

Wood substitutions include pine, cherry, maple, or birch, all of which will buff to a rich luster with the finish of your choice. Stock varies from 1" for the base to 3/4" for the sides, two-part top, door frame, and shelf supports to 1/4" for the shelves and back panel.

Dimensions shown can be used only as a guide if you want to alter the size or change the proportions to suit. The base (G) of this unit is 3-1/2" wide and 16-1/2" long; cove and bead molding are glued and nailed to the base, increasing the dimensions accordingly.

The same technique applies to the two-part top where a 4" × 16" underboard (B) is

With the exception of the hinged glass front, this collectors' cabinet bears a startling resemblance to the 19th century whatnot—a light, open set of shelves used in parlors for displaying bric-a-brac. But its origin as an early period medicine chest is underlined by its stout oak construction, a favorite stock of the time that held up well against the moisture of the bath. Possibly, the door front also contained a looking glass and served as one of the first wall-mounted shaving mirrors. As a showcase for collections, however, the cabinet is a smart choice.

MATERIALS LIST

Cove and bead molding
12-1/2 × 13-1/4" glass
Hinges
1/8"-dia. dowels
Wood screws
Wood glue

CUTTING LIST

KEY	PIECES	SIZE AND DESCRIPTION
A	1	3/4 × 4-1/2 × 17-1/2 overboard
B	1	3/4 × 4 × 16 underboard
C	1	1/4 × 16 × 17-1/4 back
D	2	3/4 × 2-3/4 × 17-1/4 sides
E	2	1/4 × 2-1/2 × 15 shelves
F	2	3/4 × 2-3/4 × 6 shelf supports
G	1	1 × 3-1/2 × 16-1/2 base
H	2	3/4 × 2 × 12-1/2 door frame
I	2	3/4 × 2 × 17-1/4 door frame

glued and screwed to a 4-1/2" × 17-1/2" overboard (A); the half-round and cove molding are added, as shown in the detail sketch. If you own or rent a router, you can make your own molding directly on the boards, but allow for the dimensional changes.

Cut the two 2-3/4" × 17-1/4" sides rabbeting the inside back edge of each 1/4" × 1/4". Secure the base to the sides with glue and countersunk screws through its underside. Cut the back (C) to fit, using glue and brads to secure it in the rabbets; the panel's top and bottom edges set flush with those of the sides. Fasten the preassembled top to the sides and backs with dowels and glue, positioning it flush with the back, and with equal overlap at the sides.

Cut the shelves (E) to fit flush with the front edges of the sides, joining them first to the supports. Then, slip the shelf unit into place at the desired height and secure it to the cabinet's sides with screws from the inside.

The door's outside dimensions should fit between the setback on the base and the top overlap with slight play. Rabbet the door frame (H, I) and install the glass. After staining and polishing, you may want to decorate the inside back panel with a fabric to complement your display. If so, staple or glue the cloth flush between shelves.

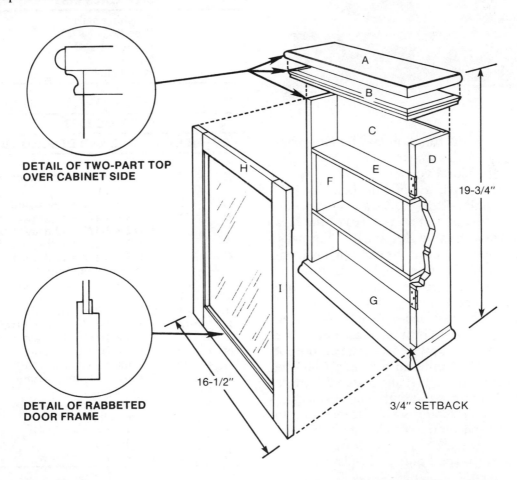

DETAIL OF TWO-PART TOP OVER CABINET SIDE

DETAIL OF RABBETED DOOR FRAME

16-1/2"

19-3/4"

3/4" SETBACK

Mirrored Chest

The frame around the mirror must have a backing (M) to help support the glass. The entire mirror assembly tilts on two wood screws that are set through knobs and uprights.

To add the finishing touch, cut the decorative scroll top (P) using the pattern provided. Nail it in place using a cleat (Q). Finish the chest to suit your taste.

MATERIALS LIST

Finishing nails
Wood screws (2)
Doorknobs (4)
Mirror
Wood glue

CUTTING LIST

KEY	PIECES	SIZE AND DESCRIPTION
A	2	1/2 × 9 × 15 top and bottom
B	2	1/2 × 8 × 13-1/2 box top and bottom
C	2	1/2 × 2-1/2 × 8 box sides
D	1	1/2 × 1-1/2 × 13 drawer front
E	1	1/2 × 1-1/2 × 12 drawer back
F	2	1/2 × 1-1/2 × 7 drawer sides
G	1	1/8 × 6-1/2 × 12 drawer bottom (masonite)
H	8	1/2 × 2 × 3 foot supports
I	4	3/4 × 1-1/2 × 1-1/2 feet
J	2	1 × 3-1/2 × 12 uprights
K	2	3/4 × 1-1/2 × 11 pivot frame
L	2	3/4 × 1-1/2 × 10 pivot frame
M	1	1/8 × 10 × 11 backing (masonite, not shown)
N	2	1 × 1 × 11 mirror frame (molding)
O	2	1 × 1 × 10 mirror frame (molding)
P	1	1/4 × 3 × 9 scroll top (plywood)
Q	1	3/4 × 1-1/2 × 9 cleat

Although its function may be somewhat altered, this shaving glass is still useful as well as decorative.

The first step is to build the box. Cut 1/4″ rabbets in the sides (C) as shown to accommodate the top and bottom (B) of the box. Assemble with wood glue and finishing nails. The top and bottom of the chest (A) are identical; a molding cutter can be used to shape their decorative edges. Use glue to secure the top and bottom to the box.

Cut the drawer pieces (D, E, F, G) to size and assemble with butt joints as shown. The detail drawing shows how each pair of foot supports (H) is mitered together. Glue the supports to the feet (I) and fasten the entire assembly to the chest with finishing nails.

The mirror requires two frames: one to enclose it and another to allow it to pivot. Cut the frame pieces (K, L, N, O) to size and assemble with wood glue and finishing nails.

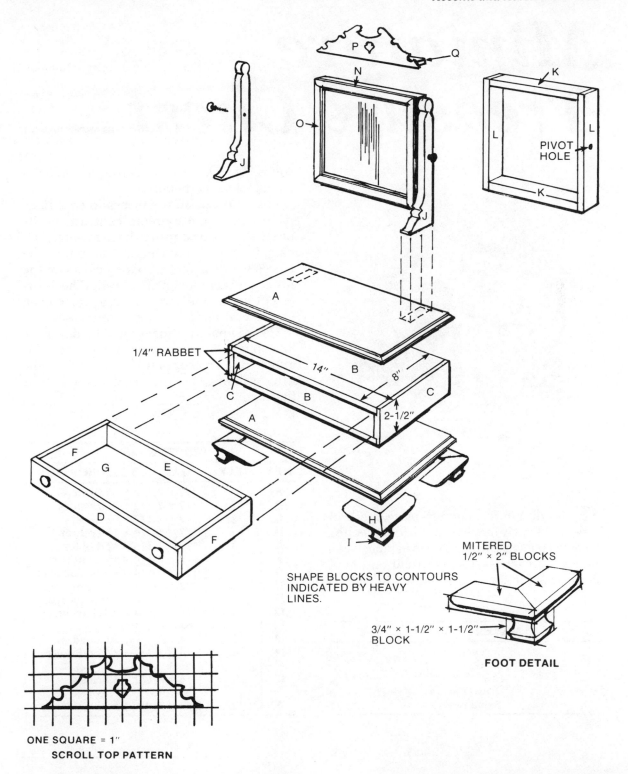

1/4" RABBET

14"

8"

B

C

2-1/2"

PIVOT
HOLE

K

L

L

K

N

O

P

Q

J

A

B

B

C

A

F

G

E

D

F

H

I

SHAPE BLOCKS TO CONTOURS
INDICATED BY HEAVY
LINES.

MITERED
1/2" × 2" BLOCKS

3/4" × 1-1/2" × 1-1/2"
BLOCK

FOOT DETAIL

ONE SQUARE = 1"

SCROLL TOP PATTERN

Miniature Treasure Chest

sories. Anywhere you keep it, it'll make a good-looking addition.

First, cut out all the pieces to size. Each piece can be cut by hand as it was in the original. (If you happen to have a router, you can dovetail the corners.) Assemble the pieces with triangular shaped cleats on the inside and countersink the brads. The drawer cutout is made with a jigsaw or coping saw after drilling the four corner holes.

The original trim edges were made with a hand plane. However, stock molding can be attached to the edges with glue and brads. After sanding, fill the brad holes before finishing.

This diminutive country piece, made of solid curly maple, once held someone's treasured jewels. Reproduced in pine, it can house your jewels, too. Or use it on top of your desk for stationery and writing acces-

MATERIALS LIST

Screws
Brads
Brass hinges
Drawer knob
Wood glue

CUTTING LIST

KEY	PIECES	SIZE AND DESCRIPTION
A	1	1/2 × 7-1/2 × 12 front
B	2	1/2 × 7-1/2 × 7-3/4 sides
C	1	1/2 × 7-1/2 × 12 back
D	1	1/2 × 6-3/4 × 11 bottom
E	1	1/2 × 7-3/4 × 12-1/4 top
F	1	1/2 × 2-1/4 × 13 front trim
G	2	1/2 × 2-1/4 × 8-3/4 side trim
H	1	1/2 × 6-3/4 × 11 inside shelf
I1	1	1/4 × 2 × 9-1/4 drawer front
I2	1	1/4 × 1-3/4 × 8-1/2 front backing strip
I3	2	1/4 × 2 × 7 drawer sides
I4	1	1/4 × 1-3/4 × 8-1/2 drawer back
I5	1	1/4 × 8-1/2 × 6 drawer bottom
J	2	3/4 × 3/4 × 7 drawer runners

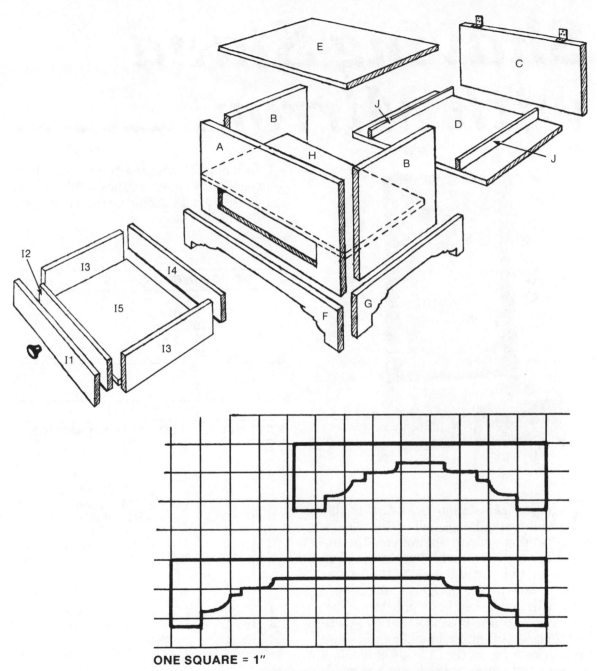

ONE SQUARE = 1"

FRONT AND SIDE TRIM PATTERNS

Shaving Stand with Mirror

Construct the chest and drawers with butt joints and miter joints as shown. Wood glue and finishing nails should be used to make a sturdy finished piece.

MATERIALS LIST
1/4"-dia. dowels (2)
Doorknobs (4)
Drawer pulls (4)
Finishing nails
Mirror

CUTTING LIST		
KEY	**PIECES**	**SIZE AND DESCRIPTION**
A	2	1/2 × 2 × 20-1/2 uprights (molding)
B	2	1/2 × 1 × 12 mirror frame
C	2	1/2 × 1 × 19 mirror frame
D	1	1/2 × 8 × 18-1/2 top
E	2	1/2 × 3-1/2 × 9 sides
F	1	1/2 × 9 × 18-1/2 bottom
G	2	1/2 × 2-1/2 × 9 dividers
H	2	1/2 × 3 × 4-1/4 drawer fronts (molding)
I	2	1/2 × 2-1/2 × 4-1/4 drawer backs
J	4	1/2 × 2-1/2 × 8 drawer sides
K	2	1/2 × 4-1/4 × 8 drawer bottoms
L	1	1/2 × 3 × 8 drawer front (molding, not shown)
M	1	1/2 × 2-1/2 × 8 drawer back
N	2	1/2 × 2-1/2 × 8 drawer sides
O	1	1/2 × 8 × 8 drawer bottom
P	8	1 × 1-1/4 × 2-1/2 feet (molding)

Strong, clean design is evident in this shaving stand, especially in the two uprights (A) that support the mirror. The uprights are made from 1/2" molding cut as shown in the pattern. Use 1/4"-diameter dowels to secure the uprights to the chest.

The two detail sketches highlight the special features of the project—four two-piece feet (P) made of mitered molding stock and three drawer fronts (H, L) made of molding stock and rabbetted at the joints. The molding you choose for the drawer fronts will, in turn, determine the curvature you'll want to duplicate for the sides (E) and the dividers (G).

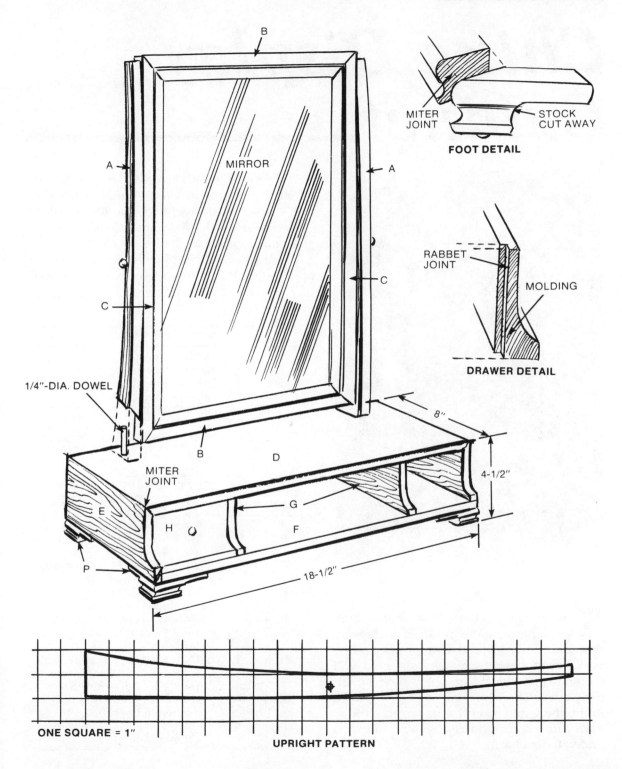

B

MITER
JOINT

STOCK
CUT AWAY

FOOT DETAIL

A

A

MIRROR

C

C

RABBET
JOINT

MOLDING

DRAWER DETAIL

1/4"-DIA. DOWEL

8"

B

MITER
JOINT

D

4-1/2"

E

G

H

F

P

18-1/2"

ONE SQUARE = 1"

UPRIGHT PATTERN

China Display Cabinet

Very little work is involved. The entire cabinet is made from knotty pine lumber. Use 1"-thick stock, except for the doors, which have a 3/4" × 1" frame and a standard trim molding nailed to the inside edge. Refer to the diagrams for cutting the scroll design on the side (B) and top (A) pieces and assemble

MATERIALS LIST

Staples or tacks
Welded wire fabric
1/4"-dia. dowel
Felt or plastic cloth
Finishing nails

CUTTING LIST

KEY	PIECES	SIZE AND DESCRIPTION
A	1	3/4 × 6-3/4 × 16-1/2 top
B	2	3/4 × 5-1/2 × 28-1/2 sides
C	1	3/4 × 5-1/2 × 18 bottom
D	1	3/4 × 1 × 19-1/2 bottom trim, front (cove molding)
E	2	3/4 × 1 × 6-1/4 bottom trim, sides (cove molding)
F	1	3/4 × 12 × 16-1/2 back
G	2	3/4 × 5-1/2 × 16-1/2 top and middle shelves
H	1	3/4 × 4 × 16-1/2 bottom shelf
I	4	3/4 × 1 × 6-5/8 door frame
J	4	3/4 × 1 × 12 door frame
K	4	3/4 × 3/4 × 6-5/8 door frame (trim molding)
L	4	3/4 × 3/4 × 10-1/2 door frame (trim molding)

This antique cabinet is an outstanding example of colonial craftsmanship and design. In colonial days, if you owned some very fine and expensive plates or china, you would proudly display them in such a cabinet. It was the best way of dressing up a home then, and it serves the purpose today even more appropriately, because time has added to its charm.

the cabinet as shown. The welded wire fabric is stapled or tacked to the back of the doors, and the bare ends are covered with felt strips or plastic cloth. Small plugs cut from doweling are glued over the nail heads at the sides, to add the look of authentic pegging.

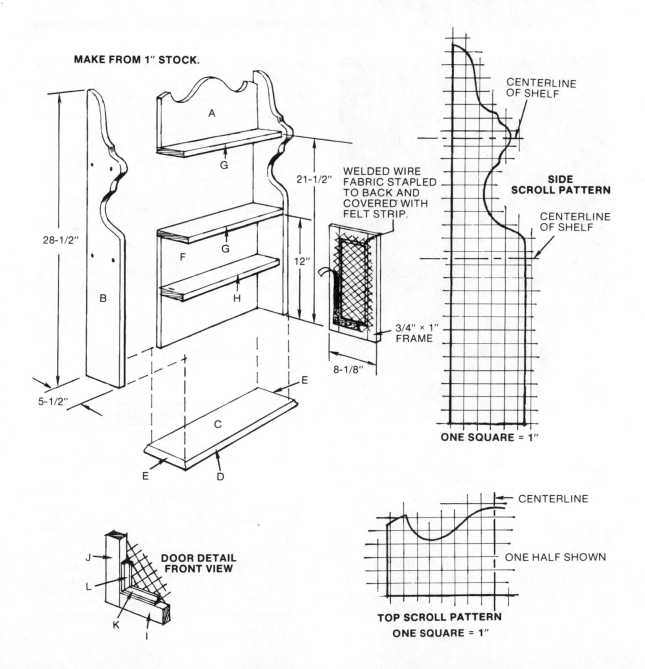

MAKE FROM 1" STOCK.

28-1/2"

5-1/2"

A

B

G

F

G

H

C

D

E

E

21-1/2"

12"

WELDED WIRE FABRIC STAPLED TO BACK AND COVERED WITH FELT STRIP.

3/4" × 1" FRAME

8-1/8"

CENTERLINE OF SHELF

SIDE SCROLL PATTERN

CENTERLINE OF SHELF

ONE SQUARE = 1"

J

L

K

I

DOOR DETAIL FRONT VIEW

CENTERLINE

ONE HALF SHOWN

TOP SCROLL PATTERN
ONE SQUARE = 1"

Wishing Well Planter

one block to each of the four straight sides of the floor board. Then glue and nail on the next layer of four blocks at 45° angles to the first as shown. Repeat the process until you've built a wall nine blocks high.

The two roof supports (C) are beveled at the tip to accommodate the gabling of the roof. Both are notched for a lap joint with the crossbars (D); the notches should be made approximately 6-1/2" from the tip of the crossbars as shown. The crossbars are also beveled to fit the angle of the roof (E).

The completed roof supports are glued and nailed to the walls. Note that they do not extend all the way to the floor. The plywood roof is glued on last and is held in place with finishing nails driven through the support frame. A suggestion: Scorched fir will show a more pronounced grain than the pine that's pictured in this example.

Here is a planter that can find a home on top of an end table, coffee table, or other piece of country furniture.

To construct the wishing well planter, begin by making the floor from 1/4" plywood. Cut off the corners at 45° angles, leaving 4" of straight edge on each of the four original sides. The walls are built with pine blocks scorched with a propane torch before assembly to achieve a rustic look. First glue

MATERIALS LIST

Finishing nails
Wood glue

CUTTING LIST

KEY	PIECES	SIZE AND DESCRIPTION
A	1	3/4 × 6-1/2 × 6-1/2 floor (plywood)
B	36	3/4 × 3/4 × 4 wall blocks
C	2	3/4 × 1 × 16 roof supports
D	2	3/4 × 3/4 × 11 crossbars
E	2	1/4 × 7-1/2 × 10 roof

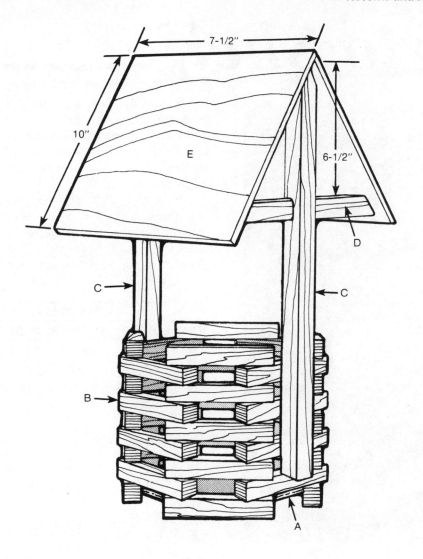

Curio Shelf

can be handled with a scroll or jigsaw. More intricate joining techniques, using rabbet, dado, and groove cuts, can be accomplished with a full array of power tools. Choose the method that pleases you best. Both types of joints are shown.

Cut the top (A), bottom (B), and divider (C) equal in size and bevel one side of both the top and bottom pieces along the front and sides. Cut five identical pieces for the shelves (G) and the top and bottom inserts (F). Then

CUTTING LIST		
KEY	**PIECES**	**SIZE AND DESCRIPTION**
A	1	3/4 × 4-1/4 × 20-1/2 top
B	1	3/4 × 4-1/4 × 20-1/2 bottom
C	1	3/8 × 4-1/4 × 20-1/2 divider
D	2	3/8 × 3-3/4 × 24-3/4 upper sides
E	2	3/8 × 2-3/8 × 3-3/4 lower sides
F	2	3/8 × 3 × 18-1/2 inserts
G	3	3/8 × 3 × 18-1/2 shelves
H	1	3/8 × 3/4 × 19-1/4 top trim
I	1	3/4 × 18-1/2 × 24-3/4 upper back
J	1	1/4 × 2-3/8 × 18-1/2 lower back
K	2	3/8 × 2-3/8 × 3-1/2 drawer dividers
L1	2	3/8 × 2-3/8 × 5 drawer fronts
L2	4	3/8 × 2-3/8 × 3-1/8 drawer sides
L3	2	3/8 × 2-3/8 × 4-1/4 drawer backs
L4	2	1/4 × 2-3/4 × 4-1/4 drawer bottoms
M1	1	3/8 × 2-3/8 × 7-3/4 drawer front
M2	2	3/8 × 2-3/8 × 3-1/8 drawer sides
M3	1	3/8 × 2-3/8 × 7 drawer back
M4	1	1/4 × 2-3/4 × 7 drawer bottom

This typically country background piece will enliven any Early American setting with its mellow charm, and then go further by offering display space for your valued bric-a-brac.

The unit lends itself to two methods of construction. Simple hand tools, such as a saw, hammer, nail set, and glue, are all you need if butt joint techniques are used throughout the construction. The scrollwork

cut the sides (D, E). The top trim (H) is attached to the top insert. The backs (I, J) are made by joining random pieces of beveled tongue-and-groove pine stock, or by cutting shallow grooves into plywood. Note that the shelves, inserts, and drawer components will have different length and width dimensions

if other than butt joint construction techniques are used.

Drawers may be simple butt-joined boxes as shown in the small drawer illustration. More intricate joining techniques such as rabbeting, which is shown in the large drawer illustration, can also be used.

MATERIALS LIST

Drawer knobs
Brads
Finishing nails
Wood glue

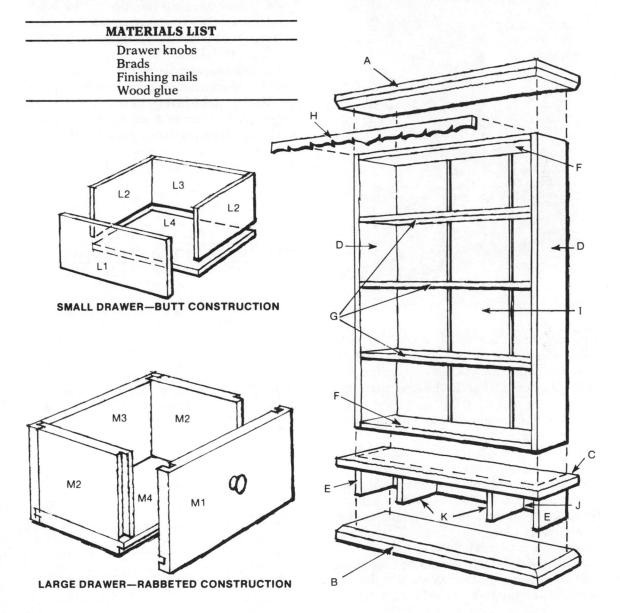

SMALL DRAWER—BUTT CONSTRUCTION

LARGE DRAWER—RABBETED CONSTRUCTION

Spice Cabinet

the lower divider (D), the lower shelf (E), and the sides (C). Add the two inner dividers (G), the top shelf (F), and the top (I). The top is needed for more than just appearance; it is used to mount the cabinet on the wall. Finally, secure the shelves (H).

The drawers are made to a loose fit. While a rabbeted edge on the drawer fronts (J, N) is illustrated, tight-fitting butt joints may be substituted. Add the backing (R, S) to prevent the drawers from pushing through. Then round all sharp edges slightly with a rasp to provide an antique look.

This reproduction of a country spice cabinet can be put to many uses. In your kitchen it may serve its original purpose for spice storage. In the sewing room it is a storage place for buttons, thread, and bindings. In your shop it may serve as tackle box or toolbox.

When used ornamentally, the open center can be an advantage. On a papered wall, the exposed paper becomes a framed picture. With a mirror behind it, the cabinet can be a frame for the mirror, or the glass may reflect some object placed on the shelf, such as a ceramic item or small flower vase.

Assemble the cabinet from the bottom up, using butt joints secured with wood glue and brads. Make the two-tiered base (A, B), add

CUTTING LIST		
KEY	**PIECES**	**SIZE AND DESCRIPTION**
A	1	1/2 × 4-3/8 × 21-1/4 base
B	1	1/4 × 3-7/8 × 20 base
C	2	1/4 × 4 × 22-1/2 sides
D	1	1/4 × 3-1/16 × 3-7/8 divider
E	1	1/4 × 4 × 20 shelf
F	1	1/4 × 4 × 20 shelf
G	2	1/4 × 4 × 16 dividers
H	8	1/4 × 3-7/8 × 4-1/2 shelves
I	1	1/4 × 3 × 20 top
J	2	5/16 × 3 × 9-3/4 drawer fronts
K	4	1/4 × 3 × 3-3/4 drawer sides
L	2	1/4 × 2-3/4 × 9-1/8 drawer backs
M	2	1/4 × 3-1/2 × 9-1/8 drawer bottoms
N	10	5/16 × 3 × 4-3/8 drawer fronts
O	20	1/4 × 3 × 3-3/4 drawer sides
P	10	1/4 × 2-3/4 × 2-3/4 drawer backs
Q	10	1/4 × 3-1/4 × 3-3/4 drawer bottoms
R	1	1/8 × 3-1/2 × 10 backing
S	2	1/8 × 5 × 20 backing

MATERIALS LIST

Brads
Doorknobs (14)
Wood glue

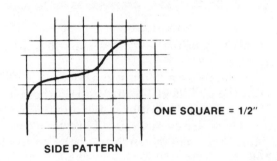

ONE SQUARE = 1/2"

SIDE PATTERN

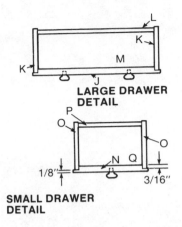

LARGE DRAWER DETAIL

SMALL DRAWER DETAIL

King-Size Spice Cabinet

The conventional spice cabinet is decorative but usually not large enough to accommodate all the flavorings and condiments used in the kitchen. In this project the cabinet has been enlarged so that it can hold everything needed.

Use the pattern to cut the sides (A). Cut the four shelves (B, C, D, E) and bottom (F). Secure the shelves and bottom so that the rear edge of each is 3/8" in from the back edge of the sides. Use 2d finishing nails, driving them through the sides into the shelves and bottom. Countersink all nail heads.

Nail the back to the shelves using 4d finishing nails.

Use the pattern to cut the top (H).

Cut the dividers (I) to size and set them in place between the bottom shelf and the bottom. These are evenly spaced and held with 2d finishing nails driven through the bottom shelf and bottom.

Attach the drawer fronts (J) to the front edge of the bottoms (M) with 2d finishing nails. Secure the sides (L) in a similar manner, nailing to the bottoms and the sides of the fronts. Add the backs (K) so that they fit on top of the bottoms between the sides. Nail through the base and sides into the back.

Cut the drawer pulls (N) out of 1/2" × 3/4" stock; each one is 1-1/2" long. Round the front edge with a wood file. Attach the pulls to the drawers with No. 5 × 3/4" wood screws. Countersink the heads.

Using a wood file, round the edges of the entire cabinet to create the appearance of age. Fill all holes with wood filler and sand the entire surface with 220-grit paper until smooth.

MATERIALS LIST

2d and 4d finishing nails
No. 17 × 1/2" brads
No. 5 × 3/4" wood screws
Wood filler
220-grit sandpaper
Wood glue

KEY	PIECES	SIZE AND DESCRIPTION
CUTTING LIST		
A	2	3/8 × 7 × 28 sides
B	1	3/8 × 2-3/8 × 35-1/4 shelf
C	1	3/8 × 2-5/8 × 35-1/4 shelf
D	1	3/8 × 4 × 35-1/4 shelf
E	1	3/8 × 6-5/8 × 35-1/4 shelf
F	1	3/8 × 6-5/8 × 35-1/4 bottom
G	1	3/8 × 30 × 35-1/4 back
H	1	3/8 × 5 × 35-1/4 top
I	4	3/8 × 4-1/2 × 6-3/8 dividers
J	5	3/8 × 4-1/8 × 6-5/8 drawer fronts
K	5	3/8 × 3-3/4 × 5-7/8 drawer backs
L	10	3/8 × 4-1/8 × 6-1/2 drawer sides
M	5	3/8 × 5-7/8 × 6-1/8 drawer bottoms
N	5	1/2 × 3/4 × 1-1/2 drawer pulls

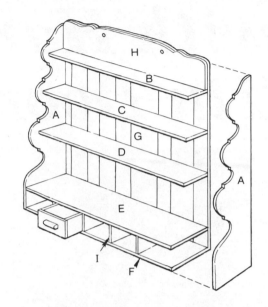

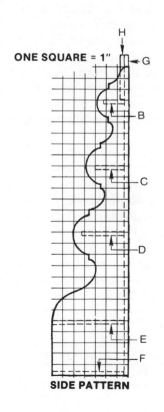

ONE SQUARE = 1"

SIDE PATTERN

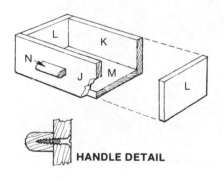

HANDLE DETAIL

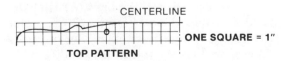

CENTERLINE

ONE SQUARE = 1"

TOP PATTERN

Spice Cabinet with Hammered Tin Door

This cabinet can be used to hold spices in the kitchen or toiletries in the bathroom.

Cut the top curve of the back (A) using the pattern provided, and bore a 1/2"-diameter hole for hanging the cabinet. Cut the sides (D) and shelves (E) to the sizes indicated in the cutting list. Use the pattern to cut the curve at the bottom of each side. Then notch the side pieces as shown to receive the back.

Nail the sides to the back, then nail and glue the shelves in place.

Cut the top (B), center it on the cabinet with a 1/2" overhang on each side, and attach it with nails and glue. Cut the frame pieces (C, G), and glue and nail them to the front of the cabinet. The frame pieces will overhang the edges of the cabinet.

Cut a 1/8"-wide groove, 3/8" deep on the inside edges of the door stiles (I) and rails (H) to receive the door front (J). Make a pattern of the design on the tin. Tape the pattern to the tin, and use a scratch awl and hammer to punch out the pattern. Aluminum or copper may be substituted for the tin.

Assemble the door with the tin inserted. Use glue to join the stiles and rails. If necessary, cut thin splines or shims to insert in the door grooves and hold the tin firmly. When the glue dries, do the final fitting of the door. Attach hinges 1-5/8" from the top and bottom of the door. Attach the doorknob about 6" up from the bottom of the door.

Attach the wooden latch to the frame, slightly above the knob. Drill a hole in the center of the latch and countersink the brass wood screw.

MATERIALS LIST

Doorknob
Brass wood screw
Finishing nails
Brass butt hinges
Wood glue

CUTTING LIST

KEY	PIECES	SIZE AND DESCRIPTION
A	1	1/2 × 10-1/2 × 17-3/4 back
B	1	1/2 × 4-1/4 × 11-1/2 top
C	2	1/2 × 1 × 10-5/8 frame
D	2	1/2 × 3-5/8 × 16-7/8 sides
E	2	1/2 × 3-5/8 × 9-1/2 shelves
F	1	1/4 × 1/2 × 1 latch
G	2	1/2 × 1 × 11-7/8 frame
H	2	1/2 × 1 × 8-1/2 rails
I	2	1/2 × 1 × 9-3/4 stiles
J	1	20 ga., 7-3/8 × 10-1/2 door front (tin)

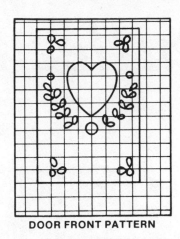

DOOR FRONT PATTERN

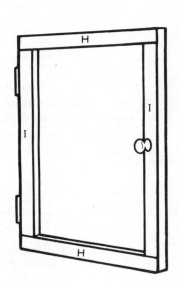

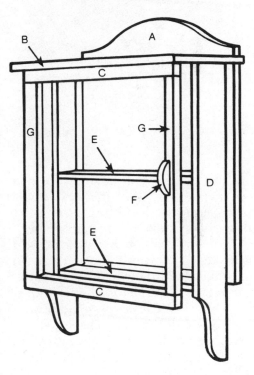

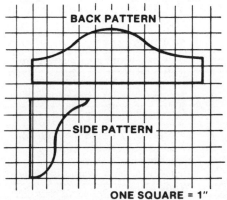

BACK PATTERN

SIDE PATTERN

ONE SQUARE = 1"

Bulletin Board_____

This oak bulletin board keeps pen and paper close for the next important message, and is a handy organizer with room for a calendar and shopping coupons.

Start construction by ripping 3/4"-thick oak to a 1-1/2" width. Cut the side (A) and bottom rail (B) to the indicated length.

Join the lower rail to the sides with a half-lap joint. A radial arm saw or table saw with a dado blade will cut the joint easily.

Because of the curve in the top rail (C), cut it to its overall width and length. The radius will be cut later.

Now, join the top rail to the sides using a miter joint strengthened with a spline. Cut the miters, then run a 1/4"-wide × 1/2"-deep groove in each end. The groove can be cut using a router mounted upside down in a router table, or a table saw with a 1/4" dado blade. Make the splice from oak because it will show.

Dry-fit the frame to make sure all the joints fit snugly, then glue and clamp the assembly.

Enlarge the top rail's design. Cut the rail to shape, then smooth the rail with a rasp or sandpaper.

Rout a 1/4" roman ogee design around the outer edge of the top and sides. Do not edge the bottom rail. Now, rout all around the inside of the assembly with a 1/4" rounding-over bit.

Give the frame a thorough sanding.

Next, run the rabbet in the frame for the insulation board (H) and cork liner (G). Insulation board will accept pins and tacks easier than plywood.

Enlarge the detailed design for the tray sides (F) and transfer it to 3/8"-thick oak. Cut the tray sides to shape and sand it.

Cut the tray front (D) and tray bottom (E) 1-1/4"-wide from 3/8"-thick oak. Round

MATERIALS LIST
No. 4 × 1-1/4" wood screws
Hanger brackets (2)
150-grit sandpaper
200-grit sandpaper
Wood glue

CUTTING LIST		
KEY	**PIECES**	**SIZE AND DESCRIPTION**
A	2	3/4 × 1-1/2 × 12 sides
B	1	3/4 × 1-1/2 × 20 bottom rail
C	1	3/4 × 4 × 20 top rail
D	1	3/8 × 1-1/2 × 18 tray front
E	1	3/8 × 1-1/4 × 18 tray bottom
F	2	3/8 × 2 × 5 tray sides
G	1	1/16 × 12 × 18 cork liner
H	1	1/2 × 12 × 18 insulation board

over the top edges of the tray front and the showing edges of the tray side's with a rasp and sandpaper.

Give the sides, front and bottom, a thorough sanding, then glue and clamp the tray together on a flat surface. Attach the tray to the frame with No. 4 × 1-1/4″ wood screws.

Cut the insulation board and cork to size. Glue the cork to the insulation board with wood glue. Lay a piece of scrap plywood or particleboard on the cork and place heavy weights such as bricks on the plywood. Let it cure for 24 hours.

Apply your favorite finish to the oak. Then install the cork/insulation board using a few small brads. Attach two hanger brackets to the top rail and your bulletin board is complete.

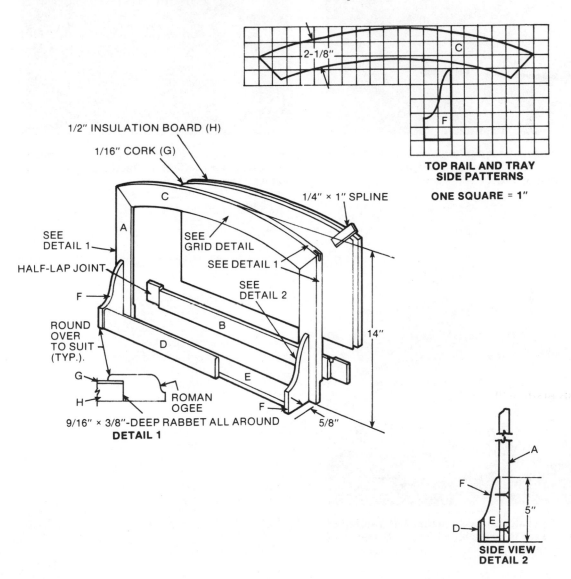

2-1/8″ · C · F

TOP RAIL AND TRAY SIDE PATTERNS

ONE SQUARE = 1″

1/2″ INSULATION BOARD (H)

1/16″ CORK (G)

C · A · 1/4″ × 1″ SPLINE

SEE DETAIL 1

SEE GRID DETAIL

SEE DETAIL 1

HALF-LAP JOINT

SEE DETAIL 2

F

ROUND OVER TO SUIT (TYP.).

B · D · E · F

14″ · 5/8″

G · H · ROMAN OGEE

9/16″ × 3/8″-DEEP RABBET ALL AROUND
DETAIL 1

A · F · E · D · 5″

SIDE VIEW DETAIL 2

When cutting the miter joints on both side pieces (A), use a stopblock on the miter gauge, as shown, to insure they are the same length.

Glue the cork (G) liner to the insulation board with carpenter's adhesive. Then place scrap plywood on top and add weights.

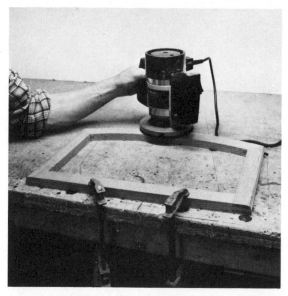

Rout a decorative edge along the top (C) and sides (A). Use a roman ogee bit with pilot. Do not rout the bottom rail; this is where the tray is attached.

Wine and Cheese Tray

Make entertaining on the patio or deck easier and more enjoyable by bringing your guests wine and cheese on this pine serving tray. It has its own convenient birch cutting board and holders that keep the glasses from sliding about when the tray is moved.

Begin construction by cutting all pieces to the appropriate dimensions. Cut the handles (A) as shown, marking the location of the hand-holds, then drilling two holes on both ends of the marks, and cutting out the section in between. Finish by cutting the contour on the bottom.

The handles, sides (B), and bottom (J) are butt jointed together and fastened with glue. Additionally, the bottom is fastened with brads, while the handles and sides are fastened with wood screws. Cover the counterbored screw holes with wood plugs.

Cut out the glass supports (G, I) and round over the edges with a file; then sand smooth. Nail the rectangular supports (H) onto part F and glue the rounded supports in place. Similarly, attach the divider (E) and glass supports to the serving tray with nails and glue.

Drill the 4"-diameter hole for the bottle holder with a hole saw or saber saw and affix it to the tray.

Finally, cut the birch panels for the cutting board and glue it into place.

Round over all of the showing edges of the tray and finish with a stain and/or varnish.

MATERIALS LIST

Wood screws
Brads
Wood glue

CUTTING LIST

KEY	PIECES	SIZE AND DESCRIPTION
A	2	3/4 × 7-1/2 × 15 handles
B	2	3/4 × 3-1/2 × 18 sides
C	1	3/4 × 6 × 13 bottle holder
D	3	1/4 × 2 × 7-1/2 cutting boards (birch)
E	1	3/4 × 3 × 13 divider
F	1	3/4 × 3-1/2 × 13 glass base
G	3	3/8 × 1-1/8 × 2-1/2 glass supports
H	5	3/8 × 1/2 × 3 rectangular supports
I	2	3/8 × 13/16 × 2-1/2 glass holders
J	1	1/2 × 13 × 18 bottom

ONE SQUARE = 1"

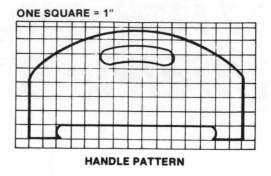

HANDLE PATTERN

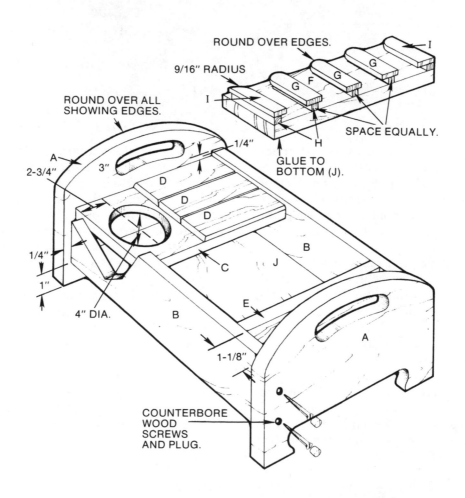

Make this tray using basic hand tools. The project is made from pine. A prominently grained wood, such as oak, will also look nice.

Glue the glass supports (G) onto the rectangular supports (H). The rectangular supports are nailed to the bottom (J).

The panel containing the bottle or wine carafe has a glued-on cheese cutting board made from three panels of birch.

Flour Box

the cleats (H, I) at an equal distance from the bottom. Use wood screws to attach the cleats from the inside.

Join the sides (E) to the back (D), then add the front (F). These joints may be made with wood screws or finishing nails, with wood glue used to provide extra support. If you cut the bottom (G) to a snug fit, it may be rested on the cleats without further attachment and can be removed at will. Attach the top (B) and the lid sides with finishing nails. Then attach the lid with brass butt hinges.

Sand the entire cabinet, then finish as desired. Stencil or paint a design on the front, or use decals.

MATERIALS LIST

Wood screws
Finishing nails
80-grit sandpaper
Brass butt hinges (2)
Wood glue

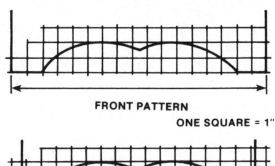

FRONT PATTERN

ONE SQUARE = 1"

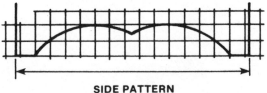

SIDE PATTERN

In Colonial times, the general store was the gathering place of the entire community. Commodities were scooped out of boxes, such as the one shown here, weighed, and sold. Shipment of flour, sugar, cornmeal, salt, and other dry stores was made in large bags, and then transferred in the store to boxes of this type for easy dispensing. The boxes were most often made by the storekeeper himself. For added attraction, the fronts of the boxes were ornamented—in this case with stenciled patterns.

Cut out all pieces to size. With the exception of the lid sides (C), round all outer edges irregularly, using 80-grit sandpaper. Attach

CUTTING LIST

KEY	PIECES	SIZE AND DESCRIPTION
A	1	1/2 × 15-1/2 × 15-1/2 lid
B	1	1/2 × 4 × 18 top
C	2	1/2 × 1-1/4 × 15-1/2 lid sides
D	1	1/2 × 15-1/2 × 37 back
E	2	1/2 × 17 × 37 sides
F	1	1/2 × 15-1/2 × 32 front
G	1	1/2 × 15-1/2 × 15-1/2 bottom
H	2	1 × 1 × 15-1/2 cleats
I	2	1 × 1 × 13-1/2 cleats

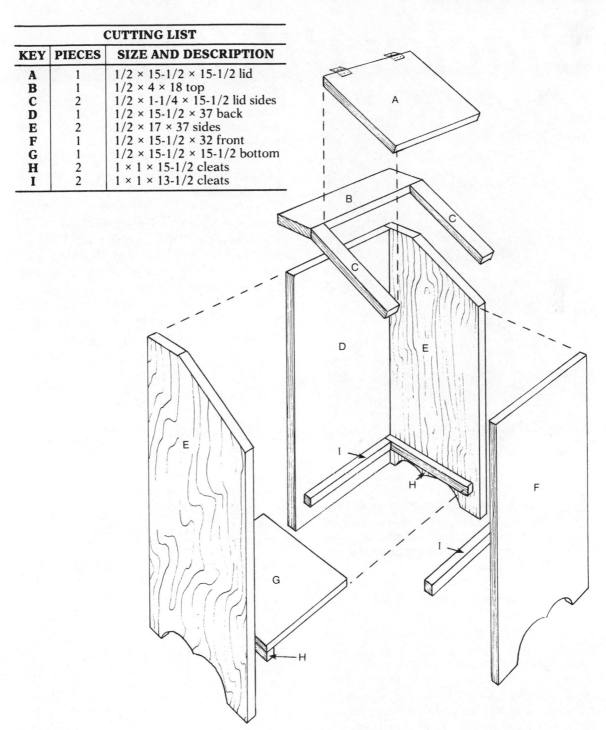

Blacksmith's Box

wide board. Use counterset wood screws and cover the screw heads with wood plugs glued into the recessed holes, as shown in Detail A.

Next, insert the center shelf (D), holding it in place similarly. Add the shelf trim (F) with glue and brads.

Attach the inserts (I, J) to the top (E) by gluing them and tacking them with brads driven into them through the top. Then attach the top to the sides with finishing nails. Miter the trim strips and attach them with glue and brads.

Use a wood rasp or router to round all the curves and lightly round the sharp edges irregularly. If you apply a decal, give it a coat of thin, low-luster varnish, then wax the entire piece with two coats of paste wax.

This piece is quite rare and hard to find in its original state, but it can still be reproduced easily. It can serve as a magazine rack, a catchall, or a knickknack stand beside a favorite chair.

The model shown was salvaged long ago and ornamented with a Pennsylvania Dutch design. You may omit this detail or, if you prefer substitute an inexpensive floral decal after finishing.

Cut out all pieces to size, then join the sides (A) to the ends (B). For the sides, you may not be able to find single boards of the width mentioned in the cutting list. If not, join two boards with glue and dowels to form the

MATERIALS LIST

Finishing nails
Brads
Wood screws
Wood plugs
Wood glue

CUTTING LIST

KEY	PIECES	SIZE AND DESCRIPTION
A	2	3/4 × 15-1/2 × 16 sides
B	2	3/4 × 4-1/2 × 11 ends
C	1	3/4 × 9-1/2 × 15-1/2 bottom
D	1	3/4 × 8 × 9-1/2 center shelf
E	1	3/4 × 8 × 11 top
F	2	3/8 × 1-1/2 × 11 shelf trim
G	2	3/8 × 1-3/4 × 8-3/4 top trim
H	2	3/8 × 1-3/4 × 11-3/4 top trim
I	1	3/8 × 1 × 11 top insert
J	2	3/8 × 1 × 3-5/16 top inserts

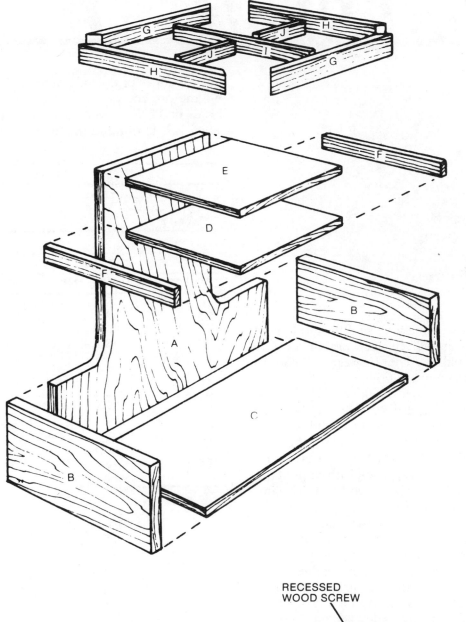

RECESSED
WOOD SCREW

3/8"-DIA.
DOWEL PLUGS

DETAIL A

Wall Shelf

This attractive wall shelf has unlimited uses—it will fit into practically any room to hold anything from an ivy plant to fancy condiment containers.

It is made of 3/8"-thick solid cherry, except for the 1/8" hardboard drawer bottoms (E4) and is an easy project to build. A bandsaw, scroll saw, or table saw are the only power tools that would really be useful here. Even they can be dispensed with without too much trouble. The scrollwork is fairly simple, and butt joint construction can be used instead of the methods discussed here.

After laying out one side piece (A), draw the curves with a compass according to the dimensions given in the detail sketches. Tacking the other side piece to it and cutting both simultaneously will ensure uniformity. Separate the pieces and dado each one in three places, for the shelving, with a 3/8"-wide × 1/8"-deep groove as shown. The same size groove is also made in the center of the two lower shelves (B1).

The drawers have conventional tongue-and-groove joint construction. Sand the curved edges of the sides and back. Assemble the project with glue and either 1-1/4" brads or 1" No. 4 wood screws. Highly polished 1/2" knobs add the final touch.

MATERIALS LIST

1/2"-dia. drawer knobs
1-1/4" brads or No. 4 × 1" wood screws
Wood glue

CUTTING LIST

KEY	PIECES	SIZE AND DESCRIPTION
A	2	3/8 × 6-1/2 × 13-1/2 sides
B1	2	3/8 × 6-1/2 × 7-1/2 bottom shelves
B2	1	3/8 × 4 × 7-1/2 top shelf
C	1	3/8 × 2-1/4 × 6-1/2 shelf divider
D	1	3/8 × 8 × 15-5/8 back
E1	2	3/8 × 2 × 3-7/16 drawer fronts
E2	4	3/8 × 2 × 6-3/8 drawer sides
E3	2	3/8 × 1-1/2 × 3-1/16 drawer backs
E4	2	1/8 × 3-1/16 × 6-5/16 drawer bottoms

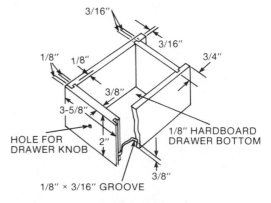

3/16"
3/16"
1/8" 1/8"
3/4"
3/8"
3-5/8"
1/8" HARDBOARD DRAWER BOTTOM
HOLE FOR DRAWER KNOB
2"
1/8" × 3/16" GROOVE
3/8"

DRAWER DETAIL

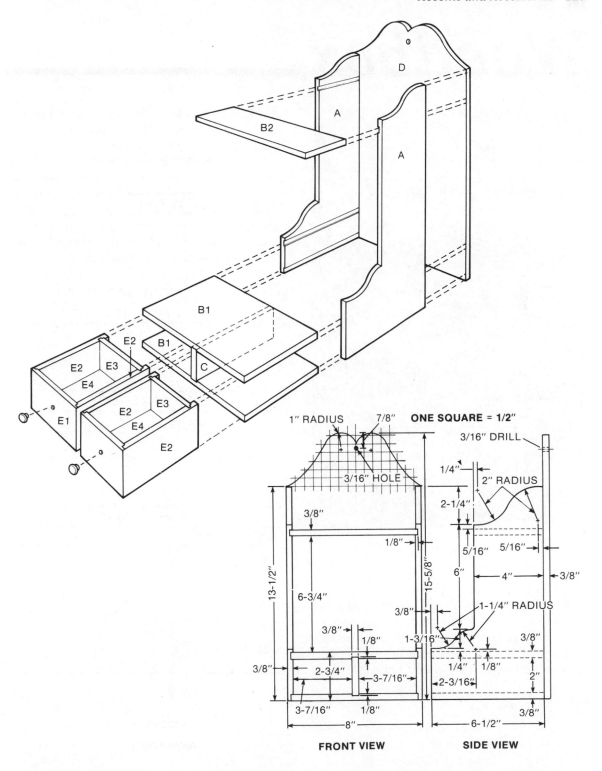

A

D

A

B2

B1

E2

E2   E3

E4

B1

C

E2   E3

E1   E2

E4

E2

1" RADIUS   7/8"   **ONE SQUARE = 1/2"**

3/16" DRILL

3/16" HOLE

1/4"

2" RADIUS

2-1/4"

3/8"

1/8"

5/16"   5/16"

3/16" DRILL

13-1/2"

15-5/8"

6"   4"   3/8"

6-3/4"

1-1/4" RADIUS

3/8"

3/8"

3/8"   1-3/16"   3/8"

1/8"

2-3/4"

1/4"   1/8"   2"

3/8"   3-7/16"

3-7/16"   1/8"   2-3/16"

8"   6-1/2"   3/8"

FRONT VIEW   **SIDE VIEW**

Woodbox

There's something warm and wonderful about having an old woodbox around. This box, made about 1825, has an uncommon feature: a removable towel rack set into sockets in its top. The box was undoubtedly positioned between a dry sink and stove; but if it had to be placed in a very small space elsewhere, it was a simple matter to remove the rack.

You can build this piece easily using butt, rabbet, and dovetail joints as shown in the drawing. Secure the sides (B) and front (C) to the bottom (A). Attach the back boards (D) as shown in the detail drawing. All edges of the box opening are chamfered to prevent splintering when wood is dumped in.

Use 1/2"-diameter dowels to connect the towel rack uprights (F) and crosspieces (G) and to secure the towel rack to the top (E). Note that the edges of the crosspieces are chamfered.

MATERIALS LIST

1/2"-dia. dowels
No. 6 × 5/8" brass wood screws
Wood glue

CUTTING LIST

KEY	PIECES	SIZE AND DESCRIPTION
A	1	3/4 × 11 × 28-1/2 bottom
B	2	3/4 × 12 × 36 sides
C	1	3/4 × 14 × 30 front
D	4	3/4 × 9 × 30 back boards
E	1	3/4 × 8 × 30 top
F	2	1 × 1-1/2 × 26 towel rack uprights
G	2	3/4 × 3/4 × 24 towel rack crosspieces

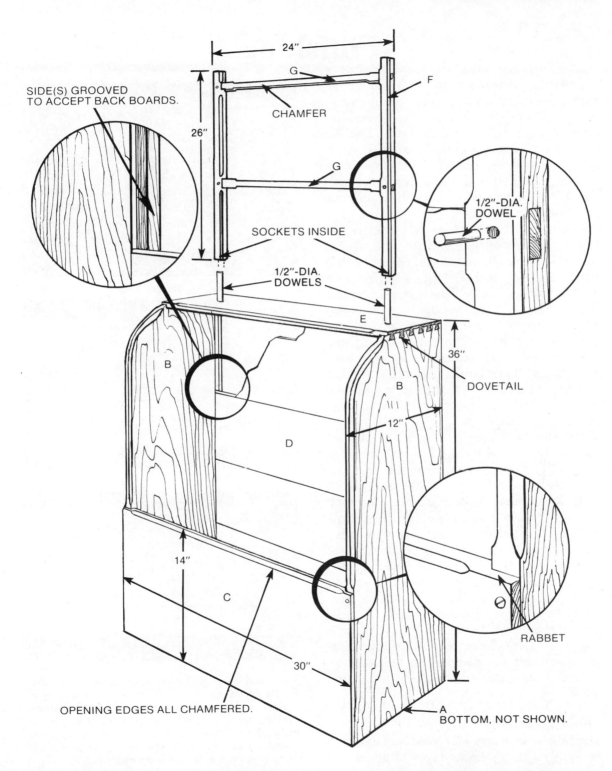

SIDE(S) GROOVED
TO ACCEPT BACK BOARDS.

24"

26"

G

F

CHAMFER

G

1/2"-DIA.
DOWEL

SOCKETS INSIDE

1/2"-DIA.
DOWELS

E

36"

B

B

DOVETAIL

12"

D

14"

C

RABBET

30"

OPENING EDGES ALL CHAMFERED.

A
BOTTOM, NOT SHOWN.

Finishing

Finishing means exactly what you would expect—it is the last step in completing your project. However, it deserves some serious consideration before you even start. The design, intended use, and the wear to which a piece will be subjected affect the choice of a finishing method, and they may require that some finishing steps be taken in the course of construction.

Finishing frequently evokes images of lengthy and painstaking work with stains, fillers, sealers, etc. All of the pieces in this book have designs that merit such effort, but do not restrict yourself to it in your initial considerations. Many products on the market will simplify the job and still provide an attractive finish. They run the gamut from combination sealer-stains and colored varnishes to synthetic laminates and paint. Your choice will depend on the quality of the wood you use and the effect you want and are willing to work for.

An important point is the principal purpose to be served by the finish. A finish is used for two reasons: to enhance the piece's attractiveness and to protect its looks against wear and abuse. A particular finish might not serve both equally well. In furniture-making, as in nature, form must follow function. No hard natural law prevents using a particular finish on any given furniture design, but the roar of the crowd will let you know that a Chippendale-quality finish on a kitchen cutting table makes as little sense as a natural pine finish on an elegantly-crafted hall table. The information on the following pages will help you decide what finish to use before you get started and guide you in doing it.

Choosing Wood
You first need to consider what kind of wood you will be using. Some types of wood are

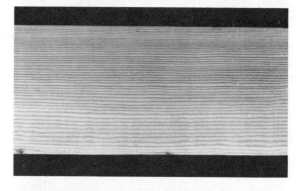

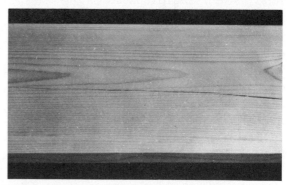

Tone and grain patterns vary widely among different types of wood. Whatever wood(s) you choose, make sure the lumber is of good furniture-making quality. While the board shown in the third photo would be acceptable for many commercial uses, the split makes it unsuitable for most furniture and cabinetry applications.

more readily available, less expensive, and easier to work with than others. Certain types will take stain better than others. Some should not be stained, either because the natural qualities are already very attractive (cherry, cedar, rosewood, and teak, for example) or because the wood is not adaptable to stain (examples are fir, spruce, poplar, and white and sugar pines).

Pines are probably the most commonly used wood for country-styled furniture. They are easy to work with, and you can count on the lumberyard having them. They are generally receptive to stain, but vulnerable to chipping and denting in use. The light natural tone permits the use of any color stain, and the use of the right tone can create a reasonable resemblance to many other woods. Oak and walnut, however, are two popular woods they will not resemble. Even if you can match the tone, the grain pattern of pine will come nowhere near matching the distinctive grains of these woods. Similarly, stay away from lower-grade pines if you are attempting to replicate other woods— the knots will give you away.

Hardwoods such as oak, hickory, and fruitwoods are harder to find, but are also popular choices. They will not absorb much stain, and unless the wood is bleached, lighter stains are ineffective on them. Dark stains are usually used to highlight the grain patterns. If you cannot find hardwoods at your lumberyard, a good place to look for them is a millwork shop.

Hardwoods such as teak and rosewood are so dark and hard that neither bleaching nor staining will have much effect on them. But then, after going to the trouble and expense of obtaining them, it is not very likely that you will want to display anything but the natural tones.

At the other extreme are plywood and particleboard. Their greatest attractions for the home craftsman generally are availability and price. The fact that plywood can be obtained in smaller thicknesses than other woods makes it particularly useful for panels, and both are useful for concealed pieces

Concealing the exposed plys on the edge of a plywood board is a simple matter with wood tape. Simply peel off the paper backing and press the tape against the edge. It can be trimmed with a hobby knife.

requiring strength. However, special precautions, such as veneering or laminating, must be taken to conceal any exposed edges on either, and any exposed particleboard surface, if the piece is being stained. Plywood sheets can also be purchased with various surface veneers, including oak and cherry. Stained particleboard will look only like stained particleboard. With care, plywood can be stained to look like something other than plywood, especially if a darker stain is used.

Once you know what kind of wood will be used and the kind of wear to which it will be exposed, you can decide which finishing method—staining, painting, or laminating or combinations of them—to use. Pay attention to the setting in which the piece will be used. Clashing furniture styles, and even room decor, can take away from a good finishing job, while shortcomings will be less noticeable if the piece complements its surroundings.

Removing Imperfections

The first step for wood that is to be painted or stained is to remove any surface imper-

Small dents can be removed by steaming them out before the wood is finished. A few drops of water, a soft cloth, and a hot iron is all it takes.

Larger dents, nicks, and scratches, and nail or screw holes can be removed by filling them with wood putty before finishing the wood. Be sure to sand the patch smooth and flush with the rest of the surface after the putty dries.

fections. Small dents are removed by steaming with a hot iron and several layers of moist cloth. Joints are filled with a wood putty or filler, with special attention being given to end grains and plywood edges. Similar treatment is given to scratches, cracks, and nail or screwholes which will not be concealed with wood plugs. A finish other than a veneer or laminate tends to highlight flaws rather than hide them. If you want a weathered or rustic look, less attention is needed here.

Sanding

After the imperfections have been corrected, the wood is ready for sanding. The most important element here, for both a sander or hand-sanding, is the paper. The least expensive sandpapers are those with flint abrasives, but they dull very quickly. More commonly used are sandpapers with garnet, aluminum oxide, or silicon carbide abrasives. They cut faster and last longer than flint. If you have a lot of sanding to do, you will recover the additional expense besides avoiding the frustration of frequently having to change papers. Silicon carbide and garnet both tend to fracture easily and are better suited to softwoods than hardwoods.

Sandpaper grades run from super fine to very coarse, based on the number and size of the grit. The table below lists the grades, including the numerical equivalents formerly used, and their applications.

Sanding is done either parallel to the grain or at a slight angle to it. The grain runs lengthwise through the length and long sides of a board, and through the narrow dimension at the ends. For hand-sanding, use uniform, overlapping strokes with a sanding block. With coarse-grade papers, sand at an angle in order to level ridges and remove glue and other stains. Glue removal is especially important if the wood is to be stained because glue prevents absorption of the wood stain and causes a spotty finish.

Sandpaper Grades and Applications			
Grade	**No.**	**Size**	**Use**
Super fine	400	10/0	Final polish after all the finishing is completed
Extra fine	240 320	7/0 9/0	Light sanding between finishing coats
Very fine	180 220	5/0 6/0	Final preparatory sanding before application of finish
Fine	120 150	3/0 4/0	Final preparatory sanding before painting
Medium	60 80	1/2 0	Intermediate sanding to remove roughness left from previous sanding; light stock removal
Coarse	40 50	1-1/2 1	Intermediate sanding to remove roughness left from previous sanding; heavy stock removal
Very coarse	24 36	3 2	Initial sanding, heavy stock removal, and smoothing extremely rough wood

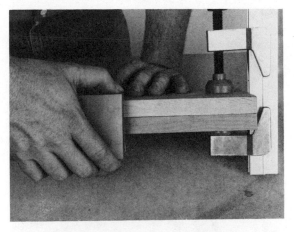

For a smooth joint between two adjoining boards, sand them with the facing sides clamped together.

On open-grained woods, such as oak and chestnut, medium-grade paper is also sanded at an angle to avoid enlarging the pores during light stock removal. In all other instances, sanding is done parallel to the grain. Smoothing the ends will take a good bit of effort, but the ends will eventually achieve a quality equal to the rest of the board. Give the corners an extra stroke or two to soften them for better paint and varnish adhesion and to make them less vulnerable to chipping and splintering. Keep your strokes short at the edges to avoid rounding off the edges, and be sure to sand smooth the interior surfaces for a smooth fit before joining two boards side to side. Remember that if sanding is done improperly, even if you cannot see the flaw before the finish is applied, chances are good that it will be apparent after the finish is on.

The sanding block is used to get the smooth finish that finger-pressure alone will not provide. If you are using a homemade block instead of one manufactured for the purpose, wrap a piece of felt, sponge rubber, or old carpet to the sanding surface before attaching the paper. This provides the resiliency needed to absorb low and high spots without skipping. To sand contours such as the edges of tabletops and furniture legs, you probably will have to hold the paper in your fingers because a block will not fit into the contours. In some circumstances a contoured block can be made for use. Because it is difficult to sand contours as smoothly as the rest of the wood after a piece is assembled, a fine finish will probably require that only the finishing sanding should be left until after assembly. The rest should be completed beforehand.

If you are finishing turned or contoured pieces such as stair railings, table legs, cabinet ledging, at least some of the sanding will have to be done by hand. To get a smooth finish, use only as much paper as will fit inside the contour being sanded, and be sure to sand in the same direction as the grain.

Power-sanding can be done with a vibrating, belt, or disk-type sander. The vibrating or finishing sander operates in either a straight-line or an orbital direction. Straight-line sanding takes time and does not remove much material, but it results in perfect smoothness. It is excellent for final sanding and for sanding veneers.

Orbital-sanding is used for smoothing wood to size and for preliminary rough and medium sanding. However, because its cross-grain motion can cause swirl marks in wood, it should never be used for final sanding.

Belt sanders operate only in a straight-line direction. Because they cut very rapidly, belt sanders should not be used for sanding veneers. Unlike straight-line sanding with a finishing sander, however, belt sanders are excellent for removing stock.

Disk sanders have a circular motion and are effective only for rough sanding and, with a buffing pad attached, for polishing a finished surface.

Whenever possible, power-sanding, like hand-sanding, should follow the wood grain, because swirling scratches are difficult to remove. Many wood-finishing experts believe that final sanding should be done only by hand.

When turning the sander on or off, remove it from contact with the wood. Once the sander is on, keep it moving to avoid creating ruts in the wood. Hand pressure should not be applied. The natural weight of the hand and the sander's weight are all the pressure normally required. Applying more pressure will slow the sander's operation and cause the paper to clog more quickly, although a heavier sander will smooth the surface faster.

It is not always necessary for every grade of paper to be used, or that they all be used in succession. Using a coarser paper than the job requires actually makes needless work because the scratches it leaves will have to be removed. However, do not skip more than one grade in succession. For example, while you can often expect satisfactory results by going from very coarse to medium to fine, etc., you will probably see only poor results going directly from very coarse to fine. Use open-coat papers (papers with less than 70% of the surface covered by abrasive) on softwoods; the concentration of abrasives which makes closed-coat papers cut faster also clogs them up faster on softwoods. Wet-sanding between the finish coats (stain, sealer, etc.) will contribute to a still smoother finish, but make sure the paper is water resistant.

Scraping
One other method favored by many experienced woodworkers is scraping wood.

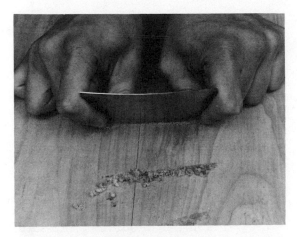

Metal scrapers are a good way to get a fairly smooth surface without a lot of sanding. However, they take practice to be used efficiently, and fine sanding will still be required to get a high-luster finish.

Be sure to test a stain on an unexposed surface of the piece, or on a scrap piece of the same type of wood, before staining the piece. No single stain usually has the same effect on the tone and grain pattern of different woods.

Where coarse sanding to remove stock will leave scratches in the wood which will themselves have to be removed, scraping shears the wood off in thin, smooth layers. Because fewer steps are needed, scraping is quicker and cheaper than sanding. Even for a fine finish, scraping saves time by allowing you to go right to the use of a fine-grade paper.

Scrapers come in various shapes to fit different wood surfaces, but learning how to use them efficiently does take practice.

Staining

After sanding, the wood is ready to be painted or stained. Many kinds of stains are available, as well as an almost unlimited range of colors because stains of the same type can be mixed to achieve more desirable tones. Stains are classified according to their bases: water, oil, alcohol, or lacquer thinner. They are available either already mixed in their base or in powders to be mixed with the base by the user. However you decide to proceed, do not presume that the color listed on the label is going to give you the tone you

want. Stains of the same name by different manufacturers, and even from different batches by the same manufacturer, frequently differ, and they will invariably produce different tones on different types of wood. To get the exact shade you desire, test the stain on scrap or unexposed wood. If you are going to mix stains to get a shade closer to what you want, mix only stains of the same type in small batches of only a teaspoonful or so in order to avoid waste.

To accentuate wood grain, stain darkens it by absorption into the wood's pores. The greater the penetration, the darker the color; the darker the wood, the darker the stain will make it. This presents two problems to achieving an even tone in wood furniture: different pieces of the same type of wood do not always have the same natural tone; even on the same piece of wood there will be hard and soft spots with different absorption qualities. It also means that water molecules are put into the wood with water-based stains and raise the grain fiber. This last circumstance requires that the wood be sanded again after a water stain is applied. The problem of uneven coloring requires two separate approaches.

First, adjoining pieces of wood should match each other's natural tones as nearly as possible, unless a contrast is intended. This can be handled by carefully selecting each piece for tone before you cut it. The second problem is especially significant on plywood, but exists on every piece that has an exposed end. End cuts and the white areas on plywood are more absorbent than the surrounding wood grain and, as a result, will be made darker by staining. To solve the problem, apply a thin coat of glue size or a mixture of shellac and linseed oil to the ends. This will decrease the amount of stain that can be absorbed. If the stain turns out too light on that area, follow with a fine sanding and another stain coat, repeating until the tone matches the rest of the wood. The entire plywood surface gets the same treatment.

Both stains and paints can be applied either by spraying or brushing. In either event, stain or paint should be applied in thin coats that are allowed to dry before a succeeding coat is applied. Applying a heavy coat can lead to an uneven finish, or one that is darker than desired. The same rules for application govern spray staining as govern spray painting. Use long strokes with the grain when brushing on stain. Move from the areas which will be least seen when the piece is completed to the ones which will be most visible, butting succeeding strokes against the still-wet edges of the prior strokes. Butting against dry edges may leave overlap marks. Wherever possible, apply the stain with the surface horizontal; where it is not possible, apply the stain from the bottom up. Make certain to work the stain into all pores, especially on open-grained woods, to avoid a spotty finish.

If you find that the stain you have applied is too dark, it can often be lightened with an

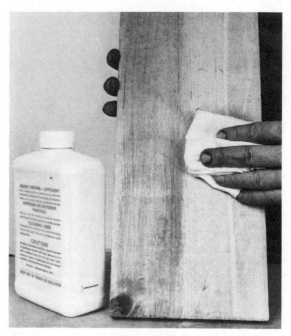

If a stain coat has been applied in too dark a shade to suit you, use a clean cloth dampened with mineral spirits or turpentine to lighten the shade.

extra-hard wiping with clean rags or a rag saturated in mineral spirits or turpentine. Never use sandpaper except for light touch-up work; even a partial cut through will show up lighter than the surrounding wood.

Bleaching can be used if the entire piece is too dark and to lighten many naturally dark woods. Household bleach and ammonia can be used by applying it full strength over the wood with a sponge or fiberbrush, washing it off after about 15 minutes and repeating the process until the wood is lightened as nearly as possible to the shade you want. Commercial wood bleaches are also available. After the bleach has been rinsed from the wood, allow the wood to dry for about 48 hours before proceeding with the staining. Of course, the wood fibers will have to be sanded down after the wood has been wet.

Once you have the desired color, filler should be applied to prevent the final finish

Bleach does a good job of lightening the natural shade of a wood so that it can be stained to match other pieces. Commercial wood bleaches are available, but household bleaches also do a good job.

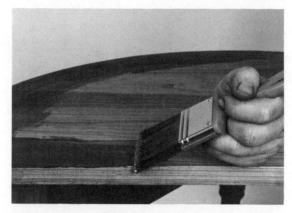

Varnishes and shellacs are brushed on by cutting in the edges of the piece first, then applying a thin coat, with the grain, over the entire surface.

coat from sinking into the wood and producing ripples. Fillers should be as transparent as possible. Paste fillers are normally used on open-grained wood and liquid fillers on woods that are close-grained. The filler is first brushed against the grain then, while it is still wet, applied with the grain. For a fine finish, it will be necessary for all the pores to be filled level.

Finish Coats

The final finish coat can be either shellac, varnish, lacquer, oil, or wax. Whichever you choose, do not apply it until the wood has been brushed with a tack rag to remove any particles that could mar the finish. Shellac is easy to work with and is either white or orange. The orange gives a deeper grain tone, but also tends to create an amber tint. It is mixed with denatured alcohol for application, generally in equal amounts of each element. A disadvantage is that if alcohol is spilled on it, the finish will be destroyed. However, a coat of wax will help delay the action of alcohol against the shellac for a brief time. Shellac is built up in thin coats brushed first with and across the grain

around the edges of the board, then across the grain, and finally with the grain. After each coat dries (about an hour), it is sanded before the next coat is applied. A thin coat of shellac is also used as a sealer over penetrating oil stains if a varnish finish will be used, because varnish will draw an oil stain out of the wood.

Varnish has several advantages over other finishes. For one thing, the availability of colored varnishes can eliminate the use of a stain. Simply brush it on the same as any varnish after the wood has been sanded and. filled. Another advantage is that a good varnish finish is alcohol and water resistant. A third advantage is the availability of many varnishes in high-gloss, semigloss (satin), and flat finishes. Do not use a spar, or marine, varnish on indoor furniture because its weather-resistant quality comes from a resilience that feels soft and sticky indoors.

If a varnish stain is being used on bare wood, the first coat should be thinned in a 4:1 mix with turpentine. It is important that each coat dry thoroughly (8 to 24 hours) before applying the next one because light sanding is done between coats to remove any bubbles or dust that accumulate. The harder the coat, the smoother the sanding. Also, be sure to run the tack cloth over the coat after each sanding. Each coat should be thin; heavy coats will settle, but take longer to dry and accumulate more dust. Like shellac, varnish is applied by first cutting in the borders of the piece, followed by brushing across the grain, and completing the coat by brushing it with the grain. Wherever possible, the coat should be applied horizontally to prevent the coat from running.

Lacquers are available in flat or glossy finishes and can be brushed or sprayed on after the piece has been sanded. Stain must also be applied before a lacquer coat if the piece is not being given a natural finish. Advantages of a lacquer finish are its extremely hard and durable qualities and its fast drying time to complete hardness. However, it will dissolve and lift many spirit and oil stains, and even the natural colors in woods such as mahogany, rosewood, and amaranth can be weakened by it. Water and nongrain-raising stains are unaffected by lacquer, and a sealer coat of shellac will avoid problems with the others. Sanding is not needed between succeeding coats of lacquer because the preceding coat tends to dissolve into the subsequent one. Any imperfections in the finish afterward can be removed by rubbing down the surface with fine steel wool and wax after the lacquer has dried for about 48 hours.

If the lacquer is to be sprayed on, use light coats to avoid runs. For brushed-on coats, do not work the brush back and forth. Instead, wet the brush enough to cover a full length of the board; brush in one direction, and reverse on the next stroke. Overlap the strokes only slightly. Do not apply lacquer in a damp atmosphere, or blushing (a white deposit) may appear in the coat.

Oil finishes are considered by many to be the most beautiful; properly applied, they make the wood almost impervious to water,

heat, scratches, and most stains. They also take plenty of patience because a good oil finish takes months—not days—to complete, and requires what often seems to be an endless amount of hand rubbing. Anywhere from four or five to as many as twenty coats may be needed for a lustrous, soft finish. The oil should be allowed to soak into the wood for several days between the first and second coats; between the later coats, several weeks will be needed, with the time increasing after each coat.

To determine whether the wood is ready for the next coat, place your hand on the surface for a few minutes. If the surface becomes oily, it is not dry enough for the next coat.

Apply the oil generously with a soft cloth, rubbing it into the wood with both hands. After about 20 minutes, wipe off the excess oil. Use as many clean cloths as needed, and be sure to remove excess oil trapped in crevices. Follow this with a vigorous rubdown with a coarse linen or wool cloth. The sur-

Apply the stain in a smooth, even coat. "Wiping gel" stains, which are available on the market, can stain a piece in spotty shades if applied unevenly.

face should be rubbed in sections, allowing 10 to 20 minutes to each section. Coats should be applied until all dull spots have been removed, then once a month for a year, then yearly. If the surface is sticky, it means that all the excess oil has not been rubbed off.

Wax can add life and reduce caring for a finish, but it should not be used alone because it will be damaged by greases, oils, water, and heat. Paste waxes are best; best of all are carnauba waxes, which can be obtained from furniture, hardware, or paint stores. Rub on wax to a 2′- or 3′-square area at a time. If the manufacturer specifies that wax should be applied with a damp cloth, wipe off any remaining moisture before polishing. After the wax has dried for about 10 minutes, the area can be polished by rubbing in a brisk circular motion with a soft cloth, followed by long strokes along the grain. Be sure to blend adjacent spots together. Succeeding coats can be applied after about an hour. To test whether the prior coat has dried, try to make a thumbprint on the surface. If the print can be seen, more rubbing is necessary.

You can feel confident, whatever finish you choose, that with patience, care, and attention to the directions above, your project will last longer and look better. And isn't that what you wanted in the first place?

Credits

Text

David Ackerman, William Beyer, Gary Branson, Monte Burch, George Campbell, Rosario Capotosto, Al Gutierrez, Gene Hamilton, Katie Hamilton, Ed Jackson, Jack Marlow, Marlyn Rodi, David A. Warren, D. R. Watson

Photographs

George Campbell, Rosario Capotosto, Kathleen Childers, Matt Doherty, Grignion Studios, Inc., Al Gutierrez, Gene Hamilton, Katie Hamilton, William Laskey, Jack Marlow, Michael Myers, Marlyn Rodi, David A. Warren, D. R. Watson, A. J. Wyatt

Illustrations

George Campbell, Ron Chamberlain, Mike Garbenck, Tim Himsel, Eugene Thompson

Photographic Styling

Virginia Howley

Furniture Design

Terry Redlin, William Ress, Marlyn Rodi

Some of the projects in this book are available in kit form. For complete information about kits, write to Cohasset Colonials, Cohasset, Mass. 02025 or Shaker Workshops®, P. O. Box 1028, Concord, Mass. 01742.

Rodale Press, Inc., publishes RODALE'S PRACTICAL HOMEOWNER™, the home improvement magazine for people who want to create a safe, efficient, and healthy home. For information on how to order your subscription, write to RODALE'S PRACTICAL HOMEOWNER™, Emmaus, PA 18049.

Miller